THE
Civil War
STATE BY STATE

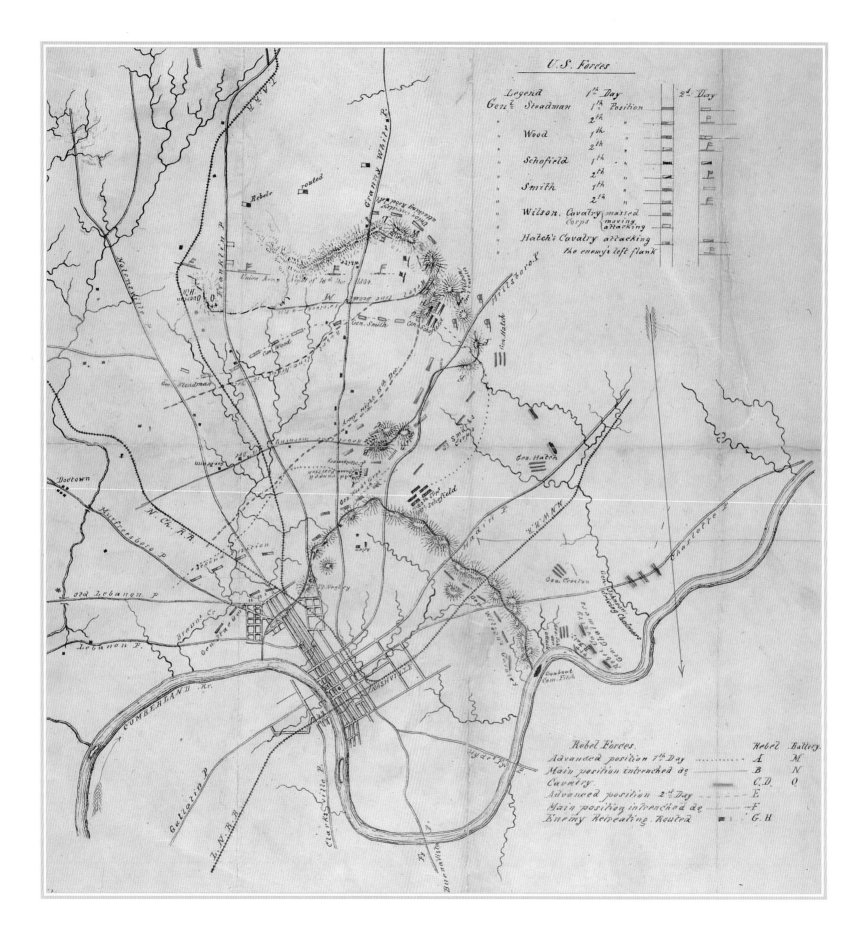

THE
Civil War
STATE BY STATE

PAUL BREWER

THUNDER BAY
P·R·E·S·S

San Diego, California

To my father, Chester (1919–1980), a true soldier in blue.

Thunder Bay Press
An imprint of the Advantage Publishers Group
5880 Oberlin Drive, San Diego, CA 92121-4794
www.thunderbaybooks.com

All notations of errors or omissions should be addressed to Thunder Bay Press, Editorial Department, at the above address. All other correspondence (author inquiries, permissions) concerning the content of this book should be addressed to Salamander Books Ltd., Salamander Books Ltd., The Chrysalis Building, Bramley Road, London W10 6SP, United Kingdom.

ISBN 1-59223-054-7

Library of Congress Cataloging-in-Publication Data
available upon request.

Printed in Singapore
1 2 3 4 5 08 07 06 05 04

CREDITS
Project Manager: Antony Shaw
Designer: Cara Hamilton
Production: Don Campaniello
Picture Research: Louise Daubeny

CONTENTS

SEEDS OF CONFLICT

"The fault of the free states in the eyes of the South is not one that can be atoned for by any yielding of special points here and there. Their offense is that they are free."
—James Russell Lowell, writer and editor, February 1861.

The Civil War emerged out of the nature of the republic itself, with its perpetual tension between the powers of the federal authority and the states, made worse by the diverging needs of different regional economies.

Left: A commercial map, by D. van Nostrand from New York, of Richmond, Virginia, and its defenses, in 1864. The concentric circles indicate distances from the city center. On April 2, 1865, following the evacuation of the Confederate government and its remaining gold reserve from Richmond, the city finally fell to Union forces.

INTRODUCTION

"These United Colonies are, and of right ought to be, free and Independent States."
—Declaration of Independence, 1776

The words of Virginia delegate Richard Henry Lee's motion of June 7, 1776, encapsulated the legal question that underlay the most bloody conflict in the history of the United States of America. Was the Union established by thirteen British colonies on the Atlantic coast of North America a permanent one or one that could be terminated by one of the constituent states? The United States emerged out of a very British kind of ad hoc organization, the Continental Congress. When the crisis between the government of London and the Britons of North America arose in the early 1770s, the different colonies sent representatives as independent entities. There was no constitution or other legal sanction to this body, which came to regard itself as a convention of independent "states." It had to invent itself as it went along, forcing compromise on colonies that had deep cultural differences and experienced generations of rivalry. Although the Declaration of Independence was formally signed into law on July 4, 1776, a plan of confederation had been drawn up by a committee of thirteen delegates and presented to Congress days before. This project eventually took the form of the Articles of Confederation, first presented to Congress in April 1777 for discussion, finally approved in November 1777, and ratified by all the states by March 1781. Formally the United States of America had established a legal structure to govern themselves. This document explicitly stated, "and the Union shall be perpetual; nor shall any alteration at any time hereafter be made in any of them; unless such alteration be agreed to in a Congress of the United States, and be afterward confirmed by the legislatures of every State." However, it also included the following: "The better to secure and perpetuate mutual friendship...the free inhabitants of each of these States...shall be entitled to all privileges and immunities of free citizens in the several States." Thus, while the Union was perpetual, its people were citizens not of the United States, but of their individual states. A free person was a citizen of Massachusetts or South Carolina, but not of the United States.

The Articles of Confederation provided for an imperfect union. Administrative problems led to a new governing document for the United States, the Constitution. Unfortunately for the future, while the new document included the statement concerning shared rights among the citizens of the different states, it removed the wording about a perpetual union subject to agreement by the Congress. (Interestingly, the war's bloodshed might have been averted had this wording been retained, as at least it provided a political approach to dealing with secession.)

The United States comprised a vast territory when their former British rulers finally recognized their independence in 1783. Economic life in New Hampshire was markedly different from that in Georgia. In Europe, the only comparably sized state was Russia, a despotic monarchy. The four Southern states—Virginia, North and South Carolina, and Georgia—relied heavily on large farms, using slave labor imported from Africa to generate an agricultural surplus that could be exported to bring in an income. In the Northern states, farms were mostly family operations that created a subsistence income for their residents. In some ways, the two sections were not far apart, since both relied on agriculture, but they had organized it in different ways.

This changed as the Northern states embraced a transportation and industrial revolution, which sought to substitute home-manufactured goods for imports, and to ship them to markets using canals and roads. The effect of this was to plug the family subsistence farms

Left: *Slaves sweeping outside a plantation house. Regardless of what has been said since, in prewar United States, both sides identified the reason to go to war as slavery. Southern politicians identified the mounting intolerance in Northern states toward the South's "peculiar institution" as the justification for secession.*

Right: Thomas Jefferson—patriot, philosopher, and president—was in some ways the ideologist of the secessionists. His support for the Kentucky and Virginia resolutions during a constitutional crisis in the 1790s suggested that states could determine the constitutionality of laws.

STATES &c.	Length	Breadth	Area	Population
Maryland	212	123	14.000	380.546
Virginia	448	233	70.300	974.622
Kentucky	328	183	40.110	406.511
North Carolina	472	188	50.500	555.500
Tennessee	400	104	43.000	261.727
South Carolina	236	210	33.380	415.115
Georgia	303	259	60.000	252.433
Mississippi T.	390	278	88.680	40.352
Louisiana	300	242	41.000	76.556
Missouri T.	1491	896	983.250	20.845
West Florida	151	88	6.112	20.000
East Florida	410	200	50.457	
Bahama Islands				15.000

into a wider market, making it possible for them to raise crops for sale and using the money earned to buy what they previously grew to feed themselves. Having more cash at their disposal, these farmers enlarged the market for manufactured goods, and something of a "virtuous circle" emerged, as a growing market encouraged industrial growth. The Northern states also put a much higher premium on mass education than the South, and this produced a knowledgable workforce that could contribute to the pace of technical development through little (and even big) innovations to their working practices. The more dynamic Northern economy was more attractive to immigrants.

Northerners and Southerners had been aware of their different societies even before the Revolution. What they had in common, however, seemed more important than what separated them. This changed over the decades, especially after the end of the slave trade in 1808 at least officially closed the Southern economy to further importation of slaves from West Africa. The difference took political form in 1819, when both Maine and Missouri petitioned Congress for admission to the Union. An attempt by a Northern

Left: *A map of the southern United States during the War of 1812 shows the progress of statehood. Mississippi and Alabama remain territories, while Louisiana is now a state of the union. The Floridas are Spanish possessions still, although during the war US troops occupy parts of west Florida out of military necessity. The development of the cotton gin would help make much of these lines viable for a cotton-growing plantation economy and give a financial justification for large-scale human slavery.*

congressman to provide for the gradual emancipation of the slaves in Missouri as a condition of admission provoked a crisis only resolved by the Missouri Compromise of 1820. Under this, slavery was banned in the parts of the Louisiana Purchase north of the latitude 36' 30°N (with the exception of Missouri). For some Southerners, this was an outrage. A slave was property, like furniture, and the Compromise was no different than trying to ban Southerners from taking their furniture to Iowa.

The problem with this point of view was that Congress had established an important precedent for having the power to regulate slavery in territories of the United States. A land ordinance passed in 1787 had banned slavery from the Northwest Territory (modern Ohio, Michigan, Indiana, Illinois, and Wisconsin). The first Congress to meet under the new Constitution in 1789 reaffirmed its predecessor's decision. Congressmen from the South had voted in favor.

A possible solution to the question of what to do when Congress passes a law to which the citizens of a state object arose in 1828. In that year, Congress passed an exceptionally high tariff on raw materials, which could potentially damage the Southern economy. A similar case had arisen in 1798, when Thomas Jefferson had supported resolutions in Kentucky and Virginia to declare a law affecting freedom of the press illegal on the grounds of exceeding the authority granted the federal government in the Constitution.

South Carolina's political leader, John C. Calhoun, used this precedent to support his view that a state could protect its citizens by declaring a Congressional law null and void within its own territories. In 1832, South Carolina did just that and provoked a crisis. The state threatened to secede if something was not done about the tariffs. Union military forces were sent to forts in Charleston and only a political compromise crafted by Kentucky Senator Henry Clay solved the problem.

The power of Congress over slavery in the territories finally came to a head after the Mexican War added

Left: *A bridge under construction on the Nashville, Chattanooga & St. Louis railroad during the Civil War. The spread of railroads across the United States helped make the family farms of the North economically competitive with the plantation-based agricultural economy of the South. Railroads and canals allowed farms to sell their produce to markets hundreds of miles away. The North embraced railroads with great enthusiasm and had a considerably more extensive network than the South.*

Texas and California, and much territory in between, to the United States. Here was an area where slavery could flourish; it was here that Representative David Wilmot of Pennsylvania proposed to ban slavery in a proviso to the congressional measure appropriating to pay Mexico millions for the new territory. Instead of voting on party lines, Democrat versus Whig, the US Congress split on sectional lines, North versus South, and then passed the proviso.

While both parties had contained pro- and antislavery elements, the debate in the country over the Wilmot Proviso gave impetus to a new party committed to the abolition of slavery. The Free-Soil Party brought together Northern antislavery Democrats and Whigs into a combination with the minor Northern abolitionist Liberty Party. Although it had little impact on the result of the presidential election of 1848, the party secured enough seats in the House of Representatives to prevent either Whigs or Democrats from having a majority there. As a consequence, voting on sectional lines began to occur regularly there as Northern Democrats and Whigs sought to recover electoral ground lost to the Free-Soilers.

These sectional lines were not as clear cut as the state boundaries delineated. Settlement patterns that dated back prior to the Revolution made the North something of a patchwork quilt of opinion. New England (with the partial exception of Connecticut) was the most solidly abolitionist area of the country. Upstate New York and northern Ohio had been heavily settled by families with a New England heritage, and this was fertile ground for Free-Soil and antislavery politicians. The New England diaspora spread into Michigan, Wisconsin, northern Indiana, Illinois, and out to Minnesota. By contrast, the southern areas of Ohio, Indiana, and Illinois had been settled early on by Southern families who may not have been slaveholders, but otherwise had little in common with New England culture. A third stream of settlement emerged from a crescent that embraced Philadelphia and the Susquehanna Valley of Pennsylvania, through New Jersey and New York's Lower Hudson Valley, and into Connecticut. Their settlements were scattered across the states around the Great Lakes, and abolition was not a major political theme here. New immigrants from Germany and Ireland who were drawn to all parts of the North—both the big cities of the Atlantic coast and the rural lands of the Midwest—contributed a fourth stream of Northern settlement, and again one that was not stirred by a call to abolish slavery. (A smaller flow of immigrants from the British Isles found homes in the South, where they embraced Southern values.)

Thus, there was an identifiable battleground in the North, where political combat between proslavery and antislavery voters was fiercely waged. It embraced Connecticut, the Lower Hudson Valley of New York, New Jersey, Pennsylvania, Ohio, Indiana, and Illinois. This was a traditionally Democratic region, just like the South. As long as these areas could be held to the Democratic side, the South's political advantage in the struggle with abolition would remain. But a new political issue arose at just the wrong time for politicians in the South.

The numbers of Germans and Irish coming to the United States increased dramatically after 1846, and many of them were Catholics. While Low Church Protestant religion in the North fueled the demand for abolition, the conservative Catholic church was more concerned with the fate of souls in the next world, than the condition of their bodies in this. The Catholic church's priorities rested on creating a network of churches and schools that would maintain the faithful in their creed. This was an affront to the traditionally militant antipapist feeling of American Protestants and a burgeoning anti-immigrant "nativist" sentiment blossomed in the same Northern areas where the abolitionists battled proslavery sentiment for control of the Whig and Democrat parties. Nativist politics simmered away until it erupted in 1854. A nativist American Party won a stunning victory in the election

for the post of governor in Massachusetts, with the support of the Free-Soil candidate. However, nativism appealed in the South as well, and the legislature of Tennessee fell to American party control in 1855, among other political victories.

The nativist political movement appealed to many members of the Whig Party. It had been the Democrats, rather than the Whigs, who traditionally embraced the newcomers in the Northern cities, where the immigrants found work in the same kind of jobs as native-born mechanics. The Whigs already had problems with the tension between its Free-Soil and proslavery wings, and nativism suggested a way of avoiding the problem. Unfortunately, nativism just went into the mix of forces pulling at the fabric of the Whig Party, with nativist and antinativist Whigs being found on both sides of the divide over the slavery question.

The Whig Party, pressed by the Free-Soilers and the nativists, fell apart under the strain. Its Southern wing effectively merged with the nativists. In the North, many Whigs found a new home in a new party that had already attracted converts from the Whig cause.

The stimulus to this new party came from an act of Congress passed in May 1854. The Kansas-Nebraska Act, in organizing two new territories from the lands of the Louisiana Purchase, repealed the Missouri Compromise. Northern Whigs were horrified, while Northern Democrats also objected, in spite of New Hampshire Democrat President Franklin Pierce's endorsement of the act. The Northern wings of both parties fractured irreparably. In each state, antislavery Whigs, Democrats, and Free-Soilers began uniting in caucuses under a variety of names. The name Republican eventually merged as the favorite. This new Republican Party attracted most of the Whigs, although anti-Nebraska Democrats were somewhat more circumspect. However, the warning signs were there for political strategists in the South who were all well aware that slavery would only survive as long as they could control the Democrats in the lower North.

The tools for the destruction of the proslavery coalition were contained in the greatest victory achieved by Southerners since the annexations following the Mexican War. The Kansas-Nebraska Act specified that the question of slavery would be left open for the settlers of the relevant territory to provide. Some Northerners organized settlement of Kansas by parties of Free-Soil farmers. Slaveholders in Missouri feared being outflanked and promoted settlement of their

Above: *In 1836, settlers in Texas achieved independence from Mexican rule, and the defense of the Alamo came to symbolize the sacrifice made to this cause. The Unites States war with Mexico (1846–48) then resulted in the acquisition of much of this territory that slaveholders believed would suit their way of life.*

own. But they took the competition a stage further by organizing bands of "border ruffians" who crossed the border into Kansas and, through intimidation and fraudulent voting, secured proslavery majorities in the territorial legislature.

Free-Soilers responded by organizing their own government. The federal government backed the proslavery interests, but it was not enough. In November 1855 a Free-Soil settler was murdered by a proslavery man. Arms arrived from the North for the Free-Soilers. One Free-Soil settler, the militant abolitionist John Brown, murdered some settlers from slave-holding states in May 1856. A low-intensity guerrilla conflict between the two sides created the image of "Bleeding Kansas."

The two sides of the great conflict were now clearly defined. The free states encompassed the most industrialized part of the nation's economy. They had more railroads, more factories and factory workers, more big cities, more immigrants, and better education. The slave states had manipulated their political advantages for two generations since the Compromise of 1820, but these had now slipped away. Their last hope, to co-opt the Northern nativists via the American Party collapsed after the election of 1856 over the issue of Kansas, as the party could no better bridge the immense gap between proslavery and antislavery sectional feeling than the Whigs had.

The crisis that had rumbled on for forty years finally came to a head in 1859–60. In October 1859, John Brown attempted to start a slave insurrection that would create a guerrilla army of runaways hiding in the Appalachian Mountains. They would be armed by the seizure of the Federal arsenal at Harpers Ferry, Virginia, with twenty men. However, the plan went awry; after capturing the arsenal, a force of federal troops captured Brown and his small band of followers. Brown was then hanged. Through his speeches at his trial and sentencing, Brown became an abolitionist martyr, convincing Southerners that the Northerners would sooner or later compel them to free their slaves.

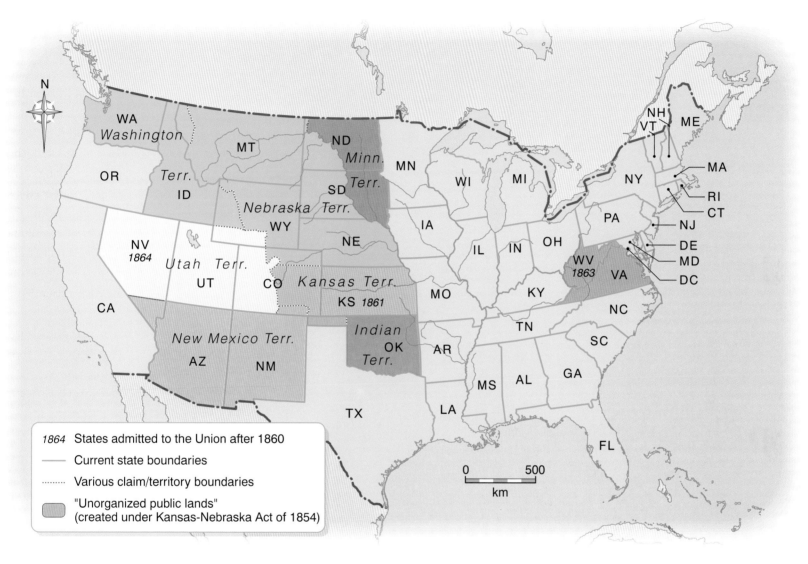

1864 States admitted to the Union after 1860

—— Current state boundaries

······· Various claim/territory boundaries

"Unorganized public lands" (created under Kansas-Nebraska Act of 1854)

0   500
km

Since 1800, the government of the United States had been dominated by men from the Southern states. During the sixty years since then, the office of president had been held by a Southerner for about forty years. Many Supreme Court justices had also been Southerners. However, in 1860, all this looked to be changing. Growing population in the Northern states and the admission of more Free-Soil states had shifted control of Congress northward. The election of a Free-Soil president in 1860 would be a signal that the levers of power that remained in Southern hands, the Court and the White House, could soon be wrested from them.

The presidential election of 1856 was a four-way contest between the Republicans, a Democratic Party split into Northern and Southern factions, and a group of former Whigs known as the Constitutional Union Party. Republican candidate Abraham Lincoln carried all the states of the North except New Jersey. The slave states split among Northern Democrat Stephen Douglas, Southern Democrat John Breckinridge, and Constitutional Unionist John Bell. Breckinridge carried ten of them. The worst fears of slaveholders had come to pass, with a majority of states now being Free-Soil, and the White House in the hands of a Free-Soil candidate. Was the Union permanent and perpetual, or could a state choose to leave it? Now was the time to settle the matter. "And the war came," as Abraham Lincoln was to say in March 1864.

Above: *A map of the United States in 1860.*

Opposite: *The firehouse at Harpers Ferry is the sole remaining structure of the great armory that was frequently the target of campaigns on both sides during the first two years of the war. It was the site of John Brown's last stand during his futile attempt to seize weapons from the armory in order to equip an insurrectionary slave army in 1859.*

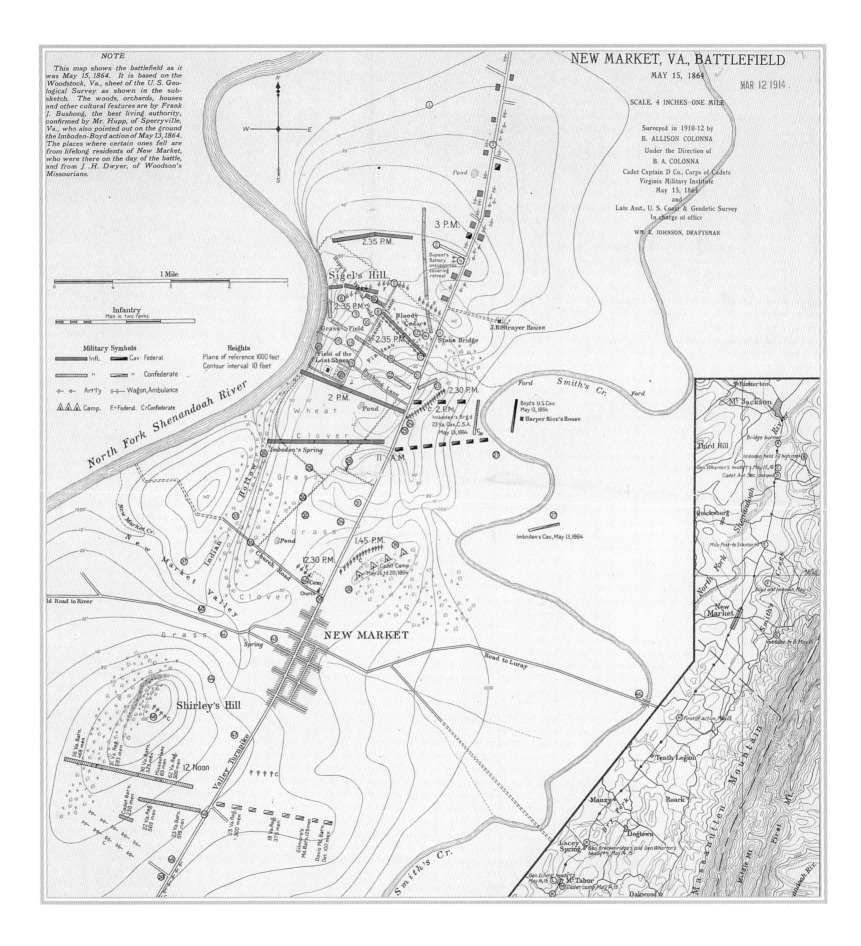

NEW MARKET, VA., BATTLEFIELD

MAY 15, 1864

MAR 12 1914.

SCALE, 4 INCHES ONE MILE

Surveyed in 1910-12 by
B. ALLISON COLONNA
Under the Direction of
B. A. COLONNA
Cadet Captain D Co., Corps of Cadets
Virginia Military Institute
May 15, 1864
and
Late Asst., U. S. Coast & Geodetic Survey
In charge of office

WM. E. JOHNSON, DRAFTSMAN

NOTE

This map shows the battlefield as it was May 15, 1864. It is based on the Woodstock, Va., sheet of the U. S. Geological Survey as shown in the sub-sketch. The woods, orchards, houses and other cultural features are by Frank J. Bushong, the best living authority, confirmed by Mr. Hupp, of Sperryville, Va., who also pointed out on the ground the Imboden-Boyd action of May 13, 1864. The places where certain ones fell are from lifelong residents of New Market, who were there on the day of the battle, and from J. H. Dwyer, of Woodson's Missourians.

1 Mile

Infantry
Men in two ranks

Military Symbols
Inft.   Cav. Federal
"   "   Confederate
Art'l'y   Wagon, Ambulance
Camp.   F.=Federal   C.=Confederate

Heights
Plane of reference 1000 feet
Contour interval 10 feet

3 P.M.

2.35 P.M.

Sigel's Hill

2.35 P.M.

Grass Field

Field of the Lost Shoes

Bloody Cedars

Stone Bridge

J. B. Strayer House

2.35 P.M.

Plateau

Bushong Lane

2 P.M.

Wheat

Clover

Pond

2.30 P.M.

C. 2 P.M.

Ford   Smith's Cr.   Ford

Boyd's U.S. Cav.
May 13, 1864

Harper Rice's House

Dupont's Battery unsupported covering retreat

Imboden's Brig'd
23 Va. Cav., C.S.A.
May 13, 1864

Imboden's Spring

11 A.M.

North Fork Shenandoah River

New Market Cr.

Hollow

Grass

Grass

Clover

Pond

Imboden's Cav., May 13, 1864

Indian Valley

1.45 P.M.

12.30 P.M.

Cem.

Church

Church Road

Cadet Camp
May 16, to 20, 1864

NEW MARKET

Id Road to River

Grass

Spring

Shirley's Hill

26 Va. Reg. 668 men
51 Va. Reg. 593 men
30 Va. Reg. 373 men
Missourians 615 men
62 Va. Reg. 500 men

Cadet Barn 230 men

22 Va. Barn, 569 men
23 Va. Barn, 519 men

23 Va. Reg. 300 men
18 Va. Reg. 375 men

Gilmore's Md. Barn 125 men
Davis Md. Barn, Det. 100 men

12 Noon

Valley Turnpike

Road to Luray

Pinkerton

Mt. Jackson

Third Hill

Bridge burned

Imboden held by high crest

Gen. Wharton's head'qr's, May 15, 16
Cadet Art. Sec. camped

Quicksburg

Shenandoah River

North Fork

Boyd and Imboden, May 13

New Market

Smith's Creek

Imboden to B., May 15

Massanutten Mountain

First Action, May 15

Tenth Legion

Mauzy

Roark

Dogtown

Lacey Spring

Gen. Breckenridge's and Gen. Wharton's head'qr's, May 14, 15

Mt. Tabor

Cadet camp, May 14, 15

Gen. Echols' head'qr's May 14, 15

Oakwood

Dry Fork

Smith's Cr.

THE STATES

The war touched every state of the Union. In the Deep South, the experience of war was direct and harsh and ultimately revolutionary. In the far west, distant and unfelt. The North learned of war largely through long lists of casualties and new taxes. The border area in between suffered divided communities and even families, and military campaigns in the early stages of the war.

Left: *A 1914 map of the battlefield of Newmarket, Virginia, on May 15, 1864. It is typical of the many battlefield maps produced after the war compiled and drawn under the direction of Cadet Captain B. A. Colonna, one of 247 Virginia Military Institute cadets who fought with distinction in the engagement.*

ALABAMA

"I can inform you that I have seen the Monkey Show at last and I don't want to see it no more…I can't tell you how many dead men I did see…I am tired of war."

—Alabama soldier T. Warrick's letter to his wife, January 1863

Alabama was admitted as a state on December 14, 1819, the twenty-second state of the Union. It was first organized as a territory in 1798 as part of the Mississippi territory. In 1817, when Mississippi became a state, Alabama was organized as a territory of its own. Following the secession of South Carolina in December 1860, Alabama authorities seized federal military installations. The US arsenal at Mount Vernon was taken on January 4, 1861, and forts Gaines and Morgan, which guarded the entrance of Mobile Bay, the following day. Then on January 11, a convention held in Montgomery voted for secession, sixty-one yeas to thirty-nine nays. Legally, Alabama regarded itself to be an independent republic until February 18, 1861, when it became part of the newly created Confederate States of America. Montgomery was in fact the site of the convention that organized the Confederate States. This body, when it first met on February 4, 1861, comprised delegates from six of the seven seceding states. The convention swiftly adopted, first, a Provisional Constitution and then, a permanent one. Both of these documents were based on the Constitution of the United States, but the permanent one incorporated some alterations. For example, the presidential term was extended to six years, at the price of not being able to stand for re-election.

Above: *A Confederate States' national flag of the first pattern, adopted while the capital was still at Montgomery. The "Stars and Bars" remained the national flag until May 1863.*

Left: *The Alabama monument at the Vicksburg National Cemetery. Nine Alabama regiments served in the garrison of the besieged city. The memorial, a bronze sculpture, was dedicated in July 1951.*

The convention elected a president and vice president under the terms of the Provisional Constitution. There were two "favorite son" candidates. The Mississippi delegation nominated Jefferson Davis (1808–89) and Georgia nominated Howell Cobb, who was serving as the president of the convention. The vote was held on February 9, and Davis won all the state delegations except that of Georgia, although once this was known the vote was made unanimous. Alexander Stephens was elected the vice president. Having been elected, Davis then selected his cabinet, and the Confederate government set about its work, keeping Montgomery as the new republic's provisional capital. Montgomery remained the capital until, on April 27, 1861, the newly seceded state of Virginia offered the city of Richmond to the Confederate States as a permanent capital. Montgomery was a small town in comparison, with limited facilities for the central government, and the offer was accepted. The move was made on May 21, and the city of Montgomery then reverted to its former status as a state capital.

One of the key elements in the strategy for the survival of the Confederate States was to gain recognition from other nations, in particular the great powers of Western Europe, France and Britain. One

Above: *One of the rooms of the Confederate White House in Montgomery.*

benefit in this was to offer favorable commercial terms related to trade.

On March 16, 1861, Alabamian William Lowndes Yancey (1814–63) led a diplomatic mission to Europe, part of which included offers of low tariffs to those who recognized the confederacy. Yancey was a powerful spokesman for the cause of secession in the prewar South. He had helped foment the split in the Democratic Party in 1860 that produced Northern and Southern candidates for president.

Yancey's delegation scored an important early victory when the British government issued a proclamation of neutrality on May 13, 1861. By recognizing the Confederacy as having "belligerent

rights," this document enabled the Davis administration to secure loans and to commission privateers. This good start proved a false dawn, as although Yancey was welcomed by London society, pressure from the Union government limited the number of personal interviews he had with the British foreign minister to two. Nor did Yancey ever manage to gain the objective of Confederate diplomacy, which was recognition of the Confederate States of America as an independent nation. Even more minor, but still valuable victories, such as the denouncement of the Union blockade of Rebel ports, eluded him.

Yancey became increasingly bitter, and in January 1862, after two new commissioners had finally reached Britain, he resigned as an emissary. He returned to Alabama, where he had secured election to the Confederate States' Senate. There, he pursued anti-administration politics, seeking to limit the ability of the president to make appointments without Congressional approval and higher payments for goods requisitioned by the Rebel army from Southerners. He died at home, between Congressional sessions.

Ship Number 290, built by Laird Shipbuilders of Birkenhead in northwest England, was made possible by the belligerent status that may have been secured by Yancey's mission to London. Launched in May 1862 under the name *Enrica*, this ship was renamed *Alabama* in August 1862 and commissioned into the Confederate navy. Although reputedly being built for Spain, the Rebel navy had ordered her from her British builders, intending to use the *Alabama* as a commerce raider against US merchant ships.

The *Alabama* had a career lasting nearly two years, and, together with the USS *Hatteras*, a gunboat sunk in a ship-to-ship duel off Galveston, Texas, on January 11, 1863, destroyed sixty-six US merchant ships in the course of it. The effect of the raiding was out of proportion to the actual number of ships destroyed by the *Alabama*, as many ships remained in port when their owners found the requisite insurance rates

needing to be paid had risen astronomically. *Alabama's* career came to an end off Cherbourg, France, when she fought a romantic ship-to-ship "joust" with the USS *Kearsarge* on June 19, 1864. The *Alabama* was in need of repairs, having been at sea for the whole of the two-year period. Also, the *Alabama* was more lightly armed, although her big guns could be used at longer range, and her two-year-old gunpowder was deteriorating. Consequently the battle was somewhat one-sided, although the *Alabama* managed to lodge a shell in the *Kearsarge's* stern post. The *Kearsarge's* cannonades were much more effective, and the *Alabama* was eventually battered into submission. She hauled down her colors and surrendered. She was already sinking,

Right: *A map of the battle of Mobile Bay, showing the approach of the Union fleet and the Confederate fleet assembled in the bay. The battle was typical of fleet engagements between the Confederate and Union navies. The Confederates relied on shore-based artillery and floating torpedoes (mines) and obstacles to reduce the odds against their outnumbered fleet, while the Union ships had to run the gauntlet of fortress-based artillery to both port and starboard.*

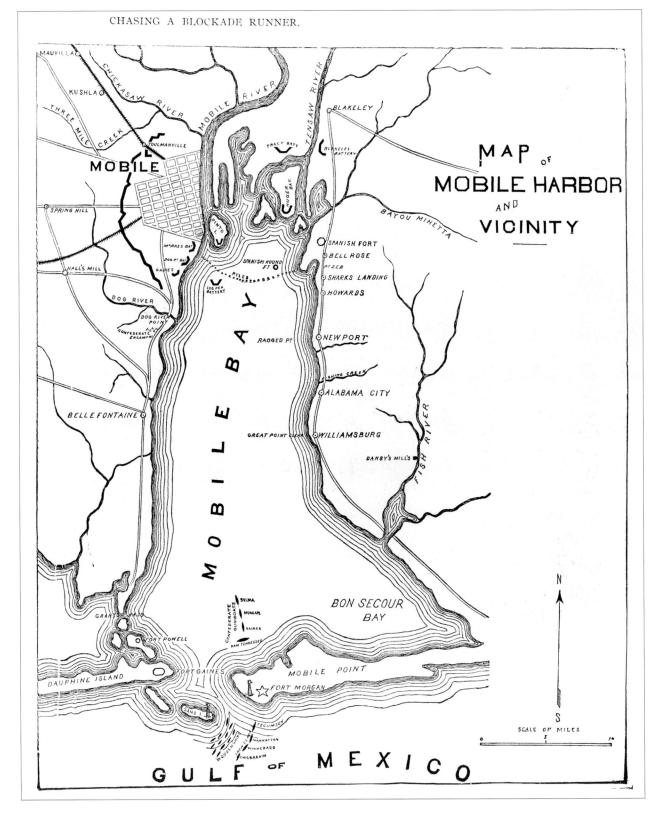

CHASING A BLOCKADE RUNNER.

MAP OF
MOBILE HARBOR
AND
VICINITY

and the wounded were transferred to the *Kearsarge* before the rest of *Alabama's* crew abandoned ship.

Alabama was the state most in the "middle" of the Confederacy, furthest from the borders with the Union. The port of Mobile was blockaded very early on in the civil war.

The most important town in the early years of the war was Decatur, through which an important east-west railroad route passed. This town was burned several times by both Union and Rebel troops during the war.

Mobile remained the most strategically significant town in the state. On more than one occasion after the fall of Vicksburg, Mississippi, in July 1863, the Union army commanders considered a strike across Mississippi and Alabama in order to seize the port. However, there always seemed to be more important targets elsewhere. Finally, on August 5, 1864, a Union fleet was sent against Mobile Bay.

The officer who was in command of the Union fleet, Admiral David G. Farragut, arranged his fleet in two lines. One line consisted of his four monitors. These would pass into Mobile Bay nearest to Fort Morgan. The second line, to port of the monitors, consisted of the Union fleet's larger steam sloops lashed to smaller vessels, some of them sidewheel paddle steamers.

Lashing the ships together in this manner shortened the line and thus the exposure of Farragut's fleet to the guns of the Confederate shore batteries. This also ensured that if one of his bigger ships was damaged by engine fire, another engine would be available to keep it underway.

The plan worked to near perfection. The only mishap occurred when the monitor USS *Tecumseh*

sank. The Confederates had placed a row of mines (known then as "torpedoes") partway across the main ship channel, one of which the USS *Tecumseh* struck. The USS *Brooklyn*, leading the other line, halted at the sight of the rapidly sinking monitor. Farragut continued on, shouting the memorable line, "Damn the torpedoes. Full speed ahead."

Once past the forts, the warships of the Union squadron had to contend with the Confederate ships defending the bay. Three of these were inadequate gunboats, but the fourth was probably the most powerful ironclad built by the Confederate navy, the USS *Tennessee*. A close-range action took place, as the Union ships attempted to sink or disable the Confederate vessel by ramming and point-blank gunfire. Round shots bounced off the armored sides of the USS *Tennessee*, and shells rarely exploded effectively. Outnumbered nineteen to one, the battering of the USS *Tennessee* eventually left the vessel unable to fight, and she surrendered. The forts were captured by the end of August, although the city of Mobile remained in Confederate hands.

Finally, close to the end of the civil war, the Union forces entered Alabama in strength. The long-proposed campaign against Mobile began in March 1865. In addition to this, a cavalry raid by the army of Tennessee was made into the north and center of the state. Mobile's Rebel garrison fled after assaults against its fortifications on April 8–9, 1865. Selma fell on April 2, and Union cavalry entered Montgomery on April 12. The remaining Confederate forces in the state of Alabama formally surrendered with the rest of the Rebel troops on May 4, 1865.

Left: *A belt buckle bearing the seal of the state of Alabama.*

ARIZONA

"My timely arrival with my command was hailed by a majority, I may say the entire population, of the town of Tucson."

—Captain Sherod Hunter, Arizona Rangers, CS Army, April 1862

The United States acquired some of Arizona in the cession made by Mexico after the end of the Mexican-American War. The southern portion, including modern Bisbee, known as the Gadsden Purchase, was bought from Mexico in 1854. The area was incorporated in the Territory of New Mexico, however, there was little in common between the Anglo Texas settlers of the northwest of El Paso and in the Gila River Valley, and the Hispanics of the Rio Grande. The cultural background of the Anglos made them sympathetic to secessionist feeling in Texas and the Eastern states. Anglos also desired to have territorial status of their own, instead of being incorporated with the Rio Grande Valley. It was unsurprising when two secession conventions held at Mesilla, New Mexico, and at Tucson, in March 1861, voted to separate from New Mexico and the United States. The Confederate Congress granted them territorial status as the Territory of Arizona.

Jefferson Davis welcomed the potential offered by Arizona's accession. The withdrawal of some Union Regular Army garrisons of New Mexico encouraged the Apache tribe to redouble efforts to discourage white settlement. A battalion recruited by John R. Baylor (1822–94), and taken into the Rebel army as the 2nd Texas Mounted Rifles, occupied Fort Bliss, Texas, and launched an invasion of New Mexico Territory. On August 1, 1861, Baylor claimed all of New Mexico Territory south of 34°N for the Confederacy. Although Mesilla was the base of Rebel operations in New Mexico, the strategic vision of a man like Baylor was drawn more to the West, and in particular Tucson. Baylor recognized his "governor-ship" as a temporary one, and awaited the arrival of Henry Sibley with more men to secure the defeat of Union forces in New Mexico. Baylor planned to take a force west to secure

Left: *The Wild West legend Kit Carson served with the 1st New Mexico Voluteer Infantry during the Civil War. In 1862, after ending the Confederate threat in New Mexico, Kit Carson and the 1st New Mexico Volunteers were assigned to military operations against the Navajo, especially in Arizona. This culminated in Carson's expulsion of 8,000 Navajo from Arizona to New Mexico in 1864.*

the road between Mesilla and Tucson. Tuscon would then serve as a base for operations in two directions. A move south, into Mexico, could secure use of the port of Guaymas, and a much harder port for the Union navy to enforce a blockade. A move west would give the Rebels the chance to test feeling in southern California.

In January 1862 the Arizona Rangers, raised by Baylor, was ordered by the now-arrived Sibley to Tucson under the command of Sherod Hunter (1834–69?). The men reached their destination in late February, and found the town full of white settlers who had fled their farmsteads to avoid Apache raids. While the Rebels had visions of securing at least part of California, actual Union possession had created the "California Column," assembling at Fort Yuma in the Colorado River Valley. This force, under James H. Carleton (1814–73), comprised some 2,500 volunteers from the Golden State. In comparison, Hunter had just sixty men. When word reached Hunter of the strong Union force, he prepared for a rapid withdrawal from Tucson, and awaited further news. Carleton sent a column of about three hundred men on the march toward Tucson. They received reports that as many as five hundred Rebels were in Tucson, and after a skirmish at Picacho Pass on April 15, 1862, retired back toward Yuma. On the way, they encountered troops from the 1st California Infantry. Reinforced they resumed the advance on Tucson. They reached Tucson on May 20, but discovered the Rebels had withdrawn to Mesilla, some six days earlier. Carleton arrived in early June. He proclaimed the creation of a new, Union, Territory of Arizona, with himself as Governor. Tucson served as a base for further New Mexico operations, but civil war combat in Arizona now came to an end.

ARKANSAS

"We have despised the enemy and laughed at their threats until, almost too late,
we find ourselves in their power."

—Washington (Ark.) Telegraph, February 26, 1862

Above: *The Confederate national flag, second pattern, carried into battle by the 9th Arkansas Infantry, which fought in many of the major battles of the Army of Tennessee, ending at the battle of Bentonville, North Carolina, in 1865, the last major action of the army in the war.*

Left: *Patrick Cleburne, the "Stonewall of the West" was born in Ireland and emigrated to the United States. Cleburne had served in the British army, and this military experience and his own talent enabled him to rise rapidly in the Confederate army. He was killed at the battle of Franklin in December 1864.*

Arkansas was part of the territory acquired by President Thomas Jefferson from Napoleon's France in the Louisiana Purchase of 1803. After the Missouri Compromise of 1820, it was the only territory of the Purchase where slavery was permitted. In 1824, the current western boundary was established for Arkansas Territory, and the part of it that is now the state of Oklahoma became Indian Territory. Arkansas was admitted to the Union as a slave state on June 15, 1836, balancing the admission of Free-Soil Michigan in January of the same year.

When the secession crisis erupted after the election of Abraham Lincoln as president in November 1860, Arkansas came closest of all the states of the "Upper South" to seceding. However, a narrow majority in its secession convention voted to remain in the Union, at least for the time being.

The call for militia volunteers after the Rebels fired on Fort Sumter led to the seizure of federal military installations in the state on the orders of Governor Henry M. Rector (1816–99) and the recall of the secession convention. Perhaps the most important post taken was Fort Smith, where the federal garrison retreated into Fort Wachita in the Indian Territory. On May 6, 1861, the secession convention voted with a single dissenter for an ordnance of secession. Arkansas was admitted to the Confederate States of America some twelve days later.

The state began recruiting troops immediately after the secession ordnance was passed and before it had even been admitted to the Confederacy. Troops drawn from the western part of the state around Fayetteville, formed a brigade commanded by Brigadier General N. B. Pearce. They were part of the force that fought at the battle of Wilson's Creek in August 1861, the first major battle in the western theater of the war. Pearce had waited at Maysville for the arrival of Rebel forces from Fort Smith and a badly-armed force under General Sterling Price that was retreating in the face of a well-equipped Union army under Brigadier General Nathaniel Lyon. Pearce helped Price by sending him some muskets, and the entire Rebel force united at Cassville, Missouri, before the battle, under Texas' Major General Ben McCulloch (1811–62). The Rebels won an important victory that forced the Union army out of southwestern Missouri, but McCulloch declined to pursue the beaten enemy, allowing the Union army to regroup at Rolla, Missouri.

The state's continuing problems with the Confederacy began in July 1861 with the appointment of Brigadier General William J. Hardee (1815–73) to organize the Confederate forces in Arkansas. Hardee was an experienced soldier, and did not like the

Above: *The CSS* Arkansas *was built at boatyards along the Mississippi River and the Yazoo. Although this was one of the smaller ironclads of the Confederate navy, it saw more combat than any other in the summer campaign of 1862 along the Mississippi River.*

amateur organizations that confronted him, many without arms or any semblance of uniform. Hardee declared his intention to fix these problems before undertaking any military operations. But when he tried to transfer the Arkansas regiments from state to Confederate control, many of the volunteers refused this change in their status, and went home. Those who remained formed a brigade that Hardee took across the Mississippi River to join the Rebel army of Mississippi, where they fought at Shiloh in April 1862, suffering heavily in a battle of heavy casualties.

McCulloch also recruited some of the original state volunteers into the Confederate army. However, he had bad relations with Price, a consequence of McCulloch's unwillingness to invade Missouri as Price wanted. The Confederate War Department appointed a new Confederate general to take charge of a Department of

the Trans-Mississippi, and established his headquarters at Pocahontas. Van Dorn had taken over command in a state that had been invaded by Union forces. In December 1861, Union Brigadier General Samuel R. Curtis (1805–66) had been ordered to drive the Rebels (effectively Price's troops) out of southwestern Missouri. He began his advance in January 1862 with considerable success. On February 17, Curtis was at Sugar Creek, Arkansas, skirmishing with Price's men. Although Price caused enough casualties to halt Curtis's advance. Curtis still managed to secure both Bentonville and, more importantly, Fayetteville, which had served as the mustering point for the Rebel forces that had advanced into Missouri the previous year.

Van Dorn received news of the fall of Fayetteville on February 23. He ordered his scattered command, which included a brigade of Indian troops under Arkansan

Albert Pike, to assemble at Elm Springs, only eleven miles from Bentonville. Van Dorn ordered his army forward on March 4, and quickly recaptured Bentonville when the Union force there evacuated the town after burning any supplies that could not be carried. The Rebels followed the retreating Union troops closely and soon found the main Union army.

Curtis had ordered his army to block the roads and construct earthworks on the side of his position at Sugar Creek facing the Rebel concentration at Elm Springs. Van Dorn recognized that his force would be unlikely to sustain a frontal assault on the Union position, and planned to attack the Union left flank on March 7. In order to fool Curtis, Van Dorn took his flanking force into position for the attack on the night of March 6–7, but left its campfires burning.

Effective Union scouting, which included Western hero Wild Bill Hickcock, detected Van Dorn's flanking move, so Curtis was not surprised by Van Dorn's maneuver. He had shifted some troops so that when the Rebel guns began firing around 10 a.m., there were Union guns able to reply. Van Dorn then launched some regimental-sized charges to eliminate the Union guns, but awaited McCulloch's assault toward Curtis's front before ordering a general advance.

McCulloch had trouble organizing his disparate command, which included the troops from Indian Territory as well as most of the Arkansas troops, but finally he pushed his division forward. The Union defenses were well organized, but the Rebel advantage in numbers ensured that the Union troops were driven back. While trying to repel a Union counterattack, McCulloch was shot dead and the Rebel advance ground to a halt. McCulloch's command withstood a number of Union attacks before withdrawing, as this time the numerical advantage swung the Union way.

Van Dorn was unaware of McCulloch's death, and waited until 2 p.m. for news from that quarter of the battlefield. He then decided to wait no longer and ordered Price's Missouri division into the attack. Price

and Van Dorn seized the position occupied by the troops moved by Curtis to counter the Rebel flank march, but night fell before either side could do much more. Under the cover of darkness they both regrouped, but the Rebels learned they were short of ammunition. Their daring maneuver had put the Union forces between the Rebels and their supplies to catastrophic effect.

The next day it was Curtis's turn to attack. The Union guns bombarded the Rebel positions. The Rebel guns replied until, one by one, they ran out of ammunition and were pulled out of the line. When only one battery was firing, the Union troops formed up. When it fell silent, they charged. The Rebel line collapsed in an embarrassing rout. By the beginning of April, Van Dorn was back in Pocahontas with his army.

He had already received order to bring his troops across the Mississippi to join the Army of Mississippi at Corinth. Van Dorn took his troops across the river, which left hardly a Rebel soldier in Arkansas, except for some state militia, who were not much value for anything but garrison duty.

Union Brigadier General Sam Curtis's victory at Pea Ridge in March had left him holding the field in Arkansas. Van Dorn and Price eventually marched away to Corinth, and the Rebels had no force in Arkansas that could oppose the Federals in the field. However, it was difficult to keep his army supplied in northwestern Arkansas, a remote area of America in 1862. He moved only slowly toward Little Rock. The appointment of Brigadier General Thomas Hindman (1828–68), a

Left: *A ten-dollar bill issued by the state of Arkansas to give its local economy some liquidity. Throughout the war the Confederacy was hampered by a shortage of specie, gold and silver coinage.*

Right: The end of the CSS Arkansas, according to Union Commander William Porter. He claimed to have destroyed the Rebel ironclad in an engagement on the Mississippi River in August 1862. In fact, the ship's engines had been badly damaged in an earlier battle some weeks before. Porter came upon the vessel, which had been set alight by her own crew, and tried to get the credit for the Arkansas' self destruction.

THE UNION GUN-BOAT "ESSEX" (COMMANDER PORTER) DESTROYING THE REBEL IRON-CLAD RAM "ARKANSAS," IN THE MISSISSIPPI.—[SEE PAGE 571.]

former congressman and veteran of Shiloh, as Rebel commander in Arkansas, and his skillful shuffling of the few troops available to him and the use of deception convinced Curtis that Little Rock would not fall easily. He also energetically recruited volunteers and conscripted the less willing in order to give himself some kind of army. Curtis, with the permission of the war department in Washington, changed his target to Helena. His army, located here, would be easier to keep supplied and better able to cooperate with the overall Union plan to take control of the Mississippi as the first stage in their conquest of the South.

Having reached Jacksonsport on the White River, Curtis was running low on supplies. Rebel batteries at Saint Charles blocked the possibility of resupply by the river. Curtis requested naval support and received it in the form of the USS *Mound City* and other vessels. The action at Saint Charles on June 17, 1862, saw the *Mound City* badly damaged when a shot blew up one of her boilers and scaled some 125 of her crew to death. But a regiment of infantry managed to turn the flank of the batteries and the Rebels abandoned them.

Curtis encountered a Rebel force at Cache River on July 7, and his troops turned initial Rebel success into a rout. Five days later, Curtis's army reached Helena, but there were still Rebel forces between him and Little Rock. The Union drive down the Mississippi had been distracted by the Confederate invasion of Kentucky in spring 1862, and Curtis chose to turn Helena into a fortress, constructing earthworks around the city.

Meanwhile Hindman had lost command of the Department of the Trans-Mississippi when he tried to impose martial law, but he gained command of a new army assembling in northwestern Arkansas, which would be used to invade Missouri. Before the Rebels could strike, more Union troops poured over the border from Missouri, led by Brigadier General James Blunt and the Kansas division.

Blunt clashed with Brigadier General John S. Marmaduke's Rebel cavalry division at Cane Hill, where it was screening the concentration of Hindman's infantry. With superior numbers, Blunt routed the Rebel cavalry before they had been able to deploy properly. Blunt sent word to Brigadier General Francis Herron, still in Missouri with the remaining Union forces, to hurry forward, while the Kansas Division established a defensive position at Cane Hill.

Hindman saw a good opportunity to defeat not Blunt but Herron. A seesaw battle ensued at Prairie Grove on December 7, with the Rebels beating off all Union attacks by nightfall. However, they were now low on ammunition and supplies and had to withdraw to Van Buren. Many of his men believed they had won and deserted in disgust.

Little Rock was finally taken on September 11, 1863, after the engagement at Bayou Fourche saw entrenched Rebel defenders driven out of their positions by Union artillery and cavalry. Fort Smith had already fallen to Union forces on August 31. The Union forces now controlled all the major towns of both northern and central Arkansas.

The last major campaign in Arkansas was the Camden Expedition of 1864. This was part of a coordinated advance from the Union enclave around New Orleans up the Red River and forces from Little Rock aiming at Camden and then Shreveport, Louisiana. On April 13, 1864, General Price attempted to halt the Union advance by attacking the rearguard of the Union column at Prairie D'Ane. Price was unable to gain any advantage, and Camden was occupied a few days later.

However, Rebel bushwhackers and guerrillas made it difficult to control the roads back to the Union supply bases, and in the end Union forces had to withdraw. On their way back to Little Rock, the Union troops were caught by Rebels while trying to cross the Saline River. The engagement on April 30 saw repeated Rebel attacks fail to stop the Union forces from crossing the river, and the Union column that had been forced to withdraw from Camden was able to reach Little Rock.

Although there were many more skirmishes in Arkansas, there were no more major engagements or campaigns. The war ended in Arkansas with the surrender of the Trans-Mississippi Department on May 26, 1865.

The most prominent Arkansan of the war was not actually born there. Patrick Ronayne Cleburne (1828–64) was born in County Cork, Ireland. After serving in the British army, he emigrated to the United States and worked as a druggist and a real estate lawyer. His prominence in his community and military experience saw him gain rapid promotion after he joined the Arkansas State Troops. By the fall of 1861 he was commanding a brigade in Hardee's division of the Army of Central Kentucky. He fought at both Shiloh and the siege of Corinth.

In December 1862 he was promoted to major general and took command of a division, where he distinguished himself at Chickamauga and in covering the retreat of the Army of Tennessee from Chattanooga. Cleburne earned the nickname "Stonewall of the West" for his excellent service on the field. Cleburne was one of a handful of Confederate officers who supported recruiting slaves to overcome the Confederacy's manpower crisis of 1863–64. After fighting in the campaign in defense of Atlanta, he advanced into Tennessee with the rest of the Army of Tennessee in Hood's attempt to capture Nashville. He was killed at the battle of Franklin, on November 20, 1864, having opposed what he regarded as a suicidal assault on the Union position.

CALIFORNIA

"The Rebel army is now the legitimate property of the Army of the Potomac."

—Joseph Hooker, shortly before he was soundly defeated by Robert E. Lee at Chancellorsville

The United States acquired the territory that encompasses the state of California under the terms of the Treaty of Guadalupe Hidalgo, signed on February 2, 1848, which brought the Mexican War of 1846–48 to an end. The population of California at this time amounted to some 15,000 white inhabitants (plus 24,000 Indians of various tribes). It was as remote from its former masters in Mexico City as it was to the new distant overlord in Washington. The discovery of gold in northern California on January 24, 1848, was the spark that transformed this situation. News reached Washington in August of that year, and as word spread across the United States, the prospect of finding wealth in the rivers of a territory reckoned to have a healthy, inviting climate, with fertile soil and plenty of land for the taking, caused a rush of population. By 1860, the population of California had increased tenfold, to 379,994.

California took a different route to statehood from the remainder of the territories taken from Mexico. On July 4, 1848, the United States officially took possession and established a military government over the state. Local civil authorities took over from the military on

Above: *A captain of the 1st US Dragoons, 1860. Perhaps the most prestigious regiment in the antebellum army, they were based in California.*

Left: *Henry "Old Brains" Halleck, who ended the war as Chief of Staff of the US Army, was perhaps a better strategist and administrator than a battlefield commander.*

December 20, 1849, and statehood was granted on September 9, 1850. One of the reasons for the unusual route to statehood followed by California was the question of whether the state would be admitted as a slave state or a free state. In December 1848, President James K. Polk recommended the extension of the Missouri Compromise 36° 30' N line to the Pacific. This would have permitted slavery in such places as Bakersfield, Los Angeles, and San Diego. The matter of slavery in the conquered territories, however, had already arisen in 1846, with the Wilmot Proviso crisis (see page 14). However, Mexico had abolished slavery some twenty years before, so the current residents of the territory had no strong enthusiasm for the institution.

Newly elected President Zachary Taylor, inaugurated in March 1849, invited California to apply for statehood, and the subsequent constitution it submitted to Congress did not permit slavery. The admission of California as a free state would upset the equal balance of senators from slave and free states, since there was no slave state awaiting admission. California was only admitted as part of the Compromise of 1850.

Service in California drew many of the officers who became prominent during the Civil War. A large US military force was based in the state, including the famous 1st Regiment of Dragoons, who served all across the Far West in the years before the Civil War. Albert Sidney Johnston, William T. Sherman, and U. S. Grant, who would face each other on the battlefield of Shiloh, were among the officers who passed through California at some time in their career. In 1861, some Californians of Southern origin sympathized with their kin and sought to add their own state, at least in part, to the Confederacy. They pinned their hopes on the fact that the commander of the Department of California, Albert Sidney Johnston, was a resident of Texas. He might have been able to hand over some of the state's military installations to secession-minded militia. Albert Johnston refused to conspire in such an act, however, and California remained resolutely pro-Union throughout the war.

With the battlefields of the war so very distant, California troops played a secondary role in the conflict. A handful of Californians fought in the battles in the east. The main military effort made against the Confederacy was California's contribution to the campaign against the Rebel attempts to seize the southern half of the Territory of New Mexico.

The Rebels had successfully taken control of much of the Rio Grande valley and of Tucson, when Brigadier General James H. Carleton (1814–73) was ordered to organize and lead a force against them. He assembled the "California Column" at Fort Yuma on the Colorado River. The column consisted entirely of California-raised troops. Apart from some small skirmishes in Arizona, these troops saw little action, and by the time they reached the Rio Grande Valley, the

Above: *John C. Fremont made his reputation by conducting surveys of trails and routes in the West used by many pioneers during the antebellum growth of the population to the Pacific coast. His military service during the Civil War, however, was unremarkable.*

Rebels had already been driven back into Texas. The march across waterless, infertile terrain was a logistical masterpiece, however. Carleton divided his column, nearly 2,500 strong, into smaller groups and sent them along slightly different routes so that there would be enough water and fodder for all. Apart from this single instance of participation in a campaign against the Rebels, California troops spent most of their wartime fighting Indians or protecting mail and telegraph routes that connected the state with the East. Carleton's troops who remained in New Mexico, for example, campaigned against Cochise and the Chiricahua Apache.

Some Californian troops did see combat in the East. A 1st Californian Regiment was organized by Edward Baker. The regiment took part in the fiasco of the battle of Ball's Bluff, Virginia, October 21, 1861. Baker was killed in the action, and the Californians made an ignominious withdrawal back across the Potomac river.

Three important Union generals were associated with California. John C. Frémont (1813–90), nicknamed "the Pathfinder" for his exploits in crossing the far West, was born in Georgia. This was ironic, since he became a leading light of the nascent Republican Party in the 1850s. He served as a senator from California and was the first of that party's candidates for president, in the election of 1856. Frémont was strongly in favor of abolition and found plenty of patronage from Republican faithfuls at the outset of the war to receive an important army post. Lincoln was compelled to appoint him one of the first four Major Generals in the Union army, and gave him command of the Department of the West. This, too, was a logical appointment, since Frémont was the son-in-law of Thomas Hart Benton, a power in pre-Civil War Missouri politics.

Frémont presented a very energetic façade, but did not have much luck on the battlefield, his subordinate Nathaniel Lyon losing the battle of Wilson's Creek (August 1861), which was followed by the capitulation of the Union garrison at Lexington, Missouri, in September. Frémont's ferocious abolitionism was his

undoing. On August 30, 1861, he issued an extraordinary decree that freed all the slaves of Rebel leaders in Missouri, imposed martial law, and placed all civil authorities under his direct control. The political firestorm that followed consumed Frémont, and eventually he was posted to the relative backwater of western Virginia. Under Lincoln's patronage, he plotted an invasion of the pro-union region of east Tennessee. This campaign was abandoned to counter the threat posed by Stonewall Jackson's army in his famous Valley campaign of 1862. Frémont suffered throughout the campaign from "the slows," a common fault among Union commanders at this stage of the war: He allowed Jackson to escape a trap, and he failed to march to the sounds of the guns of a battle nearby. When Lincoln added Frémont's corps to a new army and appointed a junior general to command, the affronted "Pathfinder" resigned his commission. Republicans opposed to Lincoln flirted briefly with winning for him the Republican nomination for president in 1864.

Frémont's successor in St. Louis was another Californian, Henry Halleck (1815–72), nicknamed "Old Brains." Halleck had been born in New York, but in 1854 left the army and settled in San Francisco. Friends in high places secured him an appointment as major general in August 1861. He was appointed commander of the Department of Missouri with his headquarters in St. Louis. Halleck earned his nickname for his various prewar writings, which included a translation of Henri Jomini's *Vie Politique et Militaire de Napoleon*, a French manual that was the standard text at West Point in classes on strategy. Halleck's war was largely spent behind the lines, and was most famous for his feuding with Grant, a general of whom Halleck had a low opinion. "Old Brains" was very lucky in succeeding Frémont. He was able to claim credit for a series of victories, including forts Henry and Donelson, the taking of Island Number 10, Pea Ridge, and Shiloh. Unfortunately, these battles were all won by his subordinates, and Halleck's own campaign, against

Corinth in April–May 1862, was fought like a textbook exercise as his army lumbered forward, allowing the Rebels to escape. Lincoln made Halleck his commander in chief, where he proved a capable administrator, but phrased his instructions in an oracular manner that enabled him to blame his subordinates when things went wrong. Grant made it a condition of his accepting overall command of the Union armies that Halleck be moved sideways to a chief of staff role.

Joseph Hooker (1814–1879), like Halleck, left the army to settle in California. This egotistical intriguer, unlike the other two Californians, spent the first part of his war in the East. He established a good reputation for himself as a fighter while in command of a division during the Seven Days' campaign in spring 1862. He was promoted to major general in May 1862, and led a corps in the battle of Antietam in September 1862. At Fredericksburg in December, he commanded the Center Grand Division. He was angered by Union Commander Ambrose Burnside's disastrous tactical battle plan and Burnside tried to remove him from command. Instead, Hooker got Burnside's job as commander of the Army of the Potomac when Lincoln overcame his suspicions of a man who had called for a military dictatorship. Hooker did much to restore the morale of the troops, disheartened by the slaughter at Fredericksburg, but when he attacked Lee near Chancellorsville, Virginia, in May 1863, Hooker seemed to lose his nerve for combat. He resigned his command when he failed to get reinforcements he requested, and was transferred to the western theater. Here he again performed well in a corps command at both Lookout Mountain, Tennessee, and Atlanta. But when he was not appointed to command of the Army of Tennessee, after the death of that army's commander, he requested to be relieved of his command.

Below: Joseph Hooker's (1814–79) Civil War career was one of ups and downs. He proved a good corps commander in several battles. As an army commander though he was totally outclassed by Lee at Chancellorsville in May 1863.

COLORADO

"They were so badly mutilated and covered with sand and water that it was very hard for me to tell one from another."

—John S. Smith, Indian agent, on the aftermath of the Sand Creek massacre of 1864

Congress created Colorado Territory out of bits and pieces of land acquired at different times. The eastern half was a part of the Louisiana Purchase, a sliver of the center was land claimed by Texas on its independence, and the western part was ceded by Mexico under the terms of the Treaty of Guadalupe Hidalgo, which ended the Mexican War of 1846–48. In 1860, the area was divided between Kansas Territory, New Mexico Territory, Utah Territory, and Nebraska Territory. However, in 1859 some of the residents of Colorado had petitioned Congress for a territorial government, and with the granting of statehood to the eastern portion of Kansas, the western part of its territory was added to a new entity, the Territory of Colorado, which largely followed its present borders.

There was never any likelihood that Colorado would become part of the Confederacy. Four regiments, plus a battery of light artillery, were raised from Colorado during the war. The first three regiments started the Civil War as infantry, but they were converted to cavalry units in 1862–63.

Colorado troops were part of the forces that repelled the Rebel invasion of New Mexico Territory in 1862. They played a crucial role in the battle of Glorieta Pass. During the first encounter between the two forces, Colorado troops, under Major John Chivington (1821–94), met and defeated a Confederate reconnaissance party trying to locate the advancing Union column.

The battle of Glorieta Pass itself occurred on March 28, 1862. Once again, Chivington was in the forefront of the fighting. The commander of the Union forces, Colorado Colonel John Slough (1829–67), sent Chivington on a flanking movement while he engaged the Rebels from the front. Slough's army fought for six hours until they were pressed back by the Rebels. Just then Chivington attacked the Rebel wagon train, capturing it and most of the Rebel supplies of ammunition. Thus, although Slough had lost the battle on the field, Chivington's success transformed the battle into a strategic Union victory. The Rebels were forced to retreat back to Santa Fe where they could draw more ammunition. The battle ended with both sides retreating back to their bases.

The rest of Colorado's involvement in the Civil War was largely spent in campaigns against Native Americans. The crisis came in 1864, and resulted in an utterly needless war that was largely the responsibility of the white settlers. The Native Americans of the region were predominantly peaceful toward whites, although toward one another long-standing feuds continued. Raiding parties prosecuting these feuds, such as that between the Cheyenne and the Utes, were none too particular about where they found their provisions. A white settler's stock was taken to eat if it was convenient. Furthermore, the problems of straying stock created the kind of misunderstandings that were exploited by settler leaders who saw the Native Americans as an impediment to progress. Colorado Governor John Evans and Colonel Chivington used this pretext to launch punitive raids that became a serious war. Chivington earned eternal infamy for his part in the 1864 Sand Creek massacre when two hundred peaceable Cheyenne and Arapaho were killed.

The 2nd Colorado Cavalry served in the Department of the Missouri in 1863–64 to protect the border of Kansas and parts of Missouri against the Rebel guerrillas who fought a war of detachment. McLane's Independent Battery also fought in the Missouri-Arkansas area, including action against Price's 1864 raid into Missouri. (See p. 145).

Left: The Civil War monument outside the capitol building in Denver. Colorado raised four regiments and a light artillery battery for the Union Army during the Civil War. Their battle honors include Glorieta Pass where they contributed to the defeat of Confederate forces in New Mexico.

CONNECTICUT

"They couldn't hit an elephant at this distance."

—Major General John Sedgwick, May 9, 1864, just before being shot by a Rebel sharpshooter

Dutch traders first arrived on Connecticut's shores in 1614. English settlers from Massachusetts Bay Colony followed them. Massachusetts declared independence from England in 1776 and was the fifth state to ratify the US Constitution.

No battles were fought in Connecticut during the Civil War. Connecticut raised thirty regiments of infantry (two of them African American), five batteries of artillery, and one cavalry regiment.

The 14th Connecticut Infantry Regiment served with the Army of the Potomac and monuments to its service stand on both the Antietam and Gettysburg battlefield parks. The 14th was mustered in at Hartford in August 1862, and was attached to the Union 2nd Corps. Within four weeks of its entering service, it was involved in the bloodiest single day's battle in American history. As part of French's Division in Sumner's corps, the 14th Connecticut advanced to the Sunken Road and stood up to some of the worst fighting on the whole battlefield. The official report by the brigade commander stated: "The men in my brigade were all new troops, hastily raised, and without drill or experience, and although under fire for the first time, behaved with great gallantry. In front of the last position held by the 14th Connecticut more than 1,000 of the enemy lie slain." The 14th also experienced the

Above: *Chasseur's pattern cap with regimental insignia, actually that of Capt. Selleck L. White, 10th Connecticut Infantry.*

Left: *Major General John Sedgwick's McClellan saddle. The Connecticut-born Sedgwick proved an exceptional corps commander, on more than one occasion being entrusted with an important independent role, as during the Chancellorsville campaign in 1863. He was shot by a Rebel sharpshooter battery in May 1864.*

catastrophic assault on Marye's Heights at Fredericksburg, being included in one of the waves that advanced to their destruction in front of the Stone Wall. Revenge for these defeats came at Gettysburg, where the 14th was positioned on Cemetery Ridge to receive Pickett's charge and engaged the flank of Pettigrew's Brigade of the Rebel army. The 14th also fought in all the major battles in Grant's Overland campaign of 1864 and participated in the siege of Petersburg. At war's end, it had suffered the highest proportion of casualties of any of Connecticut's regiments.

Connecticut also produced one of the best commanders of the Army of the Potomac, Major General John Sedgwick (1813–64). He was born in Cornwall Hollow and entered West Point with the Class of 1837. At the battle of Spotsylvania in May 1864, he was shot dead by a Rebel sharpshooter while deploying his corps artillery.

Rear Admiral Andrew Foote (1806–63), born in New Haven, attended both West Point and Annapolis. He held strongly abolitionist views. When the Civil War began he was put in charge of naval forces on the Mississippi. He worked with Ulysses Grant to capture forts Henry and Donelson in February 1862. In 1866 he was given command of the South Atlantic Blockading Squadron, but died en route.

DAKOTA

"Hell with the fires burned out."

—Brigadier General Alfred Sully's description of the Little Missouri Badlands

The Dakota Territory was carved out of Nebraska Territory and Minnesota Territory in the general reorganization of the American West by Congress in 1861. It embraced present-day North Dakota and South Dakota, the northern part of Wyoming, and most of Montana. (The Montana area was detached with the creation of Montana Territory in 1864.) Very few non-Native Americans lived in the area, mostly occupants of trading posts whose presence was valued by the Native American tribes. The few who did enter Dakota were just passing through on their way to the mines of the Rocky Mountains. The main value of the Dakota Territory was, in fact, to provide a place for Sioux and other Northern Plains tribes to continue their traditional way of life, moving them out of Minnesota where white settlement was growing rapidly.

In the months after the bombardment of Fort Sumter on April 12, 1861, most of the regular army troops in the area were withdrawn and the patrolling of the Native American frontier fell to locally recruited volunteers. Two companies of cavalry were raised in the Dakota Territory in the fall of 1861 to replace the lost regulars.

Governor Jayne opened recruiting stations at Yankton, Vermillion, and Bon Homme, towns just on the Dakota side of the Missouri River. The first of these companies, Company A, was mustered into the United States's service for three years or the duration of the war at Yankton in April 1862. Company B was organized about a year later at Sioux City, Iowa. By the time Company B entered service, a major war had broken out with Sioux Indians, initially in Minnesota. Given the nomadic way of life followed by the Sioux, it was only a matter of time before the military response to the Native American raids on settlements in western Minnesota resulted in

Left: *John Pope had much more success in the West than in the East. Pope was overmatched by the combination of Robert E. Lee and Stonewall Jackson in the East, and was badly defeated at the second battle of Bull Run. But in Minnesota and the Dakota he successfully suppressed the Sioux in 1863.*

an expedition into Dakota Territory, where the Sioux on the warpath had gone to Devil's Lake.

Two columns were sent into Dakota Territory during the summer of 1863 in search of the perpetrators of the raids. Had they been coordinated, they might have forced the Sioux further west with little loss of life. But they went in separately, encouraging the Sioux to think they could successfully attack the US troops. The four battles that ensued—Big Mound, Deep Buffalo Lake, Stony Lake, and Whitestone Hill—were catastrophic for the Sioux. Nearly five hundred Sioux warriors were killed, with the loss of perhaps fifty US soldiers.

Another punitive expedition advanced into Dakota in 1864 under the command of Brigadier General Alfred Sully. They found the Sioux encamped on Killdeer Mountain on July 28, 1864. Sully, with 2,200 men, believed himself to be outnumbered, although the Sioux afterward claimed they had no more than 1,600 braves. Sully formed a huge square out of his entire command. The Sioux attacked in traditional style, rushing up to the soldiers' lines and firing before running off again. At one point, an attack on the rear of the formation nearly broke through, but Sully rushed some of his artillery, which drove the Sioux off. After nearly a full day of fighting, the Sioux concluded they could not succeed. They formed a defensive line to give their families time to escape off the mountain. Sully mounted one of his battalions and sent it on a charge up the mountain, but the wooded terrain was too favorable to the Sioux. After scattering a number of the Sioux, the soldiers retired. Sully then bombarded the mountain until nightfall. When the Sioux retreated, they left much of their supplies and tents behind. Sully campaigned for the rest of the summer, but secured no lasting victory.

DELAWARE

"Success is not in my hands; to do my duty is."

—Rear Admiral Samuel F. DuPont

The state of Delaware was one of the original thirteen British colonies that participated in the Continental Congresses prior to the Declaration of Independence in 1776. Delaware officially joined the United States of America when its delegates to the Continental Congress signed the Articles of Confederation on February 22, 1779.

Although Delaware legally permitted slavery in 1860, and although Lincoln's candidacy ran only third here in the election of 1860, there was little likelihood that Delaware would secede. The impact of slavery on Delaware's economy was dwarfed by the burgeoning industrial power of Wilmington. Only about 2 percent of Delaware's population were African-American slaves. The governor, Democrat William Burton, invited Mississippi Judge Henry Dickinson to address a joint session of the state legislature on January 3, 1861. Having listened to his explanations of why Mississippi acted as she did, the two houses passed a resolution disapproving of secession.

Delaware's commitment to the Union cause was wholehearted. Some ten regiments of infantry were recruited, and a regiment of cavalry, plus artillery. The 1st Delaware Infantry suffered the heaviest casualties of all, serving with the II Corps of the Army of the Potomac at such battles as Fredericksburg and Gettysburg.

Many prisoners taken at Gettysburg wound up at a Delaware prison camp, Fort Delaware. They were kept

Above: *City of Wilmington, five cent note, 1862.*

Left: *Flag Officer Samuel DuPont was Delaware's most notable Civil War figure. A scion of the DuPont industrial family, Samuel DuPont played a major role in naval campaigns during the first two years of the war.*

in wooden barracks, which theoretically was a better fate than those condemned to live under canvas elsewhere in Union prisons. After the battle of Gettysburg, however, conditions at Fort Delaware deteriorated when 13,000 Rebels were packed into the fortress.

Rations were poor, and at times the prisoners were given rats by their guards to supplement their meager food. Nearly 3,000 Rebel soldiers died in captivity here. Many were buried at Finn's Point National Cemetery.

The most prominent Civil War commander with Delaware associations was Samuel Francis DuPont (1803–65) of the US Navy. DuPont had a distinguished record from his service as a naval officer during the Mexican War, helping to defeat enemy forces in California. During the against the South, DuPont initially acted on the Commission of Conference, the body that developed the strategy of blockading Southern ports. This was a crucial element in defeating the Rebels. Du Pont's major active service command was in charge of the South Atlantic Squadron. He conducted the naval part of the operations that secured and built up Port Royal, South Carolina, as a Union base in the south for the squadron. His other major engagement was an attempt to break into Charleston harbor in 1863, using a fleet of ironclads. The failure of this operation led to his eventual removal from command of the South Atlantic Squadron.

DISTRICT OF
COLUMBIA

"He is one of the thousands of unknown American young men in the ranks...the real & royal precious ones of this land, giving themselves up...in their country's cause."

—Walt Whitman's letter to the parents of Erastus Haskell, August 10, 1863

The District of Columbia first came into existence on a piece of paper. Article 1, Section 8, of the United States constitution referred to a capital district. The location of this district was a matter of some debate for the first two years of the Washington administration. At the end March 1791, Washington surveyed for the first time the proposed site of the city, along the Potomac river, between the towns of Georgetown, Maryland, and Alexandria, Virginia. During the summer and autumn of 1800, the federal government moved from Philadelphia to the site, and Congress took control of "Washington and the Territory of Columbia," as it was often known in its early years.

The District of Columbia was, strictly speaking, not a state. It had no representation in Congress. Its affairs were administered directly by the government. (Although, in 1846, the citizens of the Virginia portion of the federal district voted in a referendum to return to Virginia. The referendum was sanctioned by Congress, however.) More importantly, surrounded on all sides by the slave-holding states of Maryland and Virginia and considering itself to be a Southern city meant that the sympathies of its citizens lay more with the Southern states that seceded, than with the Northern states that defended it.

Above: *The war department (left) and navy department (right) buildings in the city of Washington. Unlike during the twentieth century wars, these departments did not expand much beyond the hundred or so workers of the antebellum years.*

Left: *Abraham Lincoln was known in Washington for his easygoing Midwestern manners. He was known to wander over to the war and navy department buildings in his carpet slippers for an informal review of events.*

Federal officials recognized this problem from the start. At Lincoln's inauguration on March 4, 1861, sharpshooters were stationed on rooftops and in the windows of the wings of the Capitol building overlooking the stand where the inauguration would take place. Artillery batteries stood at three points in the city ready to ride to Capitol Hill if necessary. Cavalry stood watch over the more important road junctions along the route of the inaugural procession. A double file of mounted men guarded the sides of the President Lincoln's carriage. This was a clear demonstration of insecurity.

All this occurred when the nearest militiaman of a seceded state stood guard over three hundred miles away. Following the firing on Fort Sumter on April 12, 1861, and Lincoln's call for troops on April 14, Virginia was propelled into the Confederacy, adopting an ordinance of secession on April 17. Suddenly, the potentially hostile militiamen were just over the river.

The federal government's most urgent need was now for troops to help defend the capital. Fortunately, the 6th Massachusetts Regiment, the best-equipped volunteer unit in the Bay State, left the very day Virginia seceded. They reached Baltimore on April 19, where they opened fire on a pro-secession crowd that

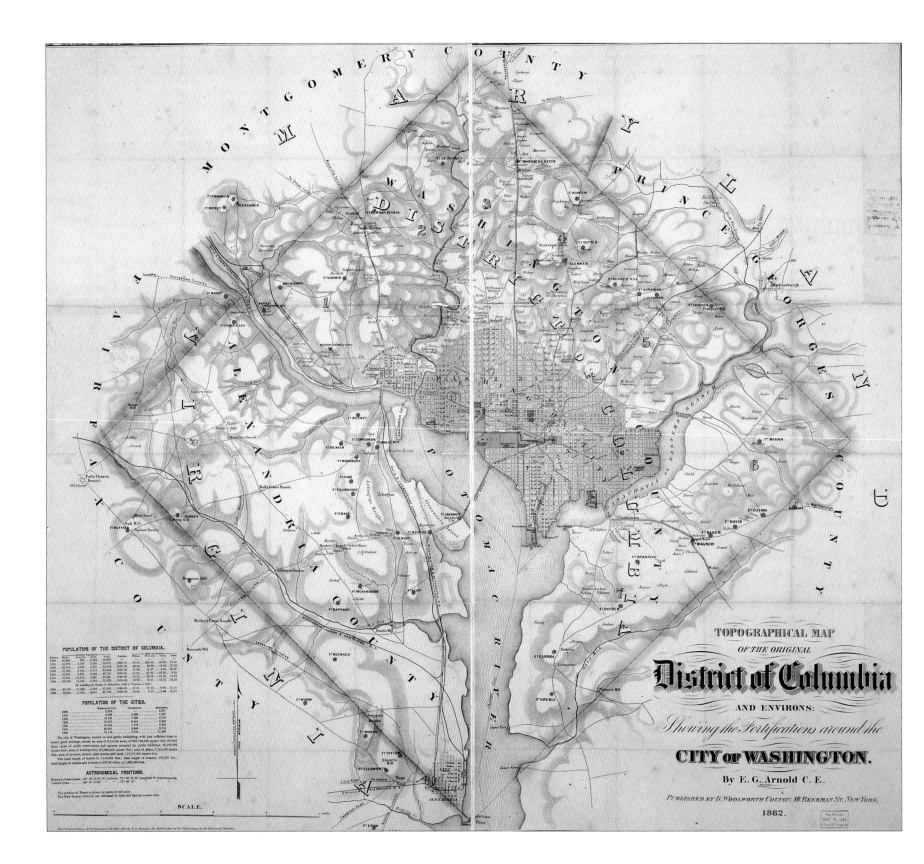

TOPOGRAPHICAL MAP
OF THE ORIGINAL
District of Columbia
AND ENVIRONS:
Showing the Fortifications around the
CITY OF WASHINGTON.
By E. G. Arnold C. E.
PUBLISHED BY G. WOOLWORTH COLTON, 18 BEEKMAN ST. NEW YORK.
1862.

endeavored to block their passage through the city. In the wake of these events, angry Marylanders tore up railroad bridges and telegraph lines that crossed their state, cutting off communications between the city of Washington and the Northern states.

Surrounded on all sides by secession-minded territory and with only a single regiment of Union soldiers quartered in the city, Washington was at its most vulnerable. General Winfield Scott (1776–68), the Union commander in chief, summoned the Union-minded militia companies of the city of Washington to put sandbags around the most defensible public buildings in the capital. On April 24, a worried Lincoln ventured the view that, "I don't believe there is any North." However the next day, the 7th New York Regiment arrived and more Massachusetts troops

reached Washington soon after. These re-established communications with the North, and the most dangerous moment in the Civil War for Washington now passed. Union troops now began to arrive in the capital on a regular basis.

Washington now turned into the central bastion of the Union war effort. As the field army assembled, the capital became a training ground for the newly enrolled regiments. Firearms and artillery were stockpiled, along with supplies of cattle and flour. The soldiers began to construct the ring of fortifications that would encircle the capital for the duration of the war. The Union high command also began to develop the strategy that would be used to suppress the rebellion of the Southern states. The plan, christened by journalists as "the Anaconda plan," was described by Scott in a letter dated

Opposite: *A commercial topographical map of the District of Columbia, compiled by civil engineer E. G. Arnold for G. Woolworth Colton. An intriguing handwritten note by one W. C. Dodge appears on the original. It states: "This map was suppressed by the Govt. because of the information it would give the rebels. I got this copy in 1862 and have had it ever since."*

Left: *Fort Corcoran in 1861, one of the sixty-eight forts erected around the city of Washington to protect the federal capital. The troops are members of the 69th New York Infantry, the "Fighting 69th," and the fort was named for its commanding officer, Colonel Michael Corcoran, standing boldly on the parapet. In the foreground are some grapeshot rounds for the fort's howitzers.*

May 3, written from Washington to one of his officers:

"We rely greatly on the sure operation of a complete blockade of the Atlantic and Gulf ports soon to commence. In connection with such blockade we propose a powerful movement down the Mississippi to the ocean, with a cordon of posts at proper points…the object being to clear out and keep open this great line of communication in connection with the strict blockade of the sea-board, so as to envelop the insurgent States and bring them to terms with less bloodshed than by any other plan."

One of the first steps taken to ensure the security of the city of Washington after the arrival of a large military force was to occupy strategic points on the Virginia shore of the Potomac River. Rebel forces had occupied Alexandria, Virginia, and also established batteries on the riverbank. On May 24, Union troops crossed the Potomac using boats and bridges and took the city from the Rebels. The Rebel militia withdrew, burning railroad bridges as they went. Several other points were seized, including Arlington, the home of former US Army officer Robert E. Lee. The newly appointed commander of the Army of Northeastern Virginia, Brigadier General Irvin McDowell, now stationed some of his troops on Virginia soil.

Very little work on long-term fortifications on the federal capital was done before the first battle of Bull Run on July 21, 1861. A substantial part of the Union force routed off the battlefield here, and it seemed as if the road to Washington was open. Had the Rebel army not been as much an amateur effort at this stage of the war as their Union counterpart, at the very least they could have laid siege to the federal capital.

McDowell's successor, Major General George B. McClellan, assessed the situation he confronted. On August 3, he decided that he faced an army of Rebels, 100,000 strong. In the face of such a force (about three times the actual Rebel strength) Washington was too weakly defended. He appointed Major John G. Barnard (1815–82) to construct strong defenses. Barnard and his engineers chose the sites of their forts with care. Roads and railroads were covered with forts. Batteries were sited to control shipping on the Potomac and fords across the river. Entrenchments were dug in between the forts for infantry to defend. A network of military roads was built to enable the rapid movement of reinforcements to threatened sectors of the lines. The development of this continued throughout the war, turning the city of Washington into a fortress.

All these fortifications were earthworks. Parapets with dry moats were heaped up to a height of as much as eighteen feet. Abatis (sharpened wooden stakes) were positioned in front, and fields of fire were cleared to a distance of two miles. The artillery pieces within were positioned to give wide arcs of fire.

At the end of the war, sixty-eight forts and ninety-three batteries connected by twenty miles of trenches and rifle pits ringed the capital. They contained 807 cannons and ninety-eight mortars. It is little wonder that the Rebels never seriously tested a position that could only have been taken with very heavy casualties.

Instead, the Confederate army focused its efforts against Washington in the field of intelligence. Even before the fighting had started, Colonel Thomas Jordan had established a network, led by Rose O'Neal Greenhow, that gave useful information about the movements of the Union troops before Bull Run. As the war progressed, the Confederacy established a "Secret Line," which smuggled information out of Washington along a network of secret agents connecting the Washington and Baltimore areas to Richmond, Virginia. Even the group centered around Rose Greenhow survived her arrest and continued to supply intelligence of the Union war effort.

The city of Washington only once came under direct attack during the war. In June 1864, Lieutenant General Jubal Early received orders from General Robert E. Lee to make a threatening move toward the federal capital from the Shenandoah Valley. Union forces were at this time close to the Rebel capital at Richmond, Virginia.

Their forces outnumbered Lee's Army of Northern Virginia by a considerable number. Lee hoped that an advance by Early on Washington would compel Union commander U. S. Grant to transfer some of the troops facing Richmond to Washington. (Grant had replaced losses in his army with most of the troops defending the forts around Washington, which he considered to be overmanned.) Once Early had defeated Union troops in the Shenandoah, he began marching on Washington. While Lee did not want Early to actually capture the federal capital, thinking it impossible, Early was more optimistic. Early's army crossed the Potomac on July 6, 1864. On July 9, he confronted a Union army at Monocacy, Maryland. The Union troops had been assembled from the raw recruits and militia at the disposal of the departmental commander, Major General Lew Wallace (better known as the author of *Ben-Hur*). Just before the battle, a division of the Army of the Potomac's VI Corps, which had been ordered to the Washington area in response to Early's sortie arrived

Below: *Lincoln Hospital's Ward 4, equipped with personal fans for each bed, which the patients could move themselves. The city of Washington became an important convalescent center for wounded soldiers, who were moved here from the field hospitals.*

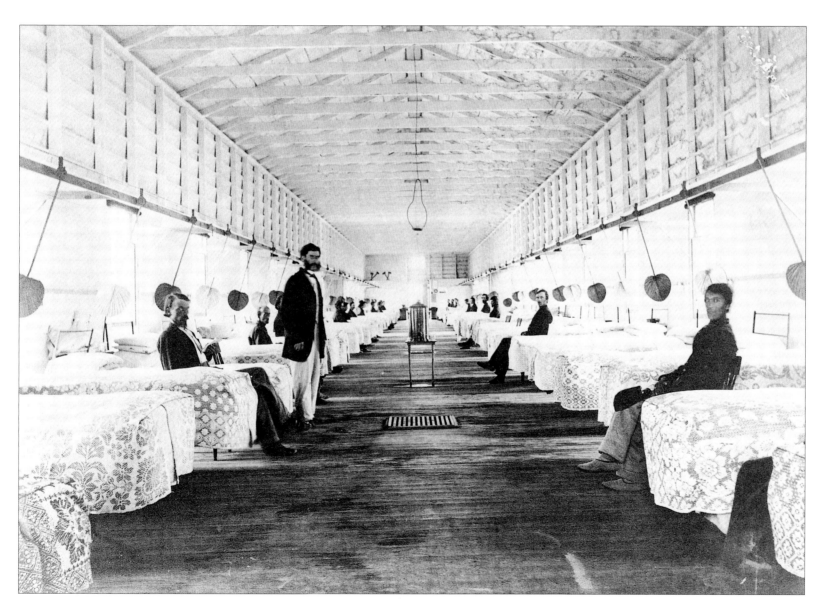

Right: The view along the gallery at Ford Theatre, showing at the end the box where Lincoln and his wife sat watching a performance of Our American Cousin *on April 14, 1865, when John Wilkes Booth shot the president.*

to reinforce Wallace. Early's army pushed these Union troops aside with a frontal attack, and the Union forces retreated. All that now stood between Early and Washington was some cavalry, with which his own mounted troops skirmished over the next two days.

On July 12, Early arrived outside the city. The fortifications appeared to him to be "feebly manned." He ordered his troops to prepare for a probing attack, but as they were forming up, a column of dust signaled the arrival of Union reinforcements who filed into Fort Stevens and opened fire with the fort's guns and sent out skirmishers. Early ordered his own troops to drive the skirmishers back within the fort, and they did so. Early was now able to perform a proper reconnaissance of Washington's defenses and then held a council of war

with his generals. They determined that in spite of the great strength of the Union position, they would assault them the next day.

In the night, however, Early received news that two more Union corps were arriving in Washington that night. Since he only had about 8,000 men, he would be outnumbered by over two to one, poor odds for an assault on a fortified position. He chose to withdraw, successfully evading his Union pursuers.

One of the witnesses of the fighting outside of the city of Washington on July 12 was President Lincoln himself. Having spent several years coordinating the movement of hundreds of thousands of men into positions where they were the target of Rebel bullets, President Lincoln took this single opportunity he had during the war to share in the danger. Foolhardily, he stood on the parapet where Rebel sharpshooters had been targeting their shots to catch a glimpse of the enemy he had encountered entirely in dispatches. Another famous American, serving as a captain in 20th Massachusetts, spotted President Lincoln and shouted, "Get down you damn fool, before you get shot." An amused Lincoln took future Chief Justice Oliver Wendell Holmes's advice.

As an extremely secure base for the Union armies, the city of Washington became an important medical center. When the war began, there were no military hospitals in the city. Those set up after Bull Run, when the first large numbers of casualties arrived, were simply large tents that were eventually grouped together as hospital camps. However, the scale of the casualties meant that more permanent accommodation was necessary. The first two hospitals taken for military use were the E Street Infirmary (Washington's only prewar hospital) and the Union Hotel. Even this was not enough, as after the spring battles of 1862, space was needed for some 20,000 wounded. Public buildings were converted into hospitals—the Patent Office, the Capitol, and even the Reynolds Barracks Hospital near the Executive Mansion. Churches, private medical

buildings, hotels, and schools also accommodated the many wounded. By the end of the Civil War there were some fifty military hospitals in Washington.

The hospitals contributed to one of the great literary works to come out of the war. The poet Walt Whitman visited many of the hospitals, offering sympathy to the wounded, listening to their stories, and bringing them fruit. His book *Drum Taps* drew heavily on what he heard during his hospital visits.

On April 14, 1865, an actor of strong Southern sympathies, armed with a knife and a single-shot derringer, put a bullet in the head of Abraham Lincoln while the president was attending a performance of a play at Ford Theatre.

President Linclon died of his wounds at 7:22 a.m. the following morning. His assassin, John Wilkes Booth, had been part of an ongoing conspiracy to kidnap or kill Lincoln. Indeed, Wilkes Booth had hoped to find General Grant attending the same performance.

Co-conspirators of his attacked Secretary of State Henry Seward at his home with a knife, stabbing him. The conspirator assigned with assassinating Vice-President Andrew Johnson lost his nerve and did not carry out his mission.

Booth was eventually tracked down and shot, while hiding in a burning barn. The surviving conspirators were arrested, and four of them were hanged in Washington on July 7, 1865.

Above: The hanging of Lincoln conspirators Mary Surratt, Lewis Powell, George Atzerodt, and David Herold on July 7, 1865. Surratt's execution was the first time the United States' government had given a woman the death penalty, which was carried out in spite of a recommendation of leniency on the part of five of the nine military judges who passed sentence.

FLORIDA

"I regard the possession of an iron-armored ship as a matter of the first necessity."

—Stephen R. Mallory, Confederate secretary of the navy

Above: *The flag of the 1st and 3rd Florida Infantry Regiment. As the war continued, many regiments were consolidated in the absence of reinforcements to bring them back up to strength. With bloody battle honors like Shiloh and Murfreesboro, the 1st and 3rd Florida was a likely candidate for such a move.*

Left: *The Florida memorial, at Chickamauga National Battlefield Park, dedicated in 1913, stands behind the memorial to Slocomb's Louisiana battery.*

In 1819 Spain ceded its colonial possession of east Florida to the United States. Three years later the Territory of Florida was organized. In 1839, the citizens of the territory applied for statehood. However, they had to wait until December 1844 for Congress to pass an act admitting them to the Union. The state of Florida was formally admitted on March 3, 1845, as a slave state.

Florida was one of the original seven states to secede from the Union, on January 10, 1861. Florida troops moved quickly to occupy federal forts and arsenals across the state. However, at Pensacola the commander of the federal garrison there, Lieutenant Adam Slemmer moved his troops to Fort Pickens, isolated from the mainland on Santa Rosa Island. Florida troops requested the surrender of the fort, but Lieutenant Slemmer refused. Like Fort Sumter, Fort Pickens presented a possible point for Rebels to fire upon the United States flag. The location of the fort, compared with Fort Sumter's situation in the middle of Charleston Harbor, however, permitted reinforcements and supplies to be landed easily from the sea. Without a strong force, backed by artillery, the Rebels were unable to take the fort.

The other key fortress retained by the Union was Fort Taylor at Key West. Key West consequently played an important role as a base for the Gulf Blockading Squadron. An ordnance storeship and supplies of coal and provisions were kept there.

On October 9, 1861, the Confederate forces attempted to capture the fort. They landed around 1,000 men on Santa Rosa Island, but the now-reinforced Union garrison was too strong for a force this size to be overcome. Most of Florida's state troops were needed to reinforce the Army of Mississippi after the defeat at the battle of Shiloh in April 1862, and Union possession of Fort Pickens was never challenged thereafter.

In early February 1864, General Quincy Gillmore (1825–88), commander of the Union Department of the South, set in motion plans to occupy Jacksonville with a large force. About 6,000 troops were allocated for the operation, and Gillmore placed Brigadier General Truman Seymour to command the expedition.

The Union troops sailed from Hilton Head, South Carolina, and landed at Jacksonville on February 7. They quickly gained control of the town and its surrounding countryside. They sent raiding parties out to Lake City and Gainesville.

General Beauregard had expected some Union attack along the Georgia or Florida coasts since mid-January, when his observers at Port Royal had seen the departure of a large number of Union vessels. Although there were few Confederate troops in Florida by early

1864, Beauregard had arranged for rapid reinforcement of the Rebel forces there with troops from the Charleston area.

An Irishman, Brigadier General Joseph Finegan, who had made his mark as an immigrant politician with links to the railroad industry in pre-secession Florida, commanded the Confederate Military District of East Florida. He had only about 1,500 men at his immediate disposal, and Beauregard advised him to avoid combat for the time being.

Shifting reinforcements to Finegan was a complicated operation. One problem was that Union forces pressed Rebel troops around Charleston and Savannah as part of a strategic plan to avert precisely what Beauregard was trying to do. No railroad ran into Florida from the rest of the Confederacy (something that Finegan might particular have felt aggrieved about), and so Beauregard's troops had to travel by train to southern Georgia and then march twenty-six miles overland until they reached a place where they could entrain on Florida's railroads. It took some two weeks for the Confederates to assemble under Finegan, but by February 20, there were 5,000 troops ready to counter any Union move.

The Union strategy had envisaged that many Floridians were skeptical about the Rebel cause and would rally to the Union if military forces arrived in the state. President Lincoln's secretary, John Hay, had arrived with the troops carrying a number of pledges of allegiance to be signed by Union sympathizers. However, the commander on the ground, Brigadier General Truman Seymour, reported on February 11 that

Below: Rebel troops at a camp at the Warrington Navy Yard, Pensacola, in 1861. The lack of standardized uniform is obvious in this photograph, with only the belts and buckles offering any kind of consistent distinguishing outfit from civilian dress.

this assessment had been far too optimistic. He wanted to concentrate his forces in Jacksonville to hold the port rather than adopt the more aggressive operational plan originally envisaged.

Brigadier General Seymour, however, seemed to change his mind after about a week and chose instead to make an advance toward the railroad bridge over the Suwanee River. On February 20, he began his movement. His first objective was Lake City, where the Confederate troops under Finegan had concentrated. Seymour and Finegan had about equal numbers of troops at their disposal.

Skirmishing between Union and Rebel cavalry began in the afternoon, and the Rebels withdrew toward Olustee Station. The railroad traversed an area of dry ground between swamps to the south and Ocean Pond to the north. Finegan had ordered the construction of some earthworks here in case of a Union advance on his Lake City position.

The cavalry skirmishing developed into a bigger engagement in front of these earthworks as both Seymour and Finegan pushed more and more troops in an attempt to find some kind of advantage. The Confederate forces achieved this goal first, when a command mix-up under fire resulted in the rout of the 7th New Hampshire. This left the inexperienced 8th United States' Colored Infantry exposed to a heavy Rebel attack. In spite of their want of training and experience, and the death of their commander, they sustained some three hundred casualties, about one-third of their strength, before giving way under pressure.

The Rebels now began a general advance across the battlefield toward the Union army. General Seymour pushed forward a brigade of New York troops, and these stabilized his front and held off the Rebels. The narrowness of the field, with swamps to one side and the waters of Ocean Pond on the other, prevented any attempt to maneuver on the flanks, and the toe-to-toe pounding both sides took caused extraordinarily heavy casualties given the size of the two forces.

Left: *A Florida three-dollar note issued in 1863.*

The Confederate advance stalled as their regiments ran low on ammunition, but once fresh supplies arrived, along with more reinforcements and General Finegan, Rebel pressure began to tell and Seymour ordered his troops to fall back. African American troops, in the shape of the 35th United States' Colored Infantry and the famous 54th Massachusetts Infantry covered the retreat of the New Yorkers and prevented defeat from turning into a rout.

The Union troops retreated back to Jacksonville, reaching there on February 22, the third anniversary of Jefferson Davis's inauguration. However, this useful port remained in Union hands for the remainder of the war. Several raids were mounted from this city against a state that was an important source of beef for the Rebels following the severing of links with the trans-Mississippi states after the fall of Vicksburg in July 1863.

The last major engagement in Florida during the war occurred at Natural Bridge on the St. Mark's River. A large Union force, numbering about 1,000, attempted to cross at Natural Bridge on March 6, 1865, after a night march. Their objective was to occupy the state capital at Tallahassee. Rebel scouts detected the movement, and a scratch force of militia, cavalry, and artillery was positioned to contest the crossing.

This force fended off the first Union attempt to cross, and Union commander Brigadier General John Newton tried to find a ford across the river. Finding no alternative, he launched another assault at Natural Bridge. The outnumbered Union troops were beaten back, and Newton withdrew, giving the Rebels a rare victory in the closing months of the war.

GEORGIA

"Our new government's foundations are laid, its cornerstone rests upon the great truth that the Negro is not equal to the white man, that slavery...is his natural and normal condition."

—Alexander H. Stephens, vice president of the Confederate States of America, March 21, 1861

Georgia, founded in 1733, was the last of the original thirteen colonies to be established in what is now the United States. Georgians were among the first to sign the Declaration of Independence. It was the first Southern state to ratify the US Constitution. Georgia was the fifth state to secede from the Union, on January 19, 1861. Some 30 percent of Georgia's delegates to the convention that voted on secession, however, opposed the ordinance.

Howell Cobb (1815–68) was a prominent Georgia politician of the pre-secession era who became an important political figure in the Confederacy. In 1859, Cobb had been the Democrats' candidate for Speaker of the House of Representatives, and was eventually elected on a plurality vote after sixty-two ballots. His election was one of the first crises of the 1850s that inexorably increased the attractiveness of secession to the slave-holding states.

When the convention to create the Confederate States of America met in Montgomery, Alabama, in February 1861, Cobb was elected that assembly's president. He was also the only candidate on the ballot for provisional president other than the eventual winner, Jefferson Davis. As a favorite son, Cobb only received the vote of his own Georgia delegation before it was agreed to make the election of Davis unanimous. Cobb received a commission as a colonel in the Georgia state troops in July 1861.

Having been elected Speaker of the Provisional Congress, however, he pursued his political duties until that body reached the end of its term in February 1862. Then, he received an appointment as brigadier general and took command of a brigade in McLaw's division of the Army of Northern Virginia. Unlike many political appointees during the war, he proved to have some talent for soldiering, and was promoted to major

general in September 1863, and given command of the District of Georgia and Florida.

One of Toombs's partners in this faction had also been his partner in the prewar Whig Party. Alexander Stephens (1812–83) had been a leading Whig congressman before secession and had been floor manager of the Kansas-Nebraska Act of 1854. Stephens was elected vice president. It was something of a compromise. Georgia was the most populous of the states that had seceded, and Stephens had been both a leading Whig and a man who switched allegiance to a Democratic candidate (albeit the Northerner Douglas) in the election of 1860. Stephens eventually joined with other critics of the administration who took a pro-civil-liberty, pro-states'-rights position against some of the "total war" measures imposed on the Confederacy: "Our liberties once lost, may be lost forever," he stated in a speech to the Georgia legislature in March 1864.

Stephens was involved in a forlorn attempt to secure some kind of compromise to save Southern honor at the end of the war. In March 1865, Stephens was appointed by Davis as part of a three-man delegation that was sent to discover what negotiated settlement the Lincoln administration was willing to offer. Davis wanted to fight on and believed that any Union offer would be unacceptable. Stephens was a leader of the movement to ask for terms. Lincoln himself came to meet the delegation. He offered them little hope, refusing to rescind his Emancipation Proclamation, although offering financial compensation. Lincoln also refused to accept anything other than a surrender of all the Rebel forces. Davis's views were vindicated.

William J. Hardee (1817–73), a Camden county native, was one of the more influential officers in the

Left: *The busy yards of the Western & Atlantic Railroad at Atlanta. Once Sherman reached Atlanta and conceived of his plan to cut loose from his lines of supply and live off the land, the city was doomed to destruction thanks to its vital role in connecting the south and west of the Confederacy with Richmond and the Carolinas.*

pre-Civil-War army. Hardee was in the West Point class of 1838, and the secretary of war sent him to study for a year with the French army immediately after graduating. He was taken prisoner early in the Mexican War of 1846–48. After the war Hardee was appointed a major in the 2nd US Cavalry. The regiment was commanded by the future Confederate generals Albert Sydney Johnston, with Robert E. Lee as Johnston's second-in-command.

Hardee was known throughout the prewar army as the author of *Rifle and Light-Infantry Tactics*, a manual that was a standard text at West Point and was read by many officers of volunteer regiments on both sides in the Civil War. During the conflict itself, Hardee commanded various units in the western theater, starting as commander in Arkansas. He proved an effective corps commander at Shiloh and Perryville in 1862. He got on badly, however, with army commander Braxton Bragg, especially after the battle of Murfreesboro (December 31, 1862–January 2, 1863). Eventually, Hardee requested to be transferred and spent a brief sojourn commanding troops in central Alabama. He returned to the Army of Tennessee in the autumn of 1863 and after the disaster at Chattanooga was offered command of it by President Davis. Hardee declined the opportunity, perhaps regarding it as a poisoned chalice. After commanding a corps in the Atlanta campaign, Hardee was

Below: *A captain of Company "A" 5th Georgia Infantry (known as the "Clinch rifles"). The company initially reflected its origins as a local militia companies by its distinctive set of uniforms. Clinch's rifles wore a green uniform, instead of the traditional cadet gray of the Rebel army.*

ROBERT TOOMBS (1810–85)

Robert Toombs was another prominent prewar politician who became a Confederate general. However, unlike Cobb he had an unhappier career. Before the war Robert Toombs had been a Whig, serving as both a congressman and a senator, who in the same election that had made Cobb Speaker of the House, refused to vote for the candidate of his own party on the grounds that the man had supported the Wilmot Proviso. Toombs also refused to support the Whig candidate for president, Winfield Scott, in the election of 1852. He had been slow to embrace secession, however. Although he had good political credentials for being a candidate for provisional president of the Confederacy, the fact that he was a Whig in an assembly dominated by Democrats counted against him. Instead, Toombs served briefly as Secretary of State in the Rebel government, where he opposed the firing on Fort Sumter. Robert Toombs left the administration of President Jefferson Davis on receiving a commission as a brigadier general in the Confederate Army in July 1861. At the battle of Antietam, his brigade fought the delaying action for Burnside Bridge that played an important role in protecting the flank of Lee's army. Toombs himself was wounded. Piqued at not receiving promotion for his actions in that battle, Toombs resigned from the army and spent the rest of the war as a leader of the anti-Davis faction in Confederate politics.

transferred to the District of Georgia and South Carolina, where he surrendered his forces just a few weeks after the battle of Bentonville where his only son, aged 16, was killed. After the war Hardee settled in Alabama, where he is buried.

Lafayette McLaws (1821–97) was from Augusta. He went to West Point, graduating in the class of 1842. He served in the Mexican War of 1846–48, although ill health sent him home early. He resigned from the army early in 1861 and was appointed colonel of the 10th Georgia Infantry. In September 1861, he became a brigadier general in the Confederate army. In May 1862, he was promoted to major general and took command of a division. He saw action in all the major campaigns of Lee's Army of Northern Virginia from the Seven Days' battles through to Gettysburg. At Antietam, his division was rushed into the line just at a point when the Union forces appeared to be about to break through, and he

stabilized the position. At Gettysburg, his men faced some of the fiercest fighting in the combat in the Peach Orchard and at Devil's Den. As part of Longstreet's corps, he fought in eastern Tennessee in the autumn of 1863. In 1864, he commanded the Military District of Georgia during the "March to the Sea," although his troops were of too poor quality to stand up to Sherman's veterans. After a brief sojourn with the Army of Tennessee in 1865, he returned to command the District of Georgia, where he was serving when the war ended.

Few battles took place in Georgia during the early years of the war. Such action as there was occurred in connection with the Union efforts to blockade southern ports. On November 24, 1861, the Union blockading fleet that had taken Port Royal in neighboring South Carolina made a move against Georgia. Troops landed at Tybee Island, in the mouth of the Savannah River. The island had originally been occupied by Rebel troops. These had been withdrawn by the commander of the Department of South Carolina, Georgia, and East Florida, Robert E. Lee, as part of his general policy of abandoning areas of Confederate territory that seemed indefensible in the face of Union naval superiority.

Upstream from Tybee Island on Cockspur Island stood Fort Pulaski, widely regarded as one of the most powerful fortifications in the world. Built of brick, its walls stood seven-and-a-half feet thick and rose to a height of twenty-five feet. The "moat" around the fort was fed by the tidal flow of the river. Several Confederate officers, including General Lee, believed that any siege operations against Fort Pulaski were

Above: *A lieutenant colonel of the 44th Georgia Infantry. Most of his equipment has come from Georgia's own resources, including a Griswold and Gunnison revolver.*

Left: *Josiah Tattnall had forty-nine years of naval experience when he left the US Navy to stay loyal to his native state of Georgia. He commanded the Rebel squadron defending Port Royal in 1861 and destroyed the CSS Virginia on the evacuation of the Norfolk Navy Yard by the Rebels in 1862.*

unlikely to succeed. Major General Joseph Totten, the Union army's chief engineer, even said of a bombardment of the fort, "One might as well bombard the Rocky Mountains."

Colonel Quincy Gillmore was the chief engineer of the expedition to Port Royal, and he had kept pace of developments in artillery. Gillmore visited Tybee Island five days after its capture and believed that if a sufficient number of rifled guns and mortars were placed on Tybee Island, Fort Pulaski could then be bombarded into submission.

The garrison of Tybee island was reinforced, and on the February 21, guns and supporting equipment began to be landed. Two-and-a-half weeks of hard work followed as the Union soldiers fought a terrain as uncompromising in its opposition as any Rebel army. Places where batteries were to be built were little more than crusts of earth atop mud. Heavy guns had to be shifted not along wharves to macadamized roadways, but landed from boats in the surf and then transported across unimproved sand and marsh. There was also danger from the guns of Fort Pulaski itself. The preparation of the batteries could have presented an easy target for guns fired from the walls, but by working at night or behind tree lines the Union soldiers finished the construction without suffering heavily. They also used camouflage to conceal the exact nature of their work during daylight hours.

The guns were ready for the bombardment on April 9, 1862, and orders were issued that afternoon with careful prescription for where each battery should aim and how fast it should fire. The main target was a point at the walls where it might have been possible to cause a fire in a powder magazine in the opposite angle. Other guns directed their shooting at the fort's own gun emplacements, in order to prevent any effective counter-battery fire.

Early in the morning on April 10, the commander of the Union Department of the South, Major General David Hunter, sent an officer under flag of truce to Fort

Left: *Men of the 48th New York Infantry fall in on the parade ground at Fort Pulaski after the fort's fall in April 1862. The fort was the key to the Rebel seaward defenses of Savannah and was thought impregnable to bombardment. But its design dated from an era of smoothbore artillery and its walls proved altogether too vulnerable to rifled batteries laboriously manhandled and emplaced in the rugged terrain to its seaward side.*

Pulaski to request the fort's surrender. This offer was declined, and the bombardment therefore commenced at 8:15 a.m. The barrage lasted thirty-three hours. The rifled guns were especially effective against the brick walls of the fort, and by nightfall on the first day, a breach had been opened. Gunfire continued through the night, with two or three guns continuing to fire in the direction of the breach to prevent working parties from making effective repairs.

The full barrage resumed the next morning, and at midday the breach in the wall was wide enough that the Union generals believed they could successfully assault it. The troops began to prepare. At 2 p.m., a white flag was hoisted over the fort, and Gillmore went forward to

Above: *The flag of the 57th Georgia Infantry uses six-pointed stars on the familiar Confederate St. Andrew's Cross. The border of the flag is pink.*

accept its surrender. Fort Pulaski remained in Union hands for the rest of the war, and its control made life difficult for blockade runners trying to enter Savannah, allowing Union ships to be redeployed elsewhere.

Following the fall of Fort Pulaski, Fort McAllister was the main defense of Savannah against the Union blockaders. The most serious attempt to destroy Fort McAllister was made on March 3, 1863, when three

monitors from Port Royal attempted a lengthy bombardment of it. After an eight-hour bombardment, the Union vessels withdrew. They had caused substantial damage to the walls and guns, but not enough to eliminate the fortress. No further attempts were made against McAllister, until it was abandoned just before the arrival of Sherman's army in 1864.

The next major engagement in Georgia occurred in September 1863. Confederate General Braxton Bragg believed that Union General William S. Rosecrans was attempting to maneuver his way to capture Atlanta. Bragg's Army of Tennessee abandoned its positions in defense of Chattanooga and withdrew into Georgia.

In Richmond, President Jefferson Davis was alarmed at the loss of Chattanooga, through which an important east-west rail route ran. President Davis ordered Bragg to respond to Rosecrans's advance by going over to the attack himself. To bolster the demoralized Army of Tennessee, Davis ordered its reinforcement by fresh troops from Mississippi and by two divisions of veterans of the Army of Northern Virginia commanded by General James Longstreet.

Rosecrans, meanwhile, had advanced beyond to Chattanooga into Georgia. However, he had pushed on recklessly. He was unsure of the location of the Rebel army, and the competing demands of aggression and concentration were rendered incompatible by the rugged nature of the terrain between Chattanooga and Atlanta. Rosecrans opted for aggression and sent his three corps on widely separated routes that made it impossible for both of the others to come rapidly to the support of the third. Major General George H. Thomas's XIV Corps had passed through the Stevens Gap in Lookout Mountain and paused at Chickamauga Creek, forming the center of the army. Major General Alexander McCook's XX Corps had swung westward through the Winston Gap into Alabama, to be the right wing of the advance. XX Corps had reached the town of Alpine, just over the Georgia state line. Rosecrans realized the danger on September 12. He pushed

forward Major General Thomas Crittenden's XXI Corps, which had initially remained at Chattanooga, into a position on Thomas's left, at Lee and Gordon's mills. He set up his headquarters at the Gordon-Lee Mansion, a house built in 1847 that today serves as a bed and breakfast residence.

Braxton Bragg had missed an opportunity to destroy part of the Army of the Cumberland through the incompetence of his subordinates and then chose to delay his onslaught until the arrival of Longstreet's reinforcements, which did not leave Virginia until September 9. Bragg's plan envisioned pushing around the northern flank of Rosecrans' line, in order to cut off the Union force from Chattanooga. Having waited for part of Longstreet's corps, the rough terrain slowed the Army of Tennessee's advance into position for the attack. Given a further day's delay on September 18, Rosecrans started shifting Thomas' and McCook's corps northward to reinforce Crittenden. Ironically, when the battle came it was provoked by Thomas. On the

Below: *An engraving showing the view from Union lines of a Rebel attack during the battle of Chickamauga, September 1863. This battle became one of the Civil War's most deadly engagements with both sides suffering some 28 percent casualties.*

Below: *Defenses at Peach Tree Creek outside Atlanta. The city was strongly fortified, but neither of the Army of Tennessee's commanders made use of them. Johnston intended to abandon the city, at least temporarily, which provoked his removal. Then Hood used an aggressive strategic plan against the superior Union numbers.*

morning of September 19, he pushed forward a couple of brigades to attack what he believed to be an isolated Rebel force. The battle, as it developed, was a confused affair, as units on both sides advanced toward the sound of the guns and fought the first enemy they came across. On both sides the organization of divisions into corps collapsed, and ad hoc arrangements for commanding sectors of the battle line created. The heavily wooded terrain also made coordination of divisional assaults almost impossible. The consequence

was that both armies were fought out by the end of the day.

However, both sides also knew that the combat would be renewed the next day. Bragg, whose persistent attempts to turn a flank had yielded no rewards, now planned a general attack all along the line. As with the fighting on the nineteenth, this went forward in an uncoordinated fashion. At 10 a.m., the Confederates struck at the left of the Union line, at Thomas' corps. Thomas demanded reinforcements

from Rosecrans, and got them. Unfortunately for the Army of the Cumberland, this opened a large gap in the center of the line. Braxton Bragg, despairing at the inability of his right wing to overcome the Union left, now told all his commanders to attack where they had the opportunity. Longstreet threw his corps forward, and part of his force entered the gap in the Union line.

The Union right, now beset on both its flanks, fled, taking with it Rosecrans, who attached himself to the fleeing troops. Thomas' force, however, held. Despite attacks throughout the day, it continued to hold, with the help of reinforcements from the Reserve Corps, whose commander, Gordon Granger marched toward the sound of the guns. By nightfall on the twentieth, the legend of the "Rock of Chickamauga," as Thomas would from now on be called, was firmly established. Thomas had prevented the Union rout from turning into the destruction of the Army of the Cumberland. He now withdrew to Chattanooga, leaving the field to Bragg's victorious army.

The carnage on the field at Chickamauga stunned Bragg into almost immobility. He had lost heavily among the horses that pulled his artillery, and this contributed to his cautious pursuit. Bragg failed to follow up the victory with a rapid march on Chattagnooga, which would almost certainly have restored that Tennessee town to the Confederacy. The focus of the war in the West now returned to Tennessee.

Georgia was secure from Union invasion as long as the Rebels besieged the Army of the Cumberland in Chattanooga. However, the breaking of that siege in November 1864 put a powerful Union force almost in Atlanta's front yard.

In General Grant's overall strategic plan for operations in 1864, Sherman's task was to destroy the Rebel Army of Tennessee, now commanded by Virginian Joseph E. Johnston. Johnston had very definite strategic ideas on how to fight a campaign. To him, cities such as Atlanta were places to be heavily fortified but lightly held, to be used as pivots around which to fight a campaign of maneuver that would draw the enemy into attacks on strong defensive positions. The terrain of northwestern Georgia half favored such a strategy. Sherman's army would have to cross a succession of parallel rivers, each of which was potentially a strong obstacle to help the defense. Furthermore, the ridges of the Appalachian chain provided another succession of defensive positions that Johnston's army could hold. Sherman had assembled three armies at Chattanooga at

Above: An 1858 Hardee hat that belonged to Colonel Francis Barlow of the 7th and 8th Georgia infantry.

Below: Union cavalry of a Missouri regiment in camp in Georgia. Union troops on the March to the Sea cut a corridor of ruin between Atlanta and Savannah, pillaging the countryside for everything they could carry or eat and burning much of what was left.

the beginning of May 1864. General James M. McPherson commanded the Army of Tennessee and formed the right wing of Sherman's forces. The Army of the Cumberland, under General George H. Thomas, comprised the center. On the left, Sherman had the Army of Ohio, under General John M. Schofield. The three armies amounted to 100,000 guns, well supported with 254 guns.

Johnston countered this with the Rebel Army of Tennessee containing two corps—John Bell Hood's and William Hardee's—and 144 guns. Shortly after Sherman began his advance from Chattanooga on May 5, Johnston was joined by a third corps under the incompetent General Leonidas Polk, adding another 20,000 men to his command. Johnston had a valuable advantage in the coming presidential election of November 1864. Sherman had to have achieved something by then to help Lincoln win a victory for the war to continue another term. If Johnston could keep his army from a serious defeat, then Sherman would fail in his objective.

Johnston occupied a very strong position outside Dalton, having deployed his army on long Rocky Face Ridge. Sherman was not a man to squander the lives of his troops without having explored other alternatives, and he sent McPherson's army toward Resaca, about

Below: The winter quarters of William T. Sherman's troops during their March to the Sea following the capture of Atlanta in the fall of 1864. In the course of this march, Sherman cut himself off from his source of supplies, planning for his troops to live off the land as they cut a path through the state of Georgia.

eighteen miles behind Johnston's position. McPherson arrived on May 9 to find a strongly entrenched position, but overestimated the number of troops holding it. A swift attack by his whole army might have cut off Johnston's line of retreat, but McPherson instead skirmished forward then pulled back. Johnston spotted what was happening, and moved three divisions from other parts of his line to reinforce the detachment covering Resaca. Then he pulled the remainder of his force back on the night of May 12–13.

When Sherman came up with the rest of his army, he tested the Resaca defenses with some probing attacks on May 14–15. Finding them strong, he tried the same maneuver again. McPherson was sent on a westward sweep, this time aiming at Kingston, on the Western & Atlantic Railroad between Rome and Allatoona, about twenty-two miles in Johnston's rear.

Johnston once again pulled out of a strong position to avoid being cut off from his "pivot," the city of Atlanta. Johnston now retreated to Cassville, counting on being able to damage the railroad sufficiently to force Sherman to wait longer for his supplies. But Sherman had plenty of engineers who got the railroad running again quickly.

At Cassville, now only some forty miles from Atlanta, Johnston decided to turn and fight. Sherman's army was divided on the march, and Johnston thought he had a chance to catch part of it with superior numbers. He prepared to attack on May 19.

Unfortunately for the Rebels, Hood came to believe that he faced the entire Union army and canceled his corps' attack. In the same way that McPherson had lost an opportunity to gain a significant advantage for Sherman at Resaca, Hood ruined Johnston's strategy at Cassville. The Rebels pulled back that night to a stronger defensive position at Allatoona Pass.

Throughout the campaign, Sherman intelligently showed an unwillingness to confront Johnston on ground of Johnston's own choosing. Allatoona Pass being so strong, Sherman figured out a way to outflank

it. It would require his men marching with their supplies instead of allowing the railroad to bring it up to them, but if it succeeded it would open a backdoor to Atlanta. Instead of part of his army, this time William T. Sherman took the whole of it on a flanking move aimed at Dallas, an important road junction to the west of Johnston's position.

Sherman could not keep Rebel cavalry from spotting the large masses of troops on the march. Johnston had encamped Hood's corps of his army in the vicinity of Dallas. Sherman underestimated the number of Confederates confronting him when his lead units reached Dallas on May 25 and ordered an attack in corps strength. Stewart's division of Hood's corps, which occupied the area in front of New Hope Church, beat this attack off. Sherman now prepared a full-scale assault. On May 27, in the battle of Pickett's Mill, Sherman sent forward Major General Oliver O. Howard's corps, reinforced by one division, against the Rebels. The corps attacked on too narrow a front and suffered heavy casualties in its repulse. The Rebels had blocked another of Sherman's flanking maneuvers, only to find him probing into Allatoona Pass.

Rainy weather turned the roads to mud and this slowed down both sides. For the soldiers on both sides, the shovel became more important than the rifle. Sherman kept using his numerical advantage to probe around the flanks of Johnston's army, while the Rebel general kept sliding his army from side to side to block each of Sherman's hook punches. The two armies were now dug in around Marietta.

Sherman was increasingly frustrated. Although he had gained a considerable amount of ground in the first

Above: *Two soldiers of Company A, 5th Georgia Infantry, the "Clinch rifles." The 5th Georgia's companies managed to avoid too much standardization of the uniforms, resulting in General Braxton Bragg referring to them as the "Pound Cake Regiment." The soldier on the right wears a dark blue tunic over his colorful shirt and light blue trousers, identical with the Union army's outfit, while the soldier on the left has the typical Rebel gray tunic and blue trousers. The blue uniform might well have caused confusion on the battlefield, and there were several incidents, during the early months of the war, of mistakes in identifying units.*

Above: *A state of Georgia issued smoothbore musket.*

weeks of his campaign, he had spent nearly a month less than twenty miles away from Atlanta. Reluctantly, he devised a new plan. Johnston's position made another flanking maneuver dangerous, since the Rebel guns on Kenesaw Mountain would be able to bombard the railroad along which most of Sherman's supplies must be brought. This time Sherman would try to punch his way through the front of the Rebel line. He understood well that many men would die, but for once he thought the possible reward outweighed the cost.

The plan was for Thomas's Army of the Cumberland to advance on a wide front against a salient in the Rebel line. The ground here was not as rugged as elsewhere, and Johnston had placed the best two divisions of the best corps in his army, Cleburne's and Cheatham's of Hardee's corps. On the Union left, the Army of Tennessee, under McPherson, would assault Pigeon Hill. A brief bombardment was conducted before the Union attacks. The whole operation failed. The bombardment was too short to do any damage and only warned the Rebels that the Union attack was imminent. Thomas's troops took too long to get into action, an hour behind schedule. At no point did the Union forces make any significant penetration of the Rebel lines. After two-and-a-half fruitless hours, Sherman called the attacks off.

Sherman now returned to looking to gain advantage through maneuver on the flanks. This time, he sent McPherson around the Confederate left, aiming for the Chattahoochee River, which he reached on July 8, only to find the Rebels there already. Once again, Johnston was forced to abandon a strong position to protect his lines of supply and retreat. However, he was confident that the Union troops would find it hard to cross the river, since he controlled all the fords and bridges near his lines. Sherman simply looked further afield than Johnston expected. He sent cavalry against some weakly held fords north of the Rebel position, this time probing around the right. The Union horse soldiers got across, and on July 9 were on the right flank of Johnston's position, some four miles from the center of Atlanta.

President Davis had seen enough. When Johnston suggested that he might abandon Atlanta, Davis fired him on July 17. The aggressive General John B. Hood was appointed in his place. Hood had been chafing under the restrictions of Johnston's defensive strategy. He would attack.

Sherman maneuvered again. He sent McPherson around the Confederate right, aiming at the town of Decatur. Hood parried this blow, while Thomas, now on the left, managed to get some of his army across Peachtree Creek. This advance opened up a gap between Thomas's forces and Schofield's Army of Ohio, now the center of Sherman's command. Hood struck hard at this gap, launching Hardee's and Stewart's (formerly Polk's) corps toward it. This attack, on July 20, was repulsed with heavy losses. Meanwhile, McPherson was able to seize Decatur, and Hood's most direct connection with Richmond was cut.

Atlanta had been heavily fortified, and Hood now withdrew within these earthworks. Sherman believed that this retirement heralded the abandoning of Atlanta, and ordered McPherson to attack from Decatur. A ferocious battle occurred on July 22, when Hood sent Hardee's corps out of the fortifications in a night march to attack the left of McPherson's command. At first the Rebels were successful, but Sherman massed his artillery to drive them back into Atlanta. In two battles over two days, Hood had lost twice as many men as Johnston had lost in ten weeks.

William T. Sherman maneuvered again. James B. McPherson had been killed at the battle of Atlanta on July 22. His army was now commanded by General Howard, who took it around to the southwest of Atlanta to cut the railroad there. Hood's scouts reported the maneuver, and Hood attacked Howard at Ezra Church on July 28. Once again, the attacking force was defeated with heavy losses, but the Union troops were kept from the railroad.

A pause of about a month ensued. Sherman appeared to have settled for a long siege of Atlanta, and the Rebel defenses and the city were kept under a steady bombardment. However, on August 25, Sherman was again on the move. At first, Hood thought that the Union troops were retreating. Then, to his horror, he found they were swinging southward, around the city, aiming for the railroad west to Montgomery, and the one south through Jonesboro. Hood had to pull Hardee's corps out of the Atlanta defenses and sent it to Jonesboro. Union troops got there first, on August 30, and repelled Hardee's attack on August 31. All the main railroads into Atlanta were now cut. Hood, who had

Below: Men of Sherman's army destroying a railroad in 1864. A popular occupation of these men was the making of "Sherman neckties." This involved heating the rails and bending them around tree trunks, as well as burning the wooden ties.

promised victory, evacuated Atlanta on September 1, and Union troops occupied the city on September 2, 1864. "Atlanta is ours, and fairly won," reported Sherman to Washington.

William T. Sherman now confronted an interesting problem. The Rebel Army of Tennessee had withdrawn to the southwest. However, its cavalry forces were still operating along Sherman's long line of supply, via the railroad through Nashville and Chattanooga. Hood's army also threatened their supply line.

The obvious target for Sherman's forces was the port of Savannah, an important harbor for the blockade runners who supplied the Confederacy with vital munitions. But the Confederate army was not protecting this. An advance on Savannah would uncover Sherman's supply line to more raids.

To move against Hood would put the Confederate cavalry in Sherman's rear, and Hood had plenty of maneuver room in Georgia and Alabama to draw Sherman on. Indeed, President Jefferson Davis had predicted that the Rebels would be able to trade space for time and secure victory in the way the Russians had overcome Napoleon in 1812.

Sherman and Grant both considered the problem, and developed a common answer. The target for Sherman had to be Savannah. Northern Georgia and the Carolinas had been largely untouched by the conflict and served as the main repository for supplies to Lee's army. A move by Sherman into this region would also potentially put him in the rear of Lee's army, should the march go on for long enough. The Union forces were in sufficient strength that their army could

be divided, a large force being held in Tennessee to prevent Hood from making an unopposed thrust against the Union occupation there. Sherman's own troops could live off the land in Georgia, since the harvest had been gathered and waited in barns and granaries to be distributed.

Sherman set off from his positions around Atlanta on November 15, having famously burned the city and destroyed the railroads in the vicinity. His army was 62,000 strong, organized into the Army of Tennessee, under Major General Oliver O. Howard (1830–1909), and the Army of Georgia, under General Henry Slocum.

The March to the Sea was largely unopposed by Confederate forces. The Rebel commanders had few troops available to throw in Sherman's way, since they believed that the damage to his supply line by Rebel troops made it difficult for him to move and that the threat posed by Hood would draw him into battle. Given the opportunity to take a long walk at the enemy's expense without too much fear of resistance, Sherman's men turned into something resembling some Hunnic horde wandering through the Western Roman Empire in the fourth century AD. Anything that could not be carried in soldiers' pockets or knapsacks to be eaten later or used as trophies for the postwar era was destroyed.

The "bummers," as they came to be known, destroyed railroads by making "Sherman neckties," heating rails and bending the consequent pliable metal around tree trunks. A penumbra of anarchy formed itself around William T. Sherman's army, as liberated slaves, Unionists out to avenge their neighbors' treason, and ill-disciplined Confederate cavalry joined in the general pillaging and destruction. While the scale of devastation in Georgia may have later been exaggerated, it was still substantial in the corridor that Sherman's forces passed along.

Confederate forces in the Carolinas were under the immediate command of Lieutenant General William Hardee, and he positioned a division on the east bank

Below: *A fifty-dollar bill issued by the state of Georgia in 1862. This was a fairly large denomination for the time, although the severe inflation experienced in the Confederate states gradually eroded its value.*

of the Oconee River in order to give some resistance to Sherman's march. General Howard sent a brigade on boats upstream of the Confederate position and outflanked it. Rebel resistance only increased at the Savannah Canal. Confederate commanders pondered what to do. Hardee only had about 10,000 soldiers and was outnumbered by about six to one.

General Pierre Beauregard, in overall command of the West, requested reinforcements from Robert E. Lee. But Lee declared that every man was needed at Petersburg. Hardee eventually was told to hang on to Savannah for as long as possible without the risk of losing his force.

Swamps and blocked roads prevented Sherman's men from attacking Savannah. A Rebel fort, Fort McAllister, prevented the Union blockading squadron from delivering supplies to Sherman via the Ogeechee river. A divisional assault captured the place on December 13, and Slocum was able to put a force across the Savannah River to threaten the Georgia port. Hardee abandoned it and, on December 23, the March to the Sea ended with the occupation of Savannah. Sherman reported to Lincoln: "I beg to present to you, as a Christmas gift, the city of Savannah, with 150 heavy guns and…about 25,000 bales of cotton." Thus ended the last major campaign of the war in Georgia.

Below: The burning of the Savannah Navy Yard by Confederate forces in December 1864 as Sherman's troops neared. The fall of Fort McAllister about a week earlier enabled Sherman's forces to end their reliance on living off the land and made possible an extended siege of the place. The heavily outnumbered Rebels abandoned it, and Savannah was presented to Lincoln as a Christmas present by Sherman.

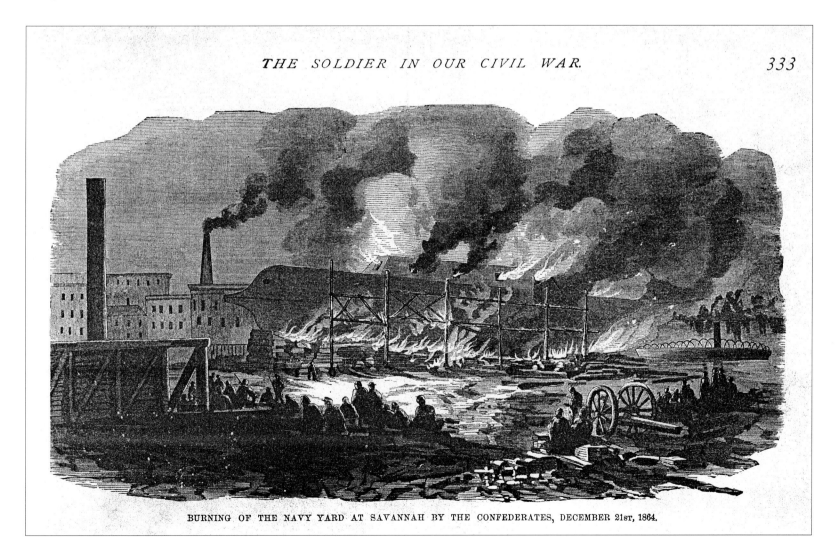

THE SOLDIER IN OUR CIVIL WAR. 333

BURNING OF THE NAVY YARD AT SAVANNAH BY THE CONFEDERATES, DECEMBER 21ST, 1864.

ILLINOIS

"Sir, the Rebels are thick up there." "Damn it, that's the place to kill them—where they are thick."

—Exchange between regimental adjutant and Major General John A. Logan of Illinois, May 16, 1863

Illinois was part of the area conceded to the United States with the signing of the Treaty of Paris in 1783, which ended the Revolutionary War. It remained an unorganized territory for four years, until Congress made it a part of the Northwest Territory. In 1800, the Northwest Territory was divided into two: Ohio and part of Michigan retained the old name; the rest became Indiana Territory. Illinois Territory, comprising today's Wisconsin and Illinois, plus northeastern Minnesota, was created by Congress in 1809. Illinois was admitted to the Union on December 3, 1818.

The Civil War history of Illinois is dominated by the two giants of the Union cause: Abraham Lincoln (1809–65) and Ulysses S. Grant (1822–85). Ironically, neither of them were born in the state. Lincoln was born in Kentucky, while Grant's family were residents of Ohio.

Lincoln's family was, in modern terms, blue collar. When Lincoln was born, they lived on a farm near Hodgenville, Kentucky. At the age of seven, they moved to Indiana. His education was legendarily poor, although he was an avid reader. With willpower and discipline he worked hard to become a lawyer. In the 1850s he was legal counsel to the Illinois Central Railroad, a pillar of the Illinois economic establishment

Above: *The monument marking the site of the death of Colonel Julius Raith, and the memorial to the 43rd Illinois Infantry at Shiloh. The 43rd was drawn predominantly from German immigrants in Illinois. It also participated in the Vicksburg campaign and later in the occupation of Arkansas.*

Left: *The interior of the Illinois monument at Vicksburg. It is modeled on the Pantheon building in Rome.*

at the time. Abraham Lincoln had already been a congressman for a single term, and in 1858 he gained nomination as the Republican candidate for senator of Illinois.

The election of Lincoln triggered the secession movement in the Deep South. Lincoln thought carefully about his strategy in handling the crisis. In his mind, the seceding state governments were preventing him from carrying out his constitutional oath to ensure that the laws of the United States were being executed. After the bombardment of Fort Sumter, he characterized the seceded states as being in a state of insurrection. During the war, he refused to treat the Rebel government or the state governors in the seceded states as representing any form of legal administration.

Nothing captured this more succinctly than an exchange of messages between Davis's administration in Richmond and Lincoln in March 1865. The messages concerned the possibility of negotiating an end to the war. Davis's message referred to entering, "Into conference to secure peace to the two countries." Lincoln referred to, "The people of our one common country," after nearly four years of war and hundreds of thousands of deaths. The question confronting Lincoln when he was inaugurated on March 4, 1861, was what

to do about the seceded states. Some in his own party counseled to let them go, because sooner or later they would come back. Lincoln's determination to compel them to return never wavered. After the bombardment of Fort Sumter, Lincoln called for 75,000 volunteers to serve for ninety days to suppress the insurrection.

Lincoln knew that this call would force the states of the upper South to decide whether to support the federal government or the seceded states, but he also relied on strong Unionist sentiment in these states to counter any movement to secede. On April 19, 1863, four days after the militia summons, Lincoln imposed a blockade on the ports of the South. (Under an 1863 decision by the Supreme Court, this became legally the date on which war broke out.) He even went so far as to suspend the writ of habeas corpus between the city of Washington and Philadelphia by executive order, a decision that was, strictly speaking, unconstitutional.

Lincoln's actions were a curious mixture of the pessimistic ally visionary and the optimistically opportunistic. Calling up militia under the terms of the law then, in effect, suggested he believed a show of force would quickly bring the Rebel states back into the Union. However, by refusing to regard the Rebel political leaders as representing anything other than an insurrectionary combination, he ensured that in the event of a long struggle their legal status under international law would be unclear.

Lincoln summoned a Congressional session for July 4, 1861. This imposed a clear deadline on military activity by the ninety-days' militia, who could not be kept under arms more than thirty days after the meeting of Congress. When the insurrection failed to collapse once Union troops advanced into Rebel-held territory, Lincoln already had legal sanction for fighting a longer war, using volunteer regiments enlisted for three years or the duration. Now the management of the conflict passed from one of policing to strategy.

Lincoln relied heavily, at least at first, on the professionals. His relationship with the army's commander in chief, General Winfield Scott, was a good one. Scott's plan to seize the Mississippi Valley dominated Union strategic thought for the first two years of the war. Lincoln never looked for an alternative strategy; his military problems lay elsewhere. From the start, he wanted a far more aggressive attitude than his generals were eager to embrace. The first commander of the Union army based at Washington, General Irvin McDowell, had to be prodded into action. McDowell was reluctant because of his army's lack of training. Lincoln had to remind him that "you are all green alike." McDowell's successor (and eventually Scott's), General George B. McClellan, also needed constant pressure from the president to take action. McClellan always overestimated the number of men the Rebels deployed against him. Lincoln never believed these estimates and eventually disposed of McClellan because he would not fight. In the West, General Don Carlos Buell (who commanded the Department of the Ohio during 1861–62) displayed many of McClellan's virtues—a good organizer and administrator, a disciplinarian— without the vice of refusing to fight. But Lincoln removed him because, while he would fight if attacked, he would not attack. McClellan's successor was a Lincoln favorite, General Ambrose Burnside. But

Below: *The river gunboat USS General Bragg at Cairo in late 1862 or early 1863. Originally a Rebel vessel, she was captured after a naval battle near Memphis in the spring of 1862. Cairo was a major Union base throughout the war, both for river craft and for supplies. Grant had his first headquarters as an army commander here.*

Burnside had no confidence in himself, could never control a battle, and consequently his subordinates lost confidence in him. Lincoln had to replace him. General Joseph Hooker, who followed Burnside, lost confidence in himself, after which Lincoln lost confidence in him. General George Meade was Lincoln's last appointment as commander of the Army of the Potomac. His predilection for defensive engagements was not shared by Lincoln. But rather than replace the one general who had delivered an incontrovertible victory over Lee, Lincoln adopted a new approach.

While the commanders in the East had added up to that sorry catalog described, Lincoln found more fruitful results in the West. After McClellan, Lincoln served as his own commander in chief until he found he had too much to do in July 1862. He brought General Henry Halleck, who had commanded the Department of the West, to Washington as commander in chief. Halleck at least constantly communicated the president's gospel of action to his subordinates. The increased energy of Union efforts on all fronts after Halleck's appointment is noticeable. Unfortunately, he was not the true author of Western success. Credit for that belonged to another Illinoisan, Ulysses Grant. Once Lincoln had recognized this and brought Grant east as commander in chief, he found a man who shared his views.

The 1864 spring campaign by the Union armies envisaged advances everywhere: by Sherman on Atlanta, by Banks from New Orleans to Mobile, by Butler on Richmond, and by Meade into Virginia. In 1862, Lincoln had written to Halleck and Buell:

"I state my general idea of war to be that we have the greater numbers, and the enemy has the greater facility of concentrating forces upon points of collision; that we must fail, unless we can find some way of making our advantage an overmatch for his; and that this can only be done by menacing him with forces at different points, at the same time."

This is precisely what Grant proposed to do. And in a conversation with one of his personal secretaries, he grimly summed up the arithmetic of the war. He found grim hope in the results of Fredericksburg, the December 1862 battle in Virginia that seems the most futile of the war, with 12,000 Union casualties to 5,000 Rebels. Ultimately Lee's army would be annihilated, while the Union force would remain "a mighty host." Grant, who would have preferred otherwise, applied this arithmetic to Lee's army in the Overland campaign of 1864, and thereby won the war.

Lincoln made many mistakes on the road to victory, and each weighed heavily on him. But his logical mind and unshakable will to see the struggle to its end ensured that he found the right formula. His assassination prevented him from realizing the fruits of

Below: *Earthwork defenses and fieldpieces mark the position of Battery A, 1st Illinois Light Artillery, during the siege of Vicksburg. Battery A also fought at Shiloh as part of Brigadier General W. H. L. Wallace's division, seven out of the fifteen infantry regiments were from Illinois. At Vicksburg, the battery was in Sherman's corps, part of Major General Francis P. Blair's division.*

his victory. Indeed, it is not inconceivable that like his successor Andrew Johnson, he might have found himself in trouble with the radicals in his own party for his conciliatory approach to the South. Johnson was nearly impeached, and Lincoln had done far more questionable things in prosecuting the war. One only needs to remember that Lincoln faced trouble over the reconstruction policy in 1864, vetoing the Wade-Davis Bill in July.

Grant's prewar career was far less noteworthy than Lincoln's. Grant's father was a tanner by trade and also owned farmland. In spite of this somewhat humble background, he was moderately well connected through his enthusiasm for literature and debate. When a vacancy at West Point occurred, Jesse Grant's acquaintance with a congressman secured the place for his eldest son. Grant entered the military academy in May 1839 and graduated as a member of the class of 1843. He was assigned to the 4th Regiment of Infantry.

Grant's early military career was a checkered one. Three years after he left West Point he was fighting in Texas and Mexico in both Zachary Taylor's and Winfield Scott's armies against Mexico. After the war he married and eventually was posted to California. Here the separation from his wife and young family led him to alcoholism that would be forever associated with his name. In July 1854 he left the army and went to Missouri where his wife Julia had a piece of farmland. He worked hard, but in the end illness forced him to sell it. In 1858 he took a job in the lead-mining town of Galena at a tannery that his father had set up for his brothers to run. Grant received a salary of $800 per year (about $17,000 in current dollars).

When Lincoln made his call for ninety-day volunteers, Grant presided over a meeting in Galena about organizing a company. He declined the company's captaincy, but agreed to go to Springfield with the company. Here he met the governor, and

Right: Confederate prisoners of war at Camp Douglas, Chicago. For the first years of the war, both sides operated a system of exchanging prisoners, or even giving prisoners parole (saying that they would not fight until exchanged). Rates of exchange were established, with for example, a major general requiring a mere thirty privates. Two reasons led to this relatively civilized system being abandoned. When the Union armies started to use African American soldiers, the Rebels refused to exchange them for white men and even sold some into slavery. The other reason: Once Grant became Union commander in chief, he opposed exchanges, which he believed reinforced the Rebel armies and consequently removed the Union advantage in numbers.

eventually found himself with the colonelcy of the 21st Illinois Infantry. However, his life changed when on August 7, 1861, he found that the Illinois congressional delegation had nominated him as one of fifty-seven newly appointed brigadier generals of volunteers. The next day he was named to the District of Southeastern Missouri. His first major battle occurred at Belmont, Missouri, on November 7, 1861, when he attacked a Confederate camp. He succeeded in taking the camp and showed considerable coolness when withdrawing in the face of a superior enemy force.

Grant strengthened his reputation in February 1862 when he captured forts Henry and Donelson in Tennessee. Six weeks later he recovered from a Rebel surprise attack at Shiloh on April 5, 1862, to defeat the enemy comprehensively in a counterattack the next day.

Grant had already displayed all the characteristics of his generalship. He was aggressive and tenacious in pursuit of an objective. He was patient and thoughtful about what his men could accomplish. He was willing to take risks, confident in his ability to deal with any obstacle, having measured carefully the resources at his disposal. His masterpiece was the campaign to take Vicksburg, Mississippi, in the spring of 1863, when he outmaneuvered two Rebel armies and laid siege to the last Confederate stronghold on the Mississippi River. The city fell on July 4, 1863.

After Vicksburg, Grant retrieved a dangerous situation for the Union forces when he broke the Rebel siege of Chattanooga in November 1863, winning a comprehensive victory. And then he was called east to take command of all the Union armies.

His strategy made full use of his greatest strength—superiority in resources. He pressed the Rebel armies hard in both the East and the West. Grant faced his toughest test against General Robert E. Lee in Virginia. Grant simply refused to acknowledge that he was beaten. He kept pushing at Lee's army, trying to find some way to get around it and to cut off its supply lines with the rest of the South. His army suffered terrific casualties, but Lee suffered badly too—with less margin to absorb heavy losses. Although Grant may have fought his army to exhaustion, that proved to be the only way to defeat a general as tenacious as himself.

Illinois unusually numbered its regiments sequentially from the last time it raised troops for United States' service. During the Mexican War, Illinois raised six regiments, and so when it raised its first six regiments for the Civil War, it started numbering them from the 7th Illinois Infantry. Illinois also had the honor of raising troops in excess of its quota.

A Southern Illinois Company was raised from the area around Carbondale and Cairo (Williamson and Jackson counties), in 1861, and at the battle of Belmont fought against other Illinois units from the same part of the state. It was the only Rebel formation officially raised from a Union state.

Left: *The Illinois monument on Cheatham Hill at Kennesaw Mountain. It was dedicated on the fiftieth anniversary of the battle, June 27, 1914. The monument stands on the Dead Angle, where a brigade of Union troops held out for six days within a hundred yards of the Rebel lines until the enemy evacuated. Most of the regiments from this brigade (3rd Brigade, 2nd Division, XIV Corps) were from Illinois.*

INDIAN TERRITORY

"[Indians] are unfit for garrison duty, and would be a terror to the Yankees."
—Colonel Douglas H. Cooper, CS Army, July 1861

The concept of an "Indian Territory" was Thomas Jefferson's. After the Louisiana Purchase of 1803 had doubled the size of the United States, Jefferson believed that the friction between settlers of European descent and the Native American tribes of the East (like the Cherokee and Creek) could be reduced by settling these people in the West. The federal government eventually conducted a mass removal from the Southern states in the 1830s, with the first large-scale settlements of Choctaws in 1833–34. Creeks, Cherokees, Seminoles, and Chickasaws joined them over the following years. These "Five Civilized Tribes" amounted to some 60,000 people in 1860.

The Confederacy had great hopes of acquiring the Five Civilized Tribes as allies in the Civil War. Their Southern heritage and embrace of slavery made them culturally more like one another, perhaps, than a Connecticut Yankee to a Tennessee resident. The Confederacy sent a transplanted New Englander, Albert Pike, to Indian Territory to secure treaties with the Native Americans. His job was helped by the withdrawal of US troops from the area's forts and the suspension of annuities paid to the Five Civilized Tribes for lands they had given up.

Although tribal leadership embraced the Rebel cause, the independent-mindedness of Native American society meant that in each tribe there were plenty who preferred to keep to the traditional link with Washington, whether out of antislavery sentiment or habit. Consequently, the war gradually spilled into the different tribes. Some of those who supported the Union fled to Northern troops in Kansas in December 1861, who were unprepared to receive 7,000 Native Americans. These people suffered terribly through the winter for want of shelter and food.

Pike organized several regiments of Native American volunteers, the most important of which was the Cherokee Mounted Regiment, commanded by Colonel Stand Watie. These formed a brigade that fought in the battle of Pea Ridge, March 5–6, 1862, and suffered heavy casualties. Meanwhile, the Indians in Kansas formed two regiments of their own, and with two regiments of white troops, they invaded Indian Territory in the summer of 1862. With most of the tribal warriors away with the Rebels, they easily occupied the Cherokee Nation capital of Tahlequah. However, this was not a lasting victory. When the white regiments withdrew, the two Indian regiments soon followed, fearing the greater numbers of the Rebel forces.

There were growing problems in the Rebel ranks, however. The hard-pressed Rebel government was unable to give the Native Americans the finances and protection required under the treaties signed. The Cherokee Council, which had pressed its leaders into an alliance with the South, voted to return to the North in February 1863. All slaves held by Cherokees were freed, and the Cherokee gave up some of their land to provide for the emancipated.

The change of heart reflected the changing military situation. From a Western perspective, the Rebels were in serious trouble. They had lost Missouri, Kentucky, northern Arkansas, western Tennessee, and New Orleans. They were also being pressed hard in Mississippi. The Union invasion of spring 1863 proved permanent. The capture of Vicksburg cut the Trans-Mississippi area off from the rest of the Confederacy. Union forces in Missouri and Kansas grew stronger. The capture of Fort Smith and other posts in Arkansas enabled Union troops to conduct regular raids against the Five Civilized Tribes. This guerrilla war lasted until the conflict in the Trans-Mississippi ended in May 1865 when the region's Rebel commander surrendered.

Left: A soldier of the 1st Cherokee Rifles, Confederate States' army. The Rebels were more successful than the Union army in recruiting Native Americans to their side, since the Union had repeatedly betrayed its promises to the tribes. They proved somewhat unreliable on campaign, and were never properly equipped.

INDIANA

"A force of sufficient strength to give the enemy a successful battle in his rear would settle all trouble about here."

—Brigadier General Jefferson C. Davis, September 13, 1861

The territory that today makes up the state of Indiana officially became part of the United States with the signing of the Treaty of Paris in 1783. In 1787, Congress organized the Northwest Territory to embrace all the United States' land north of the Ohio River. In 1800, the Northwest Territory was divided into two, with the part containing the future state of Indiana becoming Indiana Territory. In 1809 this was divided, part becoming Illinois Territory and the rest remaining Indiana Territory. Indiana Territory applied for statehood in December 1815 and was admitted to the Union on December 11, 1816. Abraham Lincoln carried Indiana in the 1860 election.

Indiana was a center of "Copperhead" feeling in the North. Copperheads were a faction of the Democratic Party that opposed the war. Centers of antiwar feeling could be found throughout the North. Each center had its own unique character. Indiana was part of the Ohio Valley area of antiwar sentiment, which owed its origins to the original settlers of the Northwest Territory, who were predominantly from Southern states. These people were known as "Butternuts" from the brownish color they dyed their clothes. They traditionally traded with merchants from along the Mississippi Valley. The war disrupted this pattern, forcing them to look to unfamiliar eastern routes

Above: *Men of the 9th Indiana Infantry in camp. The regiment served in most of the major battles in the western theater, including Shiloh, Chickamauga, Atlanta, Franklin, and Nashville.*

Left: *Brigadier General Jefferson Davis had the unhappy coincidence of sharing a name with the Rebel president, although their middle names were different. He spent the entire war in the western theater.*

and causing some economic hardship.

In 1863, John Hunt Morgan's raid into the North passed through parts of Indiana where this Southern sentiment was. Using two captured steamboats, the *J. T. McCombs* and the *Alice Dean*, Morgan led 2,000 cavalrymen across the Ohio River on July 8 at Brandenburg, Kentucky. Morgan's plan was to lead his column through unprotected territory in Indiana and Ohio where he would be able to damage the railroad and telegraph lines that connected the Union armies in the South to their supply bases in the North.

Once on Union territory, Morgan led his men northward. There was little resistance to this unexpected raid. The Home Guard of Corydon was called out to meet the Rebels, but Morgan's cavalry easily outflanked this band of boys and old men. The whole group was captured and forced to give their parole. The victorious Rebels entered the town and pillaged it. However, the experience of Corydon was not as severe as the damage to Salem, which the Rebels occupied on July 10. They imposed a heavy ransom on some local businesses, burned the railroad depot and two bridges, and looted everything that could be carried away—especially whiskey.

Morgan continued his march through the state, sending smaller columns of raiders to advance parallel

to the main force and spread the range of destruction more widely. Governor Oliver Morton called for volunteers and was able to muster thirteen regiments, as some 20,000 men responded to his call. Command was given to native son Major General Lew Wallace. The army response was already taking the field, as 4,000 men were assembled from the Union forces in Kentucky and sent after Morgan.

Morgan was already on the way to Ohio, reaching Lexington in the evening of July 10, before continuing the next day toward Paris and Vernon. Morgan found the Home Guard at Vernon waiting for him in a strong defensive position, and he bypassed the town, heading for Dupont, where they paused in the night.

At Versailles on July 12, the Rebels found the county treasury contained $5,000, which they confiscated before continuing on to the Ferris School, two miles south of Sunman. Morgan reached the Whitewater river at West Harrison early in the afternoon and had crossed over the bridge there by nightfall. Morgan's ride would continue through Ohio.

Like Illinois, Indiana raised volunteer regiments for service in the Mexican War of 1846–48, and when the time came to enroll new ones for the Civil War, it started the sequential numbering with the 6th Regiment.

The 9th Indiana Infantry started life as a ninety-day regiment, when it saw action in McClellan's West Virginia campaign. In September 1861 it converted into a three-year regiment and was part of the Army of Ohio. It fought hard at Shiloh on the second day of the battle, suffering heavy casualties. One of the young officers that day, who served with the regiment until he was wounded at the battle of Kennesaw Mountain in 1864, was the famous author Ambrose Bierce.

The 19th Indiana Infantry was one of the regiments that constituted the famous Iron Brigade, the only all-Western

brigade in the Army of the Potomac. The regiment was mustered into service on July 29, 1861, in Indianapolis. It arrived in the East on August 9, when it reached the city of Washington. Two months later, it was assigned to a brigade of three Wisconsin regiments and fought its first action in August 1862, at Brawner Farm.

The brigade as a whole gained its nickname during the Antietam campaign, when it stood up well to Confederate musketry at the battle of South Mountain on September 14, 1862. At the battle of Antietam, the 19th Indiana was part of I Corps, which fought at the northern end of the Union line, around the Cornfield and the Dunker Church. During the action they lost their commanding officer, Lieutenant Colonel Alois Bachman, an incident commemorated on the unit's battlefield monument there.

At Gettysburg, the 19th Indiana fought on McPherson's Ridge in the woods overlooking Willoughby run. They suffered heavy casualties in the afternoon when the Rebel attack in divisional strength overwhelmed their position. Only sixty-nine men of the regiment were killed or wounded at the end of the fighting that day.

The 19th Indiana saw more hard fighting in the 1864 campaign, especially in the Wilderness battle in May. Eventually it was merged with the 20th Indiana, since both regiments had lost so heavily in the fighting.

Jefferson C. Davis (1827–79) may have shared a name and a military background with the president of the Confederate States of America, but he remained loyal to the Union. Davis was born in Indiana, and enlisted in the 3rd Indiana Regiment during the Mexican War as a private. After the war ended, having been made an officer, he decided to stay in the army and remained on active duty until his death. In 1861, Davis was a member of the garrison of Fort Sumter that surrendered the fort following the Rebel bombardment. He returned to Indiana and became colonel of the 22nd Indiana Infantry. He was one of the first group of brigadier generals appointed in August 1861. He served

Below: *The 11th Indiana Infantry was a Zouave unit that wore a gray uniform and was originally raised by Lew Wallace, later the author of Ben-Hur. The red piping on an infantry uniform was unusual. In the Union army this was normally the sign of an artillery unit.*

his entire war in the western theater, starting as a divisional commander at Pea Ridge in 1862. Among the battles he fought were Murfreesboro, Chickamauga, and those of the Atlanta campaign.

Lew Wallace (1827–1905) served as a lieutenant in the 1st Indiana Infantry during the Mexican War. After the war's end, he turned to legal practice and became a prominent politician in Indiana politics. When volunteer regiments began to be raised. Governor Oliver P. Morton appointed Wallace as Indiana's adjutant general to administer the mustering in of regiments into US service. As part of this job, he was given the military rank of colonel in the 11th Indiana Infantry. For a relative amateur, Wallace had a good war. He commanded his regiment during McClellan's West Virginia campaign of 1861. In September 1861, he was promoted to brigadier general and fought under Grant in the Tennessee campaign that included the battles of Fort Donelson and Shiloh. Unfortunately, at the latter battle, he got lost on his way to the front and consequently was sent home to await orders. While waiting, the Confederate 1862 invasion of Kentucky gave him an opportunity to organize the defense of Cincinnati, which might otherwise have been occupied by the Confederates. In 1863, he organized Indiana militia to resist the raid of John Hunt Morgan. Having atoned for his mistakes at Shiloh, he was put in charge of US troops in Maryland in early 1864. When Rebel General Jubal Early approached the city of Washington in July of that year, Wallace's energetic response bought valuable time for reinforcements to be rushed from Grant's army to Washington. After the war, he became a well-known literary figure and remains remembered as the author of *Ben-Hur: A Tale of the Christ*, although more because of the motion pictures made from it than for his own writing.

Governor Oliver P. Morton (1823–1877) deserves mention as one of the most efficient of Union governors. Born in Indiana, he started his political life as a Free-Soil Democrat, a position that led him into the Republican Party. Initially elected as lieutenant governor in 1860, some political maneuvering allowed the Republicans to nominate the governor as a US senator, and Morton automatically succeeded him under the state's constitution.

When Lincoln called for ninety-day volunteers, Indiana raised twice its quota. Morton kept the extra men under arms at state expense. Such was his determination to fight the war, that when the legislature fell under Copperhead influence, Morton refused to call it into session and paid for the war with a mixture of loans from Washington and private subscription. He later served as a US senator from Indiana.

Below: *Lincoln with Lew Wallace at a camp at Antietam in September 1862. Wallace wielded considerable clout in Indiana politics, but his inexperience as a military man in his first campaign in 1862 led to his removal to rear-echelon duties. However, in 1864 his energetic moves to organize an ad hoc force that fought at the battle of Monocacy helped buy valuable time for the city of Washington, which was under threat from a raid led by Rebel General Jubal Early.*

IOWA

"The wealthy secesh rebels must be made to suffer.
They support the poor scamps who hide in the brush."

—Major General Samuel R. Curtis, October 23, 1862

Iowa was originally part of the Louisiana Purchase and unorganized until 1836, when the creation of Wisconsin Territory incorporated an area east of the Missouri River. In 1838 Iowa Territory was formed, comprising the area east of the Missouri River that was previously the trans-Mississippi region of the Wisconsin Territory. In October 1844 Iowa applied for statehood and Congress established the current boundaries of the state, omitting a considerable portion of Iowa Territory to the north. Iowa's formal admission was delayed when voters rejected the original state constitution. It joined the Union as a free state on December 28, 1846. In 1860, Iowa voted for Lincoln in the presidential election.

There were no major Civil War battles in Iowa. There was some skirmishing as guerrillas in northeastern Missouri, a strongly pro-Rebel region, crossed the state boundary to pillage. Rebel troops, part of Sterling Price's great 1864 march across Missouri, entered Davis County, but local troops were able to force them to retire.

Iowa's infantry regiments mostly served in the West, although the 22nd, 24th, and 28th Iowa fought in the 1864 Shenandoah Valley campaign. Iowa regiments were often brigaded together. Tuttle's brigade of General W. Wallace's division at Shiloh played a crucial role in the

Above: *The Iowa Monument at Grant's Last Line, Shiloh.*

Left: *The Iowa Memorial at section K, Andersonville, stands over the graves of many who died at the prisoner camp.*

battle defending the Hornet's Nest for six hours against repeated Rebel attacks. The 2nd and 7th Iowa escaped before the Rebels surrounded the defenders. The 12th and 14th Iowa could not get out and surrendered. After Shiloh, an Iowa brigade comprising the 11th, 13th, 15th, and 17th Iowa Infantry was formed. They fought at Iuka and Corinth, Mississippi, in September–October 1862, participated in the campaign and siege of Vicksburg in 1863, at Kennesaw Mountain, and in the 1864 campaign against Atlanta. They also marched to the sea with Sherman and were in North Carolina when the war ended in April 1865.

Iowa produced three major generals of note but none of them were born in the state. Samuel Curtis (1805–66) became a brigadier general of volunteers in 1861 and commanded Union forces at Pea Ridge. He was removed from command of the Department of the Missouri for political reasons and spent the rest of the war serving in the West. Grenville Dodge (1831–1916) also fought at Pea Ridge and commanded XVI Corps in the Atlanta campaign. Francis Herron (1837–1902), a captain in the 1st Iowa Infantry, fought at Wilson's Creek in August 1861. He won the Medal of Honor at Pea Ridge and was the youngest major general when promoted in 1862.

KANSAS

"Lawrence must be cleansed, and the only way to cleanse it is to kill."

—William Quantrill, Rebel guerrilla leader, August 21, 1863

The land occupied by the state of Kansas was part of the vast territory acquired by President Thomas Jefferson from Napoleon Bonaparte in the Louisiana Purchase of 1803. This area was unorganized until 1854, when the Kansas-Nebraska Act created two new territories. This was a controversial measure, as it permitted slavery in Kansas in contradiction of the Missouri Compromise of 1820, which had forbidden slavery with the Louisiana Purchase lands north of the line 36° 30'N.

In some respects, the Civil War could be said to have started in the years of "Bleeding Kansas," when Free-Soil and proslavery settlers competed to decided whether Kansas would enter the Union as a free or slave state. Their first battleground was elections for the territorial legislature. This battle was won by the proslavery forces, who stuffed the ballot boxes with the help of "border ruffians," proslavery Missourians who crossed the boundaries. Finding the law on the side of their enemies, the Free-Soil settlers, whose numbers were growing faster than the proslavery ones, tried to set up their own government. In these tense circumstances and with both sides heavily armed, it was hardly surprising that in November 1855 a proslavery man shot and killed a Free-Soil settler.

In the spring of 1856, a proslavery judge issued warrants for the arrest of five Free-Soil leaders for treason, on the grounds that they had organized a rival territorial government. A large posse from Missouri, armed with five cannons, arrived outside Lawrence, Kansas, the main center for Free-Soil settlement on May 21, 1856. The Free-Soil town allowed the posse in. The newspaper's offices were destroyed, along with several other buildings, before the posse left. The "Sack of Lawrence" brought a new player onto the stage of

Left: Lawrence, today the home of the University of Kansas, had a difficult early history. Settled by Free-Soilers, in 1856 it was occupied by a proslavery posse that vandalized a number of buildings. However, on August 21, 1863, Rebel guerrillas burned the town to the ground, killing over a hundred men and boys.

"Bleeding Kansas." Three days later, a fervent abolitionist inspired by a deeply held religion kidnapped five proslavery settlers near Pottawattomie Creek. John Brown's vengeful ferocity drove him to murder them with a broadsword.

This was the overture to the outbreak of anarchy that cost the lives of some two hundred settlers on both sides. It took the deployment of federal troops to bring the war to a temporary end. In 1858, fighting resumed when Congress rejected a proposed constitution for the territory that permitted slavery.

The outbreak of the Civil War simply continued the years of "Bleeding Kansas," although now the Free-Soil forces fought with the backing of the federal government. The territory became a free state on January 29, 1861.

The Civil War in Kansas was an ugly conflict, more a series of massacres of partisans on both sides than a conflict between bodies of soldiers. The destruction of Lawrence by William Quantrill's Rebel guerrillas on August 21, 1863, was typical. The Rebel attackers simply rode into the town, rounded up all the men and boys they could find, and killed them.

On October 25, 1864, a rare battle occurred when Major General Sterling Price's Rebel raiding column, which had marched across Missouri, entered Kansas near Kansas City, trying to evade pursuing Union forces. It was met by a Union column at Marais des Cygnes.

The outnumbered Union forces beat the Confederates through aggressive action. In fleeing their Union attackers, another Union column caught the retreated Rebels crossing Mine Creek that same day. The Union forces surrounded part of the Rebel force and captured six hundred prisoners.

KENTUCKY

"My poor Orphans! My poor Orphan Brigade! They have cut it to pieces."
—John C. Breckinridge, January 2, 1863

It could be said that Kentucky was the crossroads of antebellum America. In one of history's coincidences, it was the birthplace of both Lincoln and Jefferson Davis—and notable generals from both sides. It was a slave state, but slavery did not dominate its economy in the way it did further south.

The state's northern border, the Ohio River, offered a natural highway between Pittsburgh and points south and west. Just south of its southeastern border lay the Cumberland Gap, an important route between the original settlements of the Thirteen Colonies and the great Mississippi River valley. And the geographical position contributed to an intellectual position: Henry Clay, mastermind of so many political deals that kept North and South knitted together since 1820, came from here.

Given this background, it is hardly surprising that Kentucky's population was fairly evenly divided between Unionist sentiment and sympathy for the seceded states. Before President Abraham Lincoln's call for ninety-day volunteers, Kentucky had little thought of secession. Like Virginia, the state of Kentucky waited on developments. When they came, Kentuckians still preferred to avoid making a decision. The legislature proclaimed its neutrality and requested that neither side advance armed forces across its borders.

Thus, any taking of sides initially rested on private initiative. The governor of Kentucky, Beriah Magoffin (1815–85), sympathized with secession. Although Governor Beriah Magoffin hands were somewhat tied by the legislature's neutrality act, he actively encouraged recruiters for the Confederate army to tour his state.

Lincoln faced a delicate problem. If he advanced Union troops into Kentucky in these circumstances, he might push the state into the waiting arms of the Confederacy. However, the Confederates were acquiring recruits and supplies from Kentucky already. President Abraham Lincoln adopted a politician's popular principle: Don't do today what you can put off until tomorrow, because you never know what might come up. Union-minded Kentuckians who wanted to join the military effort to suppress the rebellion could cross the Ohio River and enlist in Cincinnati. But that was all.

While pro-Rebel Kentuckians had been quick to call for secession or at least support for the Confederacy, Unionist sentiment emerged more slowly. The clinching event that kept Kentucky officially in the Union was the state legislature elections in August 1861, after Bull Run. Unionists acquired majorities of seats in both houses, nearing three to one. It was not long before the flag of the United States once again flew over the state house in Lexington.

What secession sentiment lost at the ballot box, the Rebels tried to restore through armed force. Rebel troops from northwest Tennessee crossed the border on September 3 and seized the strategically important city of Columbus, where high bluffs overlooking the Mississippi provided a naturally strong place for batteries to control the river. The Union commander at Cairo, Illinois, Brigadier General Ulysses Grant, notified the Kentucky legislature of the Rebel move, and then advanced troops of his own to Paducah, another strategically important city that controlled the point where the Tennessee and Cumberland Rivers flowed into the Ohio. This move by Ulysses Grant's forestalled the Confederates, who already had sent a small detachment with a general into Paducah. These had to retreat in the face of far superior forces.

Left: The monument to Albert S. Johnston at Shiloh. He was the general in which Jefferson Davis placed the most confidence. Johnston was given the toughest task of the first year of the war, defending the long border of the Confederacy between the Appalachian mountains and the Mississippi. He was killed at Shiloh on April 5, 1862.

The Kentucky legislature responded to these two moves by voting to expel the Rebel invaders on September 18. But by this time a second Rebel force, commanded by General Felix Zollicoffer, had advanced into Kentucky from the Cumberland Gap area. Felix Zollicoffer's men scattered some Union militiamen at Barbourville on September 19. Zollicoffer had moved into Kentucky to cover the flank of the main Confederate force, under General Albert Sydney Johnston, which moved into the state from Nashville, Tennessee. Johnston intended to establish the Kentucky line, a string of Rebel-held outposts between Columbus on the Mississippi river through Bowling Green to Cumberland Ford in the east. With the Rebels having positioned themselves in Kentucky, and Union forces holding large bridgeheads across the Ohio River at Paducah and Louisville (which Union troops had entered in early September), both sides paused.

The Rebels continued to send officers on recruiting expeditions in parts of Kentucky where pro-Confederate sentiment might be strong, while the Union commanders incorporated the Home Guard militia into the Union army. Neither side was confident in the abilities of their amateur fighting forces, and devoted much of their efforts to training and equipping their men.

Right: A camp for militia companies at Frankfort in 1860. Kentucky's militia were not forced to choose a side right away in 1861. The state government made some attempt to remain neutral and asked both Union and Rebel governments to respect this. Rebel recruiters achieved some success in securing volunteers for their cause throughout 1861. However, Confederate forces crossed the border first, giving Union forces a chance to appear as the defenders of the state. Ultimately, more recruits joined the Union army than the Rebel one.

Lincoln's prodding compelled Union commanders to do something that winter. Lincoln wanted to send troops to the strongly Unionist area of east Tennessee, in spite of the difficulties faced in both getting them there and keeping them supplied once they had arrived. Brigadier General George H. Thomas was given command of some 4,000 men and ordered to try and do what he could.

Thomas marched into eastern Kentucky, and found that Zollicoffer's force, now under the command of

Below: *A map of one of the forts guarding Louisville, a vital base for Union armies and the rallying point for Buell's Army of Ohio during the Kentucky campaign of 1862.*

Below: *A soldier of the 4th Kentucky Infantry of the Confederate army. The regiment was part of the so-called Orphan Brigade, members of which enlisted in the Rebel army in 1861 and then never returned except as part of Bragg's army in the autumn of 1862. This brigade achieved an elite reputation in the Army of Tennessee, at the cost of heavy casualties.*

Major General George B. Crittenden, occupied an extremely ill-defended position near Mill Springs. Felix Zollicoffer, finding the enemy near, led an attack against Thomas. In the dim light of dawn, on a dark, rainy January 19, 1862, there was much confusion. Zollicoffer, whose eyesight was poor in any case, mistook a Union regiment for some Rebel troops and was shot down. The fighting continued until the Rebel attacks were beaten off.

Mill Springs was a small engagement, some 4,000 on each side. Thomas was eventually forced to abandon the advance into east Tennessee owing

to severe winter weather. Eastern Kentucky, however, was now firmly in Union hands.

The next development in Kentucky's Civil War occurred not because of any events within the state, but because of events in Mississippi. Ulysses Grant had moved his army up the Tennessee River with gunboats in February 1862. On February 6, the gunboats, backed by Grant's infantry, captured the Rebel Fort Henry on the river.

The next day, General Albert Sidney Johnston considered his alternatives. Grant's army was now between the force at Columbus, guarding the Mississippi, and Johnston's main command at Bowling Green. Grant was also in a position to threaten Nashville.

At the same time, a second, larger Union army was headquartered at Louisville under the command of Brigadier General Don Carlos Buell. If Johnston stayed at Bowling Green, he risked being trapped between Buell and Grant. Johnston had no choice but to retreat. The Rebels left Kentucky in the control of Union forces, at least temporarily.

The next major military event occurred in July 1862, when a raiding expedition entered Kentucky under the command of Brigadier General John Hunt Morgan. He left Knoxville with two regiments of cavalry on July 4, and crossed the Cumberland River on July 8.

John Morgan's command attacked a smaller body of Union cavalry at Tompkinsville on July 9, surprising and routing them. Moving quickly, he advanced to Glasgow, burning any Union stores that he found there. He continued his raid toward Lebanon, destroying bridges and telegraph lines as he went.

On July 12 John Morgan reached Lebanon and captured the town after a skirmish. What military stores he could not put to his own use he destroyed.

At Harrodsburg, Morgan's men found a warm welcome from the Rebel sympathizers there and then continued in the direction of Frankfort. On the way, he learned that a large force of Home Guard militia, along

with some regular troops, had assembled in Frankfort. Avoiding this force, he traveled via Lawrenceburg and Versailles to Georgetown, where he attempted to ambush a Union train carrying troops from Lexington. The Union forces discovered that a trap was waiting for them and stopped the train.

Georgetown proved to be another community that greeted the Rebels with enthusiasm. Brigadier General Morgan remained there for a couple of days, wreaking havoc on local arms depots and railroad bridges. He now prepared to return. On the way back, he fought the sharpest engagement of the raid at Cynthiana on July 17. The fighting lasted over an hour, but Morgan used the superior mobility of his all-cavalry force to overwhelm the defenders from different directions. The Union troops put up a stiff fight from behind stone walls and in the town's buildings, losing nearly two hundred soldiers in the fight.

Brigadier General Morgan captured over four hundred prisoners, some weapons, and horses. By now, the Union response was closing in on Morgan, but by intercepting telegraphic communications he was able to establish a safe route back toward Tennessee. On July 28, Morgan returned to the relative safety of Rebel-controlled areas at Livingston, Tennessee. The raid was a tremendous success, having caused much consternation among Union commanders, even attracting the attention of President Lincoln. Morgan lost ninety men over the course of the raid, but took over a thousand prisoners and destroyed a considerable quantity of Union supplies.

After the success of Morgan's small force in penetrating into Kentucky and finding knots of Rebel sympathizers, the commander of the Confederate Army of Tennessee, Braxton Bragg, tried the same feat on a larger scale. Using railroads to shift his forces from Mississippi to Chattanooga, Tennessee, and then marching up to Kentucky, Bragg launched some 40,000 troops toward Kentucky. The vanguard consisted of some 20,000 Rebel troops based at Chattanooga, who

advanced toward the Cumberland Gap and took it from a much smaller Union force that had occupied it in June. This force, commanded by General Edmund Kirby Smith, reached Richmond at the end of August, where they found a Union division of 6,500 recruits with no experience of combat.

A howling Rebel charge destroyed the Union force with the loss of only five hundred Confederate soldiers. Smith carried on his advance until he reached Lexington, from which he could threaten the state capital at Frankfort.

Braxton Bragg, meanwhile, had followed Smith by a more westerly route via Tompkinsville that brought him to Munfordville on September 17. Bragg now was positioned astride the main railroad line between Louisville and Nashville.

Above: *The brigade colors of the "Orphan Brigade."*

Right: *A printed poster commemorating the wartime career of Battery E, 1st Kentucky Light Artillery. It includes a list of all who served in the battery, those who died, the transferred or discharged, and even a list of deserters. The design of the poster captures the patriotic tenor of the Union states after the war. The stars and stripes is prominent, and two of the generals turned president, Andrew Jackson and George Washington, appear. Scenes considered typical of the soldier's experience are also illustrated in the margins.*

Buell had brought his army back from Nashville, but seemed to be content to remain stationary in the vicinity of his base at Louisville. The Rebels were able to inaugurate, with all proper ceremony, a Confederate governor of the state at Frankfort and seemed to be intent on taking up permanent residence in the Bluegrass State.

Lincoln, who had spent the spring urging McClellan to use the army against the Rebels in Virginia, now found McClellan's close associate Buell similarly reluctant to close with the enemy army. Buell could draw on the 55,000 troops he had brought with him from Tennessee plus a similar number of recruits training in camps around Louisville and Cincinnati. Bragg, by contrast, with only 40,000 men and little response to his florid appeals for new recruits from Kentucky, was outnumbered over two-to-one. Worse still for the Rebels, where Buell's army had concentrated its forces, Bragg's men were spread across a sixty-mile-wide front.

After all of Buell's intelligent planning, when the battle came it happened by accident. In the evening of October 7, 1862, a Union corps searching for a good source of water found one corps of Bragg's army defending Perryville. Word of the encounter between soldiers of the two sides was sent to the rival generals. Bragg urged an attack. Buell counseled delay until he could get more troops up. Bragg's subordinate, Major General Leonidas Polk, preferred the "defensive-offensive," and consequently the Rebel attack did not take place until Buell's reinforcements had arrived. Buell, in fact, was surprised that his isolated force had not been subject to a strong attack.

However, shortly after noon on October 8, Polk sent three divisions against the Union left flank. By luck, this blow fell on a part of the Union line that was occupied by inexperienced troops who, "seeing the elephant" (a contemporary slang term for combat experience) for the first time, ran away. The Union left was now exposed, and the situation would have been a lot worse

had the Union 11th Division, commanded by Brigadier General Phil Sheridan, not attacked in the center, driving the Rebels in front of them back, and entered Perryville. All this fierce fighting went on without Buell being aware of it, as a mixture of wind direction and local topography placed him in an acoustic shadow, and the booming sounds of artillery did not reach him. The chance of an attack by the Union right against a much weaker Rebel force went untaken, and a battle that could have seen the destruction of Polk's force ended at nightfall without decisive advantage to either side.

Bragg converted this tie into a loss by retiring. He had little choice, since Smith was not planning to join him, and the Army of Tennessee would be dangerously overmatched by Buell's much stronger force if Bragg remained. Bragg gave up the invasion of Kentucky and retired into Tennessee, even though his army still had a lot of fight left in it. Thus ended the last chance of a Confederate Kentucky.

When Bragg became aware that the new Union commander at Nashville, Major General William S. Rosecrans, was gathering supplies in preparation for a winter campaign, he ordered Morgan to make a raid into Kentucky to disrupt the railroads across the state. Morgan led his raiders out on December 20 from Alexandria, Tennessee.

Once again Morgan chose the route through Tompkinsville to enter Kentucky, only this time he headed in a more northerly direction, toward Elizabethtown. North of here were two trestle bridges carrying the Louisville & Nashville Railroad. Morgan's men destroyed these on December 28, 1862, and put the railroad out of operation until March 1863. Morgan returned to Smithville, Tennessee, on January 5. In the course of the raid his force had captured some 2,000 Union soldiers for a total loss in killed, wounded, and missing of ninety.

In March 1863, the Rebel cavalry of the Army of Tennessee conducted a raid into central Kentucky to secure some beef cattle for the army's stores. The

column, commanded by General John Pegram, targeted Danville, where the Union forces had a supply depot. They crossed the Cumberland river on the night of March 21–22, and reached Danville on the 25th. The Union forces retired without much of a contest, but pulled out many of their wagons. The Union commander of the district, Brigadier General Quincy Gillmore, watched carefully before requesting permission to take the field against the Rebels with a column of cavalry. By the time Gillmore took the field, Pegram was already pulling back toward the Cumberland. Pegram was more concerned with securing the cattle than contesting Gillmore, and a delaying action was fought at Dutton's Hill, near

Right: *The flag of the 1st Kentucky Infantry copied the first pattern of the Confederate national flag. The regiment served a short time in the eastern theater, before being mustered out in 1862.*

Somerset. A state historical marker notes the spot. The Rebels outnumbered the Union forces, and both sides struck with their left wings. The Rebels swept around the Union right, but this force did not move quickly enough to suit Pegram, and got caught in the rear by a detachment sent from the victorious Union left and center. The Rebels lost about two hundred men, the Union forces about thirty.

Morgan tried a third raid, in July 1863, but this time his actual targets lay north of the Ohio River. He conducted some small skirmishing in Kentucky, and this time he found the Union troops were better trained, and his casualties were significantly heavier, including his own brother Thomas.

The next significant Rebel incursion into Kentucky occurred in March 1864, when General Nathan Bedford Forrest led a raid that started in Columbus, Mississippi, and reached all the way to Paducah before he turned around to head home. The Confederate forces destroyed supplies in Paducah, but they were unable to capture the Union garrison that occupied Fort Anderson.

One last noteworthy event occurred on Kentucky soil. In May or June 1865, a group of Rebel guerrillas that had crossed from Missouri in late 1864, were caught in a barn in Spencer County. Their leader, William Quantrill, was mortally wounded in the shootout that followed. He died in a Louisville hospital.

One of the better-known Kentucky units of the war was the Confederate "Orphan Brigade," made up of regiments recruited from Kentucky at the outset of the war. It served in many major battles, including Shiloh, Murfreesboro, Vicksburg, and Atlanta, and surrendered with the Army of Tennessee in North Carolina in 1865.

Kentucky supplied generals to both sides. The best-remembered figure is John Hunt Morgan (1825–64), whose raids into Kentucky acquired a romantic quality. He had served in the Mexican War of 1846–48 as a junior officer and had settled in Kentucky afterward as a factory manager. He enlisted in the Rebel army in the fall of 1861, leading a small cavalry unit and fought at Shiloh. His skill at guerrilla warfare saw him given an independent command, but during his raid in the summer of 1863, into the states of Indiana and Ohio, he was captured. He had kept his plans to himself, thus surprising Confederate commanders just as much as Union ones. After a daring escape from a Columbus, Ohio, prison, Confederate generals were less enthusiastic about trusting him. He was killed in Greenville, Tennessee, by a surprise Union attack.

A former vice president of the United States and a candidate for the presidency, John Cabell Breckinridge (1821–75), found success as a general in gray. His personal battle honors included Shiloh, Murfreesboro, Chickamauga, and New Market.

Union General John Pope (1822–92) made his reputation in the West. He graduated from West Point in 1842, with an excellent academic record. He cemented his reputation with gallant service in the Mexican War, and was favored with command of the key Union thrust down the Mississippi river in 1861–62. His success in capturing Island No. 10 and Memphis helped him secure command of a large Union Army being assembled in northeastern Virginia in the summer of 1862. However, he was beaten by Robert E. Lee at the second battle of Bull Run in August, and was removed from command. He spent the rest of the war in the West, where he organized several expeditions against the Sioux.

Left: *Officers of the 1st Battalion, 1st Regiment, Capital Guards, and Kentucky State Guard. Kentucky remained a battleground state for much of the war as Confederate raiders, usually mounted, attacked Union army supply lines running through the state. These men were part of a unionist militia organization formed by the state's administration to combat these raiders.*

LOUISIANA

"There is but one thing that at this hour stands between you and your government—and that is slavery."

—General Benjamin F. Butler, farewell address to the people of New Orleans

Louisiana was originally part of the Louisiana Purchase of 1803. The Territory of Orleans was created in 1804, embracing the Red River valley and New Orleans. On April 30, 1812, the state of Louisiana was admitted to the Union. Louisiana voted for secession on January 26, 1861.

With a population of 170,000, New Orleans was the largest city of the Confederacy in 1861. It was one of the most important ports. It stood on the Mississippi River. For these three reasons an important early target for the Union forces. However, it was surrounded by swamps on its seaward side and too far from any Union-held territory to be reached by land. Taking the city this early in the war could only be done from the Gulf of Mexico, by sailing up the Mississippi. This was not a straightforward task. The British had famously failed in 1815, stopped by Andrew Jackson's army at Chalmette. Since then, two forts had been built at a bend in the Mississippi, forts Jackson and St. Philip, which had been seized early in the Louisianan march toward secession. Any fleet attempting to capture New Orleans would have to run past the guns of these forts. In order to hamper any such attempt, a chain supported by hulks had been stretched across the Mississippi River, sited to increase the amount of time any fleet would be exposed to the guns of the forts. Furthermore, they would have to contend with

Above: A belt buckle displaying the Louisiana state seal.

Left: Rear Admiral David Farragut was a southerner by birth, but a navy man by upbringing. His daring plan to run his fleet up the Mississippi river secured New Orleans for the Union.

a fleet of small ships that was strengthened and incorporated by an ironclad ram, the CSS *Manassas*, that had already caused damage to Union blockading ships. The CSS *Manassas* had been paid for by private subscription and was intended to be used to attack the blockading vessels off the mouth of the Mississippi. In addition to the *Manassas*, the Confederates were also building two ironclads along the pattern of the CSS *Virginia*, the CSS *Louisiana*, and the CSS *Mississippi*. However, before these problems could be dealt with, a fleet would have to pass the bar of the Mississippi river, which limited the draft of any attacking vessel to about sixteen feet.

The Union commander, Flag Officer David Farragut, was willing to try. His foster brother, Commodore David Dixon Porter, created a plan to shell the forts and then run the fleet up the river. Farragut had a lot of trouble crossing the bar, taking more than two weeks and using shallower-draft ships of his squadron to help the deeper-draft ones across. He had to leave one of his big-gun steam-and-sail ships back in the gulf, but by April 8, 1862, he had managed to get the rest of the big ships into the Mississippi.

Farragut had originally hoped to get over the bar quickly and up the river to start the bombardment of the forts using specially designed mortar vessels

commanded by Porter. But it had taken so long to get the big ships into the river that the element of surprise was lost. However, the Rebel leaders did not consider Farragut's squadron a serious threat to the "Crescent City." In fact, New Orleans was more vulnerable than they appreciated. Most of the troops protecting this part of Louisiana had been sent to fight at the battle of Shiloh, while part of the Rebel squadron guarding the Mississippi here had been dispatched to Memphis, where Union gunboats threatened the Tennessee city. The defense of New Orleans was vested in the two forts, which were about to be subjected to an extended bombardment by Union forces.

Porter's mortars went to work on April 18. They dropped anchor in the river and began firing, the shells of their big thirteen-inch guns arcing across the Louisiana sky and crashing in the vicinity of the Rebel positions. Porter's fire was effective until rifled guns in Fort Jackson got the range of one of his groups of mortar vessels. These then had to withdraw slightly. While they could still bombard the Rebels, they did so with much less effect.

For six days the mortars pounded the forts, but in the end they did little damage, partly because at nightfall they stopped, and the Rebels could repair some of the damage. Farragut concluded after six days

Below: The Union fleet runs past forts St. Philip and Jackson during the battle of New Orleans, April 24, 1862. Farragut's line formation fell into some confusion during the fighting, but the weakness of the Rebel squadron could not halt the Union ships from dropping anchor off the wharves of New Orleans that day.

that the mortars had been given a fair chance at wrecking the forts. Now it was the turn of the big ships to fight their way past them. He prepared his vessels carefully. They would steam past the forts by night in a line ahead formation, broken into three divisions. Guns were positioned on the forecastle and poop decks to give some firepower fore and aft. The sides of the ships, near their engines' boilers, were draped in anchor chains to provide some additional protection against Rebel shot.

At 2:00 a.m. on April 24, 1862, the signal to form up appeared on Farragut's flagship, the USS *Hartford*. Around 3:30 a.m. the Union's first division began sailing upriver. Some ten minutes later, the Rebel forts opened fire. The lead ship, the USS *Cayuga*, steered close to Fort St. Philip, since the Rebel guns were ranged on the center of the river. The second ship, the USS *Pensacola*, briefly engaged in a shooting duel with the fort, which had the effect of disrupting the Union line. Consequently, Flag Officer David Farragut brought his second division under way.

Once past the forts, the first division engaged the Rebel gunboats and the CSS *Louisiana* in a confusing melee. (The *Louisiana* had no engines and was moored as a floating battery off Fort Jackson.) The *Louisiana's* guns were so poorly mounted that she could do very little damage, but one Confederate gunboat did enough damage to one of the Union vessels to sink her. Flag Officer David Farragut's second division encountered the ironclads, but drove them both off, and both were later scuttled. The third division never passed the forts, as daylight made it too dangerous.

The city of New Orleans was now at the mercy of Flag Officer David Farragut's squadron. Furthermore, the Union plan envisaged landing 7,000 troops across Black Bay, under Major General Benjamin Butler. Once Butler's troops rendezvoused with David Farragut's ships at the quarantine station on April 25, the forts could be besieged. Recognizing their predicament, the garrison of Fort Jackson mutinied and half deserted.

The remainder surrendered to Porter. Farragut steamed up to the wharves of New Orleans, where he was greeted by a mob. After four days of negotiations, Farragut sent the marines to raise the Stars and Stripes over federal buildings. On May 1, Ben Butler's soldiers occupied New Orleans.

The occupation of New Orleans opened the way for campaigns and raids in Louisiana. Baton Rouge fell, and Farragut's fleet steamed all the way up to Vicksburg, Mississippi, in June. However, without a large army, he

Above: *Judah P. Benjamin (1811–84), shown here in a legal wig in his postwar career as a barrister in Britain. He served Jefferson Davis successively as attorney general, secretary of war, and secretary of state.*

Right: A plaque at Vicksburg National Military Park showing Colonel Robert Richardson of the 17th Louisiana Infantry. The regiment had fought at Shiloh and surrendered with the rest of the garrison at Vicksburg.

Far Right: The Louisiana state monument at Vicksburg National Military Park was dedicated in 1920 and disassembled after a lightning strike in 1999. In 2003 it was still undergoing restoration.

Below: The 1st Louisiana Special Battalion, the "Tiger Zouaves," at New Orleans in 1861. The colorful reputation of this unit was well deserved, drawn from a mixture of plantation aristocracy and the notorious street gangs of New Orleans. It was commanded by Major Roberdeau Wheat.

could do little against that city's powerful gun batteries. In August, a Confederate attempt to recapture Baton Rouge failed in part because the ram CSS *Arkansas* developed engine trouble that proved mortal and the ship was scuttled.

General John C. Breckinridge's assault on the Union position was initially successful. John Breckinridge, however, could not breach the final line of Union defenses. The Confederates retreated to Port Hudson. At Port Hudson they erected strong fortifications to prevent attempts by Union naval forces to advance up the Mississippi River.

Major General Benjamin Butler, meanwhile, expanded Union control to the west and southwest of New Orleans. However, Benjamin Butler's stern measures against secessionist sentiment, notably an order that permitted Union soldiers to treat any hostile woman as no better than a streetwalker, won him few friends in Louisiana. Although he made the streets of New Orleans safer and cleaner than they had ever been before through his administration, his policy of

Louisiana Tigers, *New Orleans, 1861.*

financing this through high taxes and confiscations led to his removal in December 1862.

President Abraham Lincoln appointed another political general, Nathaniel Banks, to take charge of New Orleans. During Ulysses Grant's campaign against Vicksburg, Banks was given the job of taking Port Hudson. Banks arrived outside of the city with his army on May 21, 1863, and laid siege to it. His troops' attacks on the trenches, some of which involved African American regiments, consistently failed. But the siege kept the garrison from receiving supplies, and after the fall of Vicksburg on July 4, Port Hudson in turn surrendered.

The next major campaign in Louisiana occurred as part of the general Union offensive of spring 1864. Originally, Banks was supposed to attack in the direction of Mobile, Alabama, but the presence of French troops in Mexico, propping up a civil war there, encouraged Lincoln's administration to make a military move westward in the direction of Texas. It might also be able to recover some cotton production to help put millworkers in the North back to work. The Red River campaign had as its target the city of Shreveport.

Banks was opposed by a much smaller army commanded by General Richard Taylor, the son of Zachary Taylor, president and Mexican War hero. Taylor had about 15,000 men at his disposal, a number very close to Banks, who also received support from a squadron of gunboats commanded by Rear Admiral David D. Porter.

The campaign opened on March 14, 1864, with the seizure of Fort DeRussey. Zachary Taylor fell back before Nathaniel Banks's superior numbers, waiting for reinforcements from Texas. He received little support and eventually chose to make a stand at Mansfield on April 8. Although intending a defensive action, one of Taylor's divisional commanders charged instead.

In the general advance, the Union forces were routed. The next day, another action at Pleasant Hill ended with the Union forces repelling the

Far Right: *Gunners of the Washington Artillery, a long-standing militia artillery company of New Orleans. Most of the unit served in Virginia, although one company served closer to home in the Army of Tennessee.*

Below: *Soldiers of the 2nd Louisiana Infantry, an African American unit, assault Rebel positions during the siege of Port Hudson on May 27, 1863.*

Confederates, but low water in the river and the failure of a Union force from Arkansas to reach Banks led him to retreat back to Baton Rouge. This was the end of major fighting in the state of Louisiana.

The greatest general of the war associated with Louisiana was the controversial James Longstreet (1821–1904). He was actually born in South Carolina, but after the death of his father and at the age of ten, he was taken to Alabama. Longstreet was a member of the West Point class of 1842 and served in the Mexican War. After the war he remained in the army until the secession crisis and then resigned. This resignation was followed by his appointment to the rank of brigadier general in the Confederate army.

James Longstreet fought in many of the major battles in Virginia and was also transferred to the Army

PIERRE BEAUREGARD (1818–1893)

This prominent Confederate general was born in St. Bernard parish. Beauregard had a distinguished career as a soldier in the US Army during the Mexican War and after. He was superintendent of West Point the time of Louisiana's secession and resigned immediately on receiving the news after just five days in the post. Beauregard's Civil War career took in some of the conflict's most significant events: Fort Sumter, first Bull Run, Shiloh, and Petersburg. However, after first Bull Run this prickly character found himself at the start of a war-long feud with President Davis. After the May 1862 evacuation of Corinth, Mississippi, Davis lost all confidence in Beauregard and dispatched him to command of the Department of South Carolina, Georgia, and Florida. Beauregard applied himself energetically to this post, and eventually returned to some favor as commander of the Military Division of the West, followed by a crucial role as commander of the Department of Southeastern Virginia and North Carolina, before finishing the war as the second-in-command of the Army of Tennessee. However, his difficulties with Davis limited his contribution to the Confederate cause. Beauregard always talked a good fight, promoting aggressive strategy and tactics, but his actual battlefield and campaign performances are a catalog of caution. His real skill lay in identifying good ground on which to fight and a certain strategic vision. After the war he remained prominent in Louisianan affairs.

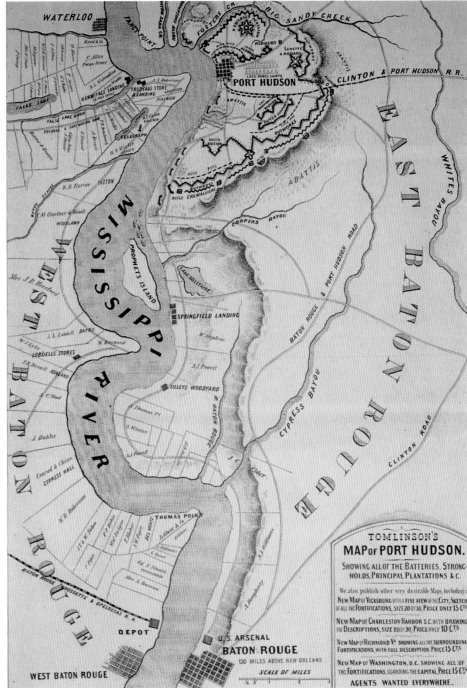

TOMLINSON'S
MAP OF PORT HUDSON.
SHOWING ALL OF THE BATTERIES, STRONG-
HOLDS, PRINCIPAL PLANTATIONS &C.

We also publish other very desirable Maps, including a
NEW MAP OF VICKSBURG with A FINE VIEW of the CITY. SKETCH
OF ALL THE FORTIFICATIONS, SIZE 20 BY 30, PRICE ONLY 15 CTS

NEW MAP OF CHARLESTON HARBOR S.C. WITH DRAWINGS
AND DESCRIPTIONS, SIZE 20 BY 30, PRICE ONLY 10 CTS

NEW MAP OF RICHMOND VA SHOWING ALL THE SURROUNDING
FORTIFICATIONS, WITH FULL DESCRIPTION. PRICE 15 CTS

NEW MAP OF WASHINGTON, D.C. SHOWING ALL OF
THE FORTIFICATIONS, GUARDING THE CAPITAL PRICE 15 CTS

AGENTS WANTED EVERYWHERE.

of Tennessee to help them gain the victory of Chickamauga in September 1863. His reputation was tarnished after the war when he was accused of being responsible for the Confederate defeat at the battle of Gettysburg. The gist of the accusation leveled against him was that he had opposed Lee's tactical plan and behaved in an insubordinate manner on July 2 by taking too long to maneuver his troops into position for the assault they made against the Round Tops. Longstreet had no confidence in attacking a position that appeared so strong and advocated a maneuver that would put the Army of Northern Virginia between the Union troops and the city of Washington, so that it would be the enemy who would be forced to attack. The matter remains a subject for debate. James Longstreet's association with Louisiana began after the war, when he settled in New Orleans.

Above: A commercial map of Port Hudson produced on July 23, 1863—only two weeks after the Union seized the city following a siege.

MAINE

*"I owe the country three years of service.
It is a time when every man should stand by his guns."*

—Joshua L. Chamberlain, February 12, 1865

Maine was originally a part of the state of Massachusetts, known as the district of Maine, so it officially became part of the United States when Massachusetts signed the Articles of Confederation in July 1778. However, the people of Maine were not happy with the government in Boston. They were heavily outnumbered in voting by the people of Massachusetts, a settled state with a large population. Maine was more of a wilderness than the Bay State, and four attempts to secure separate statehood were made over the years. In 1819, the fifth attempt succeeded, and the law admitting Maine as an independent state was signed by President James Monroe on March 3, 1820. Maine voted for Abraham Lincoln in the presidential election of 1860.

Maine's Civil War experience will always be identified with the famous 20th Maine Regiment and its commander at Gettysburg, Joshua Chamberlain (1828–1914). Chamberlain was born in Brewer, Maine. Chamberlain felt a strong urge to save the Union, and at the outbreak of the Civil War, he left his post as an academic to volunteer his military services to Maine's governor. He had been offered the colonelcy of a regiment when he applied to join the volunteers, but took instead the lieutenant colonelcy of the 20th Maine Volunteer Infantry Regiment. The regiment's first battle was Antietam in September 1862, but they only had a minor role in the center of the battlefield. Likewise, at Fredericksburg and Chancellorsville, the 20th Maine

Above: *A forage cap bearing the badge of the 19th Maine Infantry.*

Left: *Union Commander Oliver Otis Howard was badly wounded at the battle of Fair Oaks in May 1862, and his right arm was amputated. After the war, he was appointed as commissioner of the Freedom Bureau to assist former slaves. He later served in operations against the Native Americans and was superintendent of West Point (1880–82).*

avoided the worst of the fighting. So their epic contest on Little Round Top at Gettysburg on July 2, 1863 was the first serious combat it saw. Chamberlain and his men repelled an attack in brigade strength that might otherwise have turned the Union left flank and given the Rebels a decisive advantage in battle. For his services at the battle of Gettysburg, he was later awarded the Congressional Medal of Honor. Joshua Chamberlain went on to command a brigade and to receive a promotion to brigadier general. The unit went on to experience heavy combat at the Wilderness in May 1864 and Five Forks in April 1865. Ulysses S. Grant chose Joshua Chamberlain to receive the formal handover of weapons and colors at the formal surrender of Lee's Army of Northern Virginia at Appomattox on April 12, 1865.

The best-known general from Maine was Oliver Otis Howard (1830–1909). This officer, who was born in Leeds, Maine, graduated from West Point in 1854. He fought at the first battle of Bull Run and was promoted to brigadier general in September 1861.

Unfortunately, Oliver Howard's career is identified with the poor conduct of the XI Corps at both Chancellorsville in May 1863 and Gettysburg in July. Howard, a devout Protestant Sabbatarian and teetotaller, had little in common with the largely German-American corps, with its predilection for the Continental Sunday of games and parties.

MARYLAND

"Here is a paper with which if I cannot whip Bobbie Lee, I will be willing to go home."

—General George McClellan, September 13, 1862

Maryland declared independence from Britain in 1776 and became part of the United States on March 1, 1781, the last state to do so. In 1788 it became the seventh state to ratify the US Constitution.

Of all the four border states of Missouri, Kentucky, Delaware, and Maryland, the last was strategically the most significant to retain in the Union. This was not because it was especially wealthy or populous, but because it surrounded Washington on three sides. Worryingly for Lincoln, in the presidential election of 1860, Maryland had voted for the most proslavery of all the candidates, the Democrat John C. Breckinridge.

However, like all the border states, Maryland's division between pro-Union and pro-secession was largely a geographical one. The coastal counties around the Chesapeake Bay had the greatest concentration of slaveholders and were the most in favor of secession. In the west of the state, however, slaves were few and votes were for the Union. The balance of power was held by the city of Baltimore. The mayor of Baltimore in 1860 was George W. Brown, a man opposed to using force against seceding states, and the chief of police, George P. Kane, was an outright secessionist. Like most American cities at that time, violent gangs with political sympathies dominated Baltimore's streets. On April 19, 1861, when the first Union regiment bound for the city

Above: *A sword belt plate emblazoned with the Maryland state seal.*

Left: *Captain Raphael Semmes stands on the deck of his most important command, the CSS Alabama. He was born in Maryland, and as well as a career as a raider on the high seas, he also had an unusual postscript as an army officer: Commissioned as a brigadier general in 1865, he commanded soldiers during the last weeks of the war.*

of Washington, the 6th Massachusetts Regiment, passed through the streets of Baltimore because there was no direct railroad across the city, a mob with secessionist sympathies gathered and eventually turned hostile. Stones were thrown, soldiers were hit, and they replied by firing their muskets. A riot began in which four soldiers and twelve citizens died.

Maryland's authorities took measures to prevent further passage of their state by Union troops, tearing down railroad bridges. The Maryland legislature tried to establish neutrality in the struggle, but Lincoln positioned troops along the railroad line and suspended the writ of habeas corpus in that area. The army arrested Kane along with other active secessionists. In September, Lincoln went so far as to arrest members of the state's legislature. The crisis only ended with the election of a legislature dominated by Unionists in November.

Maryland avoided being a battleground until September 1862. After the second battle of Bull Run, August 29–30, 1862, the way into the North was open to General Robert E. Lee and the Rebel Army of Northern Virginia. There had not yet been a better moment in the war to make such an attempt. Most importantly, midterm Congressional elections would be held in November. To put a Rebel army in Maryland or even Pennsylvania would undermine the standing of

Right: *Camp Millington, at Baltimore, showing the carefully laid out tents of the 128th New York Infantry. Union troops marching through Baltimore in April 1861 were attacked by an anti-abolitionist mob, and afterward martial law was imposed on several areas of the state. Maryland's important strategic position in between the city of Washington, the seat of government, and the states of the North meant that it remained heavily garrisoned throughout the war.*

Lincoln's administration among Northern voters. President Davis's hope from the start of the struggle was to secure recognition from European states such as Britain and France. They would only back a cause that seemed to be winning. One more victory over the Army of the Potomac might well convey that impression. Finally, fought-over Virginia was hard-pressed to keep Lee's army in supply. With the way open into Maryland, the Rebels could subsist off countryside that had not seen much of the war, and would eat better there than by remaining in Virginia. Lee crossed the Potomac and entered Maryland on September 4.

The strategic situation confronting Lee was more perilous than the political one. He had about 55,000 men. To the east, around the city of Washington, McClellan had about 85,000 men. To the west, at Harpers Ferry, some 12,000 men defended the important railroad crossings there. Lee's line of retreat could easily be blocked by a strong detachment of troops from McClellan's command, while a slightly superior number engaged him directly. An aggressive, gambling commander might have risked such a move since the possible payoff could be the jackpot of the

destruction of Lee's force once and for all. McClellan, however, was a cautious, defensive commander. His first moves were to keep the entirety of his army between Lee and the national capital. As usual, he believed the Rebels had a numerical advantage.

Lady Luck, however, handed McClellan not one but two good cards. First, Lee developed an unwanted concern about the garrison at Harpers Ferry. He sent almost two-thirds of his army against Harpers Ferry. Control of it would not only sever the best rail route west out of Washington, it would also open a second line of supply and retreat for his army. Lee believed that McClellan would take so long to reorganize his army that not only did he have time to take Harpers Ferry, but he would also be able to approach the Pennsylvania border before McClellan would be ready to move. And so it might have proved, had a Union soldier not discovered, on September 13, three cigars wrapped in paper at his campsite near Frederick, where Lee's army had been on September 6. The paper proved to be a detailed order describing not only Lee's plan of campaign, but also the location and routes to be followed by all the divisions of his command.

Maryland

McClellan recognized the value of what he had, but not of the need to take advantage of it speedily. His excitement had been witnessed by a rare pro-Rebel sympathizer in this part of Maryland, who got word to Lee. Lee ordered the concentration of his army near Sharpsburg. A ferocious delaying action fought by Generals D. H. Hill and Longstreet at South Mountain on September 14 gave Lee a valuable extra day. When McClellan's troops started to arrive along Antietam Creek, near Sharpsburg, on September 15, Lee had already doubled the size of his force there and expected to increase it by two-thirds on the next day.

Both armies prepared for battle on September 16. Lee had 15,000 troops at his disposal, with another 11,000 almost arrived. One division remained at Harpers Ferry, which had fallen on September 15, but would be on the march as soon as possible. McClellan had some 60,000 troops at his disposal, a margin of more than two-to-one in his favor.

McClellan concocted a vague plan of a double envelopment of Lee's army. Once success had been achieved on each flank, a cavalry charge would be launched against Lee's weakened center, and split the Rebel army in two. However, the thrust against Lee's right would have to pass over Antietam Creek across a narrow bridge overlooked by heights that offered a strong defensive position. Lee kept his left wing strong, and relied on the natural strengths of the right and the rapid arrival of the division from Harpers Ferry to keep the Union forces away from the most threatened part of his position, the road from Sharpsburg across the Potomac. This was the main line for the troops returning to the army from Harpers Ferry, and Lee's army would suffer a crushing defeat if it could be taken before these arrived.

Around 6 a.m. on September 17, 1862, the bloodiest day in American military history began as General Joseph Hooker's I Corps advanced against the Rebel positions to the north of Sharpsburg. A ferocious battle now broke out in some woods and a cornfield near the

Dunker church. Union troops made uncoordinated attacks, as a seesaw battle raged for over an hour. Casualties on both sides were heavy, and whole regiments were obliterated as fighting forces. The Rebel line was near breaking point when a fresh division, commanded by General John Hood, reinforced it just in time and pushed the Union soldiers back. Hooker's corps was now the one near breaking point, and he

Above: *The memorial to soldiers from Indiana who fought at Antietam, September 17, 1862. Antietam was the bloodiest single day's battle in American history.*

summoned General Joseph Mansfield's XII Corps to his aid. It didn't seem possible, but the fighting became even more intense. The cornfield was solid with the bodies of the dead and the writhing figures of the wounded. Mansfield was killed, but his men fought on. At 9 a.m. the Rebel line grudgingly gave way and retired to a line anchored on the Dunker church. Hooker was now wounded and forced to leave the field, and the moments it took for the Union command to reorganize gave the Rebels a vital breathing space.

Fresh Union troops, General Edwin Sumner's II Corps, now entered the fray, while the Rebel line was reinforced by General Lafayette McLaws's division. One of Sumner's divisions advanced through the bloody Cornfield, but was stopped by Rebel musketry. In this part of the battlefield, the fighting was just about over.

Above: *Twin pontoon bridges span the Potomac River at Brunswick, Maryland, beside the ruins of a railroad bridge in October 1862.*

Just to the south of the Dunker church, the rest of Sumner's corps continued to advance across the farmland. D. H. Hill's troops waited for them in a strong defensive position, a sunken road between two farms. It was a natural breastwork. Hill's troops held their fire until the Union attackers were almost upon them. Then a sheet of flame and smoke erupted from the Rebel guns and the front Union ranks went down as if they had been scythed stalks of corn. The battle here raged

with the same ferocity as it had in the Cornfield. Union troops eventually forced their way into the Sunken Road, but could not proceed beyond as a Rebel counterattack drove them back into the relative shelter of the high-banked avenue. By about 1 p.m. the battle in this sector also petered out.

This left the assault on Lee's right, across Antietam Creek. The Union attack by Ambrose Burnside's IX Corps did not get underway until about 10 a.m., four hours after the battle on Lee's left. One assault was repulsed while trying to cross the narrow bridge in force. No further serious attempt was made for about an hour. Burnside awaited the arrival of a single division he had sent downstream to locate an alternative ford and get on the flank of the Rebel position on the heights overlooking the bridge. With no word of this division by 11 a.m., Burnside sent another assault across the bridge. This time it succeeded in finding purchase on the far bank, thanks to the Rebels running low on ammunition. McClellan for once ordered a rapid push forward, but Burnside wasted time shuffling his troops around for the assault. He did not move until 3 p.m. Perhaps better late than never, he gained ground steadily, until by about 4 p.m. when some Union troops gained the Harpers Ferry road. Then, in the nick of time for Lee, came word that A. P. Hill's division was arriving from Harpers Ferry. Lee pitched them into the flank of Burnside's corps, and the Union troops, the tips of their fingers just touching the outline of a decisive victory over the Army of Northern Virginia, found themselves being pushed back toward Antietam Creek. As night fell, both sides began counting the cost.

For the Army of the Potomac, 12,400 men had paid by becoming casualties. But Lee withdrew over the Potomac on September 19, retreating into Virginia. They had won a significant strategic victory. For the Army of Northern Virginia, just over 10,000 men were killed, wounded, or missing. They had saved themselves from defeat on the battlefield, but more than Gettysburg, this battle marked the high watermark of

FRANKLIN BUCHANAN (1800–74)

This naval commander from Baltimore was appointed midshipman in 1815. He spent the next forty-six years in the service of the US Navy. In April 1861, believing Maryland was about to secede, he resigned. However, when Maryland did not secede, he attempted to withdraw the resignation. The Navy Department instead dismissed him from the service, and Buchanan turned to the Confederate navy. He commanded two of the most important ironclads built by the Rebel fleet, the CSS *Virginia* in the fighting at Hampton Roads and the CSS *Tennessee* in the battle of Mobile Bay. He was wounded in both actions. He died in Talbot City, Maryland.

Left: *Emmitsburg, the location of St. Mary's College, was the headquarters of Union General Joseph Reynolds who organized the Union advance on Gettysburg and reported to General Meade on Confederate movements toward the Pennsylvania town.*

the Confederacy. Never again was the political, international, and military situation quite so favorable to its prospects of success.

The last major military action in Maryland was the battle of Monocacy on July 9, 1864, when a Rebel army defeated a Union force in Jubal Early's attempt to threaten the city of Washington.

Two of the Confederacy's most important naval officers, Raphael Semmes and Franklin Buchanan, claimed Maryland as their birthplace. Semmes (1809–77), who was born in Charles City, became a midshipman in the navy in 1826 and settled in Alabama in 1849. He resigned his commission after Alabama seceded and, in 1861, took to sea in command of the CSS *Sumter*. He then began his career as a commerce raider, attacking merchant ships flying the Stars and Stripes. He is most closely associated with the CSS *Alabama*, a British-built commerce raider responsible for sinking fifty-five vessels between August 1862 and June 1864. Semmes arranged a battle with the USS *Kearsarge* off Cherbourg on June 19, 1864. The battle was like some medieval joust, as the ships sailed a succession of circular courses as they traded shots. The *Kearsarge's* better-trained crew won. The *Alabama* went to the bottom.

MASSACHUSETTS

"A bullet had a most villainous greasy slide through the air."

—Captain Oliver Wendell Holmes Jr., 20th Massachusetts

This state was first permanently settled by English colonists in 1620. Boston, the capital of Massachusetts, became the de facto capital of New England. It declared independence from Britain in 1776 and officially became part of the United States on July 9, 1778. The state, perhaps the center of abolitionist sentiment in the antebellum United States, played a key role in the creation of the Republican Party, and voted for Lincoln in the election of 1860.

The governor of Massachusetts in 1861, John A. Andrew, was well prepared for Lincoln's call for 75,000 militia to suppress the insurrection in April 1861, and the 6th Massachusetts Volunteers were ready to travel south two days after the proclamation. However, on their way south, the lack of a connecting railroad line across Baltimore, Maryland, required them to march from one terminal to another through the streets. Many citizens of Baltimore had strongly pro-Southern opinions and gathered in the city streets to protest the use of force. The crowd turned violent, and the men of the 6th Massachusetts, having been pelted with stones and shot at, opened fire on the mob. Four soldiers and twenty-two civilians were killed.

Massachusetts' speed in responding to the call to arms reflected the important role it occupied in the

Above: *A row of mortars at Boston Navy Yard, an important base for refits of and repairs to ships of the Union navy.*

Left: *Clara Barton, born in Massachusetts, was working in in the city Washington when she saw some of the first casualties of the war, the Massachusetts soldiers wounded in Baltimore on April 19, 1861. Barton organized a nursing party, and spent the rest of the war raising funds or caring for wounded troops.*

Union war effort as a whole. The state included one important US arsenal at Springfield, and its textile and shoe factories helped to clothe the Union infantry. Boston was also, prewar, the second largest port in the United States and provided an important entry point for goods imported to sustain the Northern war economy.

As a significant mercantile city, Boston was also an important base for the US Navy. Several ships of the Civil War had been constructed at the navy yard, on the Charlestown peninsula. The USS *Merrimack*, whose hull and engines were used for the CSS *Virginia*, was one of the ships of the prewar navy that had been built there. Boston Navy Yard was also the best-equipped naval installation of all. Following the seizure of Gosport Navy Yard in Virginia, Boston boasted the largest joinery, saw mill, and mast shop available to the US Navy. It also had the largest steam engineering shops under navy control. There were nineteen ships laid down at Boston during the Civil War, including the sloop USS *Housatonic*, the first ship sunk by a submarine, and the monitor USS *Monadnock*. The navy yard was also an important base for refits and repairs and provided sailors with a taste of life on land among civilians that long spells on blockade reduced to a fond memory.

Above: *Looking more like British guardsman than American militia, this Massachusetts regiment visits New York City in 1860. Antebellum militia companies were often more social than military organizations, but Massachusetts regiments were among the best. The 6th Massachusetts responded to Lincoln's call for volunteers in April 1861 within two days.*

Massachusetts' military units played a prominent part in many of the battles of the Civil War. The 20th Massachusetts Regiment, whose ranks included future Supreme Court Chief Justice Oliver Wendell Holmes, was recruited at Camp Massasoit in July and August 1861 and fought in the disastrous battle of Ball's Bluff in October, where it suffered nearly two hundred casualties. Its battle honors also included Antietam, Fredericksburg, Gettysburg, the Wilderness, Spotsylvania, and Cold Harbor. It suffered most heavily at Antietam, where it was engaged in the fighting around the West Wood and the Cornfield, losing another 140 men. Worse still, at Fredericksburg it was both involved in the crossing of the Rappahannock in

boats on December 11, during the seizure of the town and the assault on Marye's Heights on December 13, losing another two hundred men over the two days. At Ream's Station, one of several small actions around Petersburg in the summer of 1864, virtually the entire regiment was isolated and captured by Rebel troops. Since at this time, Grant had abandoned the old system of parole and prisoner exchange, these men remained in Rebel hands for most of the remainder of the war. The regiment was reconstituted around the handful of men who escaped, but along with the replacements, they only made up three companies instead of ten.

The 20th suffered grave losses but another unit sustained even greater numbers of casualties. This unit

was 57th Massachusetts Regiment. The 57th was unusual in that it was not recruited as other regiments, but was made up of veterans of other regiments. It was raised at Worcester in late 1863 and first saw action during the Overland campaign of 1864. It suffered heavily during the battle of the Wilderness, but did not go into action until the second day, May 6, when it took part in the fighting around the Plank Road. Over 250 men were lost. Then, on May 12, the regiment was again heavily engaged in the fighting around Spotsylvania Court House, losing another seventy men. Thus, in a week it had lost almost a third of its strength and illustrated just how savage the battles of the Overland campaign were to Grant's men. To continue this hard-luck story, the 57th also took part in the battle of the Crater on July 30, 1864, when it entered the Crater with about a hundred men, all that were left after three months' of fighting. In this disaster, the 57th lost its colors and half its strength. The 57th thereafter, in spite of regular replacements, never boasted much more than two hundred on its strength. Considering that the regiment did not exist for half the war, this tale of losses in combat illustrates very clearly the demands that Grant put on his army.

The 57th's sad record is balanced by the healthy record of the 13th Massachusetts Regiment. In a conflict where the number of casualties from disease—on both sides—approached the total losses in combat, the

Left: *An artillery officer's insignia of the 4th Massachusetts Battery.*

Left: *Preserved artillery pieces mark the position of Brigadier General Daniel Ruggles' division during the battle of Shiloh. Born in Massachusetts, Ruggles was one of a number of Northerners who took the Rebel side in the Civil War. Ruggles was a graduate of West Point who spent much of his military service in Texas and resigned from the US Army in May 1861. After the war, he retired to a large estate he owned in Texas.*

13th Massachusetts Regiment had the lowest levels of loss from this cause of any three-year regiment in the entire US Army. The extremely low number of deaths through desease in the 13th Massachusetts suggests a remarkable level of attention to hygiene on the part of its men—quite a feat.

The career of the 54th Massachusetts has been deservedly given the Hollywood treatment in the film *Glory*. This was the first military unit of African Americans raised in the state, on February 21, 1863. All the commissioned officers were white men, and the regiment's commander was a former captain in the 2nd

Right: Fortifications manned by the 13th Massachusetts at Manassas Junction in 1862. The 13th Massachusetts set an exemplary record for losses from disease, a major cause of death in the armies of both sides, having the lowest of any regiment in the Union army.

Massachusetts

Massachusetts, Robert Gould Shaw. The regiment was sent to South Carolina to take part in the operations that summer against Charleston. Its first combat occurred near Secessionville, South Carolina, on July 16, 1863. Two days later, the 54th Massachusetts led the attack on Fort Wagner on Morris Island. The regiment

Left: *Robert Gould Shaw was a veteran of the 2nd Massachusetts and Antietam, when he was appointed to the colonelcy of a Massachusetts regiment to be raised from African Americans. Shaw commanded the 54th Massachusetts at the assault on Fort Wagner in July 1863, and was killed leading his men into the Rebel defenses.*

suffered over 350 casualties, including Shaw, who was killed while leading the attack. When Fort Wagner was eventually evacuated by the Rebels in September, the 54th was given the honor of being the first to occupy it. The 54th also fought at Olustee, Florida, on February 20, 1864, another Union defeat. The regiment led the fight for equal pay for African American soldiers and eventually secured full pay in the autumn of 1864.

Massachusetts contributed two of the least regarded generals of the Union army in the war, both of whom owed their rank to political influence. Without doubt, Major General Benjamin Butler (1818–93) is one of the candidates for the most incompetent general of the war. Butler was a Democratic politician who went so far as to

03

support proslavery John C. Breckinridge in the 1860 election. However, his prompt response in taking control of Baltimore in the spring of 1861 endeared him to Lincoln, who at that stage of the war was feeling especially isolated from the North.

Butler was commissioned a major general in May 1861 and sent to Massachusetts to recruit a force to be used on the Gulf Coast. He was given command of the troops who supported Flag Officer David Farragut's attack on New Orleans and became military governor of the city. However, perhaps because of his role in the 1860 campaign, the severity of his conduct toward "traitors" including hanging a man for taking down the Stars and Stripes from the US Mint Building in New Orleans. He also issued his infamous General Order No. 28, which allowed Union soldiers to treat any

woman who insulted them as a prostitute. The outrage in the South to this order contributed to President Jefferson Davis's condemning Butler as an outlaw and inviting Rebel officers to hang the Union major general should he fall into their hands.

Some of his acquaintances, including his brother, did suspiciously well financially out of Butler's administration, which contributed to his removal in December 1862. A year later he was given command of the Army of the James, based at Fortress Monroe, Virginia, where he completely missed an opportunity to seize an almost defenseless Petersburg during the spring campaign of 1864.

The fact that it took Grant some eight months of siege and many casualties to capture the place only underlines the extent of Butler's failure. Butler also lost a chance to capture Fort Fisher in his last command of the war in 1865.

General Nathaniel P. Banks (1816–94) did not plumb the depths of incompetence reached by Butler. His case was more of being overmatched by some of the better Rebel commanders. Banks's political association was originally with the American or "Know-Nothing" Party of

nativists, who were opposed to immigrants in the antebellum United States. Many American Party supporters moved into the Republican Party when proslavery advocates began to wield too much influence, and Banks was one of them.

Nathaniel Banks was appointed a major general of volunteers in May 1861 and was outmaneuvered by Stonewall Jackson in his first important field command in the Shenandoah Valley in the spring of 1862. Major General Banks replaced Benjamin Butler in New Orleans and, in 1863, eventually captured Port Hudson, which surrendered after the fall of Vicksburg and not because of Banks's military genius.

In 1864 Major General Nathaniel Banks commanded the army in the Red River campaign in Louisiana. Once again Nathaniel Banks faced a superior soldier— General Richard Taylor—who defeated Nathaniel Banks's army at Sabine Crossroads and Pleasant Hill. Nathaniel Banks retreated when a supporting column from Arkansas failed to arrive, having been itself defeated by Rebel forces there.

Above: *A surgeon of the 22nd Massachusetts. The regulation rank for surgeons was major, and much of the first professional medical attention for wounded soldiers was provided by these officers.*

CLARA BARTON (1821–1912)

This indomitable woman worked in the patent office until the outbreak of the war when she became a nurse. Her friendship with congressional politicians enabled her to find considerable support for her efforts to give aid to the wounded. Barton spent most of her time working in hospitals in Virginia and came to national prominence for her care of the wounded after the Wilderness in May 1864. She helped locate those listed as missing in action, interviewing exchanged prisoners to see who else might be in Rebel prisoner-of-war camps for families uncertain of the fate of their kin.

Several other Massachusetts men also made important contributions to American literary history in response to the Civil War. John Greenleaf Whittier (1807–92) wrote the poem *Barbara Frietchie*, and Henry Wadsworth Longfellow (1807–82) wrote *Paul Revere's Ride* in order to rouse patriotic sentiment during the Civil War.

The fascinating short story *The Man Without a Country*, penned by Edward Everett Hale (1822–1909), was perhaps the most interesting contribution to Civil War literature. It told the story of a US officer of the 1800s who damned the United States. The officer's punishment was to be banished to the decks of US Navy warships that carried him at sea until his death, never giving him the slightest piece of information about his homeland, nor even uttering the name of his native land. Published in 1863, many readers in that difficult time believed it to be a true story.

MICHIGAN

"Where in Hell is the rear?"

—General George Armstrong Custer, June 1864

The Northwest Territory was organized by Congress in 1787, after becoming a part of the United States under the Treaty of Paris in 1783. This included the present territory of the State of Michigan. In 1800, when the original Northwest Territory was divided into two, Michigan was divided between the new Indiana Territory and the reduced Northwest Territory. In 1805, the lower peninsula became Michigan Territory, and four years later the upper peninsula was added to Indiana Territory. In 1816, after Indiana became a state, the upper peninsula was added to Illinois Territory. The areas of Wisconsin, northeast Minnesota, and the upper peninsula were then added to Michigan when Illinois became a state in 1818. In 1834, the land east of the Missouri River was added to Michigan Territory, then taken away again two years later when Wisconsin Territory was created, leaving Michigan Territory with the current boundaries of the state. Michigan was admitted to the Union in 1837. Abraham Lincoln carried Michigan in the 1860 election.

Michigan's role in the Civil War economy was threefold. Its agricultural products helped to feed the Union armies. Its timber helped to construct the railroads, wagons, and bridges that connected the

Above: *Lieutenant Parker and two soldiers of the 4th Michigan, plus an orderly.*

Left: *George Armstrong Custer graduated from West Point in 1861. Born in Ohio, he was raised in Monroe, and made his reputation with Michigan cavalry regiments. In June 1863, he was promoted to brigadier general, aged 25.*

Northern economy to its armies in the field. Its mineral resources were used in the production of Union guns. Michigan also controlled a vital part of the communications network of the Northern economy because iron mined in northern Minnesota passed through the locks of Sault Ste. Marie, Michigan, on its way to the foundries of Pittsburgh.

The legendary George Armstrong Custer (1839–76) was born in New Rumley, Ohio, but his father sent his son to study in Monroe, Michigan, south of Detroit, in 1849, where the "Boy General" came to maturity. An equestrian monument at the junction of Elm Avenue and N. Monroe marks the link between the town and its best-known resident. Custer may be more notorious for his conduct during wars against the Native Americans of the Great Plains in the decade after the Civil War, but he first came to national prominence for his actions with the cavalry of the Army of the Potomac. He left West Point in June 1861, just in time to join in the campaign leading up to Bull Run, where he earned a citation for bravery.

His war career was entirely in the eastern theater, where he made an ascent in one of Thaddeus Lowe's balloons, acted as an aide to General George McClellan,

and in 1863 became the youngest general in the army when he was promoted to a brigadier general of the US Volunteers. The battles he fought at included Gettysburg, Yellow Tavern, and Trevilian Station. He was also present at the surrender of Lee's army at Appomattox Court House, and in fact acquired the desk on which the surrender was signed.

The 4th Michigan Infantry was mustered at Adrian from among militia companies based in cities in the southeastern corner of the state. It was sent east and served for three years with the Army of the Potomac. It was present at every major battle in the eastern theater between the Seven Days' battles of 1862 and the start of the Siege of Petersburg in 1864.

Like the 4th, the 7th was assembled from a variety of militia companies. The 7th was part of the Army of the Potomac's II Corps, and at the battle of Antietam was heavily engaged in the fighting around Dunker Church. The 7th was on the flank that was attacked by the Confederate division commanded by Lafayette McLaws,

and suffered terrible casualties. The general commanding the brigade, Brigadier General Napoleon Dana, reported the Rebel volleys as "the most terrific I ever witnessed." Two days before the battle of Fredericksburg, on December 11, 1862, the 7th made a crossing of the Rappahannock River under fire from Rebel sharpshooters in the town, before clearing the buildings of the enemy. This enabled a bridge to be completed and the army to begin its crossing of the river. On December 13, the 7th participated in one of the assaults on the strong Confederate position at the foot of Marye's Heights, behind a stone wall. By the time of the battle of Gettysburg, in July 1863, the 7th was reduced to barely 160 men, from an enlisted strength of nearly 900. At Gettysburg, the 7th only arrived on the second day and was posted on Cemetery Ridge. As the advanced position occupied by the III Corps (including the Wheatfield and the Peach Orchard) gave way under Confederate assaults, the 7th found itself under attack. A few well-timed volleys

Right: *Men of the 21st Michigan Regiment in camp, most wearing the slouch hats characteristic of Union soldiers in the western theater. The 21st Michigan served in General Philip Sheridan's division at the battles of Perryville, Stones' River, and Chickamauga, where it distinguished itself for its steadiness under fire and in critical situations.*

halted the Rebels, and the Confederate brigade commander, General Barksdale, was mortally wounded. On July 3, the 7th was part of the target for Pickett's Charge. The 7th was given the order to fire on the advancing Confederate column by the brigade commander (and former commander of the regiment) Colonel Hall. In his official report he said of this: "I caused the Seventh Michigan and Twentieth Massachusetts Volunteers to open fire at about two hundred yards. The deadly aim of the former regiment was attested by the line of slain within its range." In the fierce melee around the point where Pickett's charge reached its high watermark, the 7th took its share of the fighting, as Union regiments became intermingled and confused. The role of the 7th is illustrated in the Gettysburg Cyclorama.

Another Michigan regiment, the 24th, also played a dramatic role in the battle. The 24th Michigan was recruited from Wayne County and became part of the Iron Brigade, the only all-midwestern brigade in the Army of the Potomac. On July 1, 1863, the 24th was positioned with its fellow Iron Brigade regiments along Willoughby Run when the Rebel attack swept forward and around the brigade's flanks. The commander of the regiment was severely wounded and captured, although he was left behind when the Rebel army retreated on July 4. Out of 496 men who stood on the line at Willoughby Run, 316 were killed or wounded, about 69 percent. The regiment did not rout, but retreated in good order in the face of superior numbers.

The 22nd Michigan Infantry was raised from the counties north of Detroit and mustered at Pontiac in July 1862. It led a largely uneventful war in the western theater until September 1863. At this time it was part of the Reserve Corps of the Army of the Cumberland. The Reserve Corps was stationed north of the battlefield at the time of the Confederate attack on September 19th. The corps commander, Gordon Granger, organized a reinforcement of the Union 14th Corps under George Thomas. The 22nd was sent to the right of the Union

line, where it was subjected to a flanking attack by Hood's corps of the Confederate army. The Union line in the 22nd's part of the field almost disintegrated, and most of the regiment was killed, wounded, or taken prisoner. After Chickamauga, the regiment performed various rear echelon duties for the rest of the war.

The 22nd's biggest claim to wartime fame, however, is that it was the regiment of Johnny Clem, the Ohio-born drummer boy who tagged after the 22nd when it passed through his hometown in Ohio. Clem evaded capture by the Rebels at Chickamauga by shooting the officer attempting to take him prisoner. He was appointed a second lieutenant by President Grant after the war. When Clem retired in 1915, as a brigadier general, he was the last serving Civil War veteran in the army. His story was the basis of a novel and a Disney film.

Above: *A monument to the soldiers and sailors of Michigan at the site of Andersonville prison camp in Georgia. The dreadful conditions here claimed the lives of many Union prisoners.*

KILLED IN ASSAULT OF MISSION RIDGE,
NOVEMBER 25 1863.
LIEUT. SAMUEL G. TRIMBLE COMPANY D
SERGT. JOHN WESTERMAN, " B
SERGT. BENJAMIN P. TALBOT, " B
CORP. HENRY F. KOCH, " K
PRIVATE RINGIS DE GRAVE, " C
SAMUEL LOUDON, " H
JAMES PELKEY, " H
GEORGE E. LAMPHEAR, " K
PHILETUS S. BARNETT, " K
CHRISTIAN KASMIER, " K
COMPANIES F & G ABSENT ON DETACHED
SERVICE — 185 MEN ENGAGED.

MINNESOTA

"Colonel, do you see those colors? Then take them."

—General Winfield S. Hancock to Colonel William Colville, July 2, 1863

The history of Minnesota's journey to statehood is a complicated one. Only the far northeastern corner was included within the borders established by the 1783 Treaty of Paris, which ended the Revolutionary War. The remainder of the state's territory was acquired as part of the 1803 Louisiana Purchase. The northeastern part was incorporated in the Northwest Territory established by Congress in 1787. The Louisiana Purchase portion was unorganized territory until in 1836 a region known as "East of the Missouri River," which also included parts of the Dakotas, was added to Wisconsin Territory. Northeastern Minnesota had passed through several successive territories organized from the original Northwest Territory, the last of which was Wisconsin Territory. The union was only temporary, as in 1838 Iowa Territory was formed and took over east of the Missouri River. Minnesota was reunited in 1849, when Minnesota Territory was formed from leftover parts of recently admitted Iowa and Wisconsin. In 1858 Minnesota was admitted to the Union, using the current state boundary. What was left over remained known as Minnesota Territory until 1861. The state voted heavily for Abraham Lincoln in 1860 providing the president-elect his second-highest majority.

This enthusiasm for Lincoln carried on into his call for volunteers to suppress the Southern rebellion.

Above: *The USS* Minnesota *saw action at Hampton Roads in March 8, 1862, when it attempted to come to the rescue of the USS* Congress, *but ran aground. On March 9, 1862, the CSS* Virginia *came out to destroy the* Minnesota, *but found the USS* Monitor *instead.*

Left: *The monument to the 2nd Minnesota Infantry on Missionary Ridge, Chattanooga, Tennessee. The unit was among the first regiments to breach the Rebel lines here, in one of the worst routs of the Confederate army's history.*

Traditionally, the first volunteers enlisted on April 15 were Minnesota men, who became the original members of the most famous Minnesota regiment of the war, the 1st Minnesota Volunteers. The unit was part of the Army of Northeastern Virginia and the Army of the Potomac throughout the war and first saw action at the first battle of Bull Run. The regiment is best remembered for its charge at Gettysburg on July 2, 1863. The defeat of Sickles' III Corps in the fighting around the Wheatfield and the Peach Orchard left the II Corps's flank on Cemetery Ridge exposed to Rebel attack. A brigade of Rebels was advancing on the Union position, when II Corps's commander ordered the 1st Minnesota to charge in order to buy time to bring up more men. Then, 262 Minnesotans attacked 1,600 Rebel soldiers. They attacked in good order, as fast as they could. As they neared the Rebel troops, the first line of the enemy gave way, and the Union troops were able to fire into the second line. Only when reinforcements were brought up did the Rebels resume their attack, and the 1st Minnesota withdrew. Returning to Cemetery Ridge they counted forty-seven survivors. Losses had amounted to 82 percent of the men engaged, one of the highest totals in the war. The 1st Minnesota added several more major engagements to its battle honors and was still with the army at Appomattox Court House.

MISSISSIPPI

"I feel that I would like to shoot a Yankee, and yet I know that this would not be in harmony with the spirit of Christianity."

—Captain William L. Nugent, 28th Mississippi Cavalry

Most of Mississippi's territory lay within the boundaries of the United States as laid out in the Treaty of Paris of 1783. Spain claimed a part of this area, but the western boundary was fixed at the Mississippi River by the Jay-Gardoqui Treaty of 1795. The portion of the state south of the 31st parallel that touches the Gulf of Mexico remained part of Spain's territory until 1810, when American settlers there rebelled against Spanish rule and proclaimed a Republic of West Florida in 1810.

The United States claimed this land as part of the Louisiana Purchase, and eventually it was incorporated into the United States by treaty. The Territory of Mississippi was organized in 1798. The western half was admitted to the United States in 1817, while the eastern portion became the Territory of Alabama. Mississippi was the second state to pass an ordinance of secession, on January 9, 1861, having voted for Southern Democratic candidate John C. Breckinridge in the election of 1860. It became part of the Confederacy in February 1861.

The only important military event to occur in Mississippi during the first year of the war was the seizure of Ship Island on the Gulf Coast on September 16, 1861. Ship Island became an important naval station for the Union squadron blockading the Gulf Coast.

After the battle of Shiloh, the focus of operations in the Mississippi Valley shifted to Corinth, Mississippi.

Above: *A state of Mississippi $2.50 note, backed by the proceeds from the sale of cotton acquired by the state authorities for this purpose. The shortage of gold and silver in the South required emergency measures to back the currency and provide cash for circulation in the economy.*

Left: *President Jefferson Davis was outclassed by the easy-going Lincoln as a war leader. His unwillingness to suffer gladly those he saw as fools and a preference for those who told him what he wanted to hear hampered the Rebel war effort. However, he took second place to no one for his dedication to the cause of Southern independence. After the war, he hoped for a trial to vindicate himself and the Confederacy, but the federal government never obliged.*

This was a key junction for railroads in the Confederacy, where the line from the Gulf Coast joined an important east-west line. The Union commander of the Department of the Mississippi, General Henry Halleck, had made it the target for offensive operations even before the battle of Shiloh. He assembled a huge army, some 100,000 men, on the Shiloh battlefield. This was one of the largest assemblages of men during the war. This brought together the Army of West Tennessee, the Army of Mississippi, and the Army of Ohio. Halleck arrived there on April 11, 1862, and the Army of Mississippi completed the array with its arrival on April 21st.

Halleck, however, conducted a slow advance that secured him from attack by the Confederates, even though it made it difficult for him to attack himself. He took four weeks to complete a march across twenty miles, which the Confederate Army of Mississippi accomplished in three days on its advance to Shiloh. As soon as any resistance was encountered, Halleck had his men entrench themselves. They also entrenched each night.

The Confederate government's value for the Corinth was demonstrated by the effort put into reinforcing the battered losers of Shiloh. Beauregard returned with about 35,000 effective soldiers. By scraping up soldiers from the eastern seaboard, from eastern Tennessee, and even from Arkansas in the Trans-Mississippi

Department, the army was doubled in size to some 70,000 men. The problem of compressing so many men in a small area with a limited water supply became apparent as disease began to attack Confederate numbers. Typhoid and dysentery reached epidemic levels as one thousand soldiers died of disease.

Halleck's advance with the aid of the spade suggested his willingness to surround the Corinth garrison with entrenchments and subject the railroad junction to a siege if necessary. Beauregard, whose own health was badly affected by a respiratory infection, recognized that to accept a siege under such circumstances would worsen the existing medical disaster. He could either attack the entrenched Union army in the field, a risky proposition, or he could evacuate Corinth. Beauregard chose the latter and retired to Tupelo, Mississippi. He characterized his withdrawal as a victory, since it left the Confederates with a large army that could conduct an offensive against the Union forces under more favorable terms at a later date. President Davis was less impressed by Beauregard's boast of a strategic victory. When the Louisianan took unauthorized sick leave, Davis took the opportunity to remove him from command and appointed Major General Braxton Bragg in his place.

Meanwhile, developments at the south end of the Mississippi threatened the state from a new direction. The fall of New Orleans on May 1 opened the Mississippi to Union ships sailing up from the Gulf. A squadron of deep-draft screw sloops did just that and passed Vicksburg on May 18. On July 1, 1862, Flag Officer David Farragut attempted to bombard the city into submission using a fleet of mortar boats. This effort proved fruitless without support from troops approaching the city by land. He had also learned that a new ironclad was being built up the Yazoo River, at Yazoo City. The CSS *Arkansas* had began building at Memphis, but was moved to the Yazoo River after the fall of New Orleans in order to avoid any possibility of capture. Farragut was uncertain of where the *Arkansas* was located and his attempts to fix its position with reconnaissance by both land and sea had uncovered nothing. Instead, the Rebel ram paid his own fleet a visit, attempting to run past it to Vicksburg on July 17. This escapade enraged Farragut as the *Arkansas* sank one Union ram and fled to Vicksburg in spite of being the solitary target of a Union fleet numbering thirty vessels. Farragut made three more attempts to sink the *Arkansas*, but each one failed. He did not realise—and nor did the Rebels—that the last of these attempts inflicted a fatal wound on the vessel by damaging its engines. The vessel would have to be scuttled in August while trying to help Rebel troops recapture Baton

Right: *A private of the 11th Mississippi wears the characteristic long gray blouse with red frogging of official state uniforms. The 11th Mississippi fought at the far left of the Rebel line at Antietam, in the bloody combat around the Dunker Church.*

Left: *The memorial site to Lowe's Mississippi battery at Vicksburg National Military Park.*

Rouge. David Farragut himself abandoned his naval attempts to lay siege to Vicksburg and retired to New Orleans on July 26.

Both Union and Rebel forces operating in Mississippi underwent command changes in the early summer of 1862. Bragg replaced Beauregard, while for the Union forces, Halleck left for the city of Washington to fill the role of commander in chief on July 17, leaving Grant in charge of the Union forces along the Mississippi. He did not have enough forces for offensive operations. Bragg was preparing his invasion of Kentucky, while two other Rebel armies occupied Vicksburg (commanded by General Earl Van Dorn) and Holly Springs (General Sterling Price).

In September the pace of war began to gather again. Price's small army launched an attack on one of Grant's troop detachments at Iuka on September 14. Price pushed the Union force out, but left himself vulnerable to a pincer movement by two parts of Grant's army. However, the wily Price spotted the trap closing and evaded it, retiring toward Vicksburg and Van Dorn. Now the two Rebel generals combined to create a sizable army and plotted an attack on Corinth.

On October 3, the rebels reached the important rail junction and launched their assaults. The armies were fairly even in numbers, with just over 20,000 men each. On a hot day a fierce battle saw Union General William S. Rosecrans's troops hold on grimly as the Rebels seized the first line of entrenchments, but got no further. Once again, Grant attempted to trap the Rebel forces, but Rosecrans's slow pursuit allowed them to get away. Leadership changes were the main consequences of the battle. Rosecrans took over command of the Department of the Ohio. President Davis transferred General John Pemberton from Charleston, South Carolina, to take command of both Van Dorn's and Price's troops. General Joseph E. Johnston was made commander of the Department of the West in order to give some strategic direction to Rebel efforts in this critical theater.

A month after the battle of Corinth, Grant went over to the offensive. He advanced down the line of the Mississippi Central Railroad, establishing a forward base at Holly Springs. Then he pushed his army on to the Tallahatchie River and flanked Van Dorn's position there before moving on to Oxford where he halted. Here he received an unfortunate order from Halleck. He was to hold the line of the Tallahatchie and instead a force was

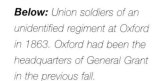

Below: Union soldiers of an unidentified regiment at Oxford in 1863. Oxford had been the headquarters of General Grant in the previous fall.

to approach Vicksburg down the Mississippi. This job was supposed to be given to Major General John A. McClernand, an Illinois Democrat who owed his rank to his political prominence. However, McClernand was campaigning at home and the telegram never reached him, so Sherman took over the four-division force that now moved down the Mississippi. The operation began on December 23, when the Union gunboat fleet sailed up the Yazoo River to cover the approach of Sherman's transports. The troops arrived on December 26 and began approaching Vicksburg from the north. The Rebel defenders of Vicksburg advanced a couple of brigades to entrench a strong line at Chickasaw Bluffs, protected on the left by the Mississippi River and on the right by Chickasaw bayou, while to the front lay an area of flooded bayous. Sherman's troops made their attack on December 29, erecting pontoon bridges to help them pass the bayous. The Rebels easily repelled the attack, causing 1,700 casualties of Sherman's forces, while losing only two hundred themselves. The second attempt to take Vicksburg had failed. McClernand now arrived and turned his attention to the capture of Fort Hindman in Arkansas.

With the bulk of his army now on the west bank of the Mississippi, Grant arrived to take personal command at the end of January 1863. The main Rebel army under Pemberton was at Grenada. Several weeks were now spent in trying to construct a series of canals that would connect various bends in the Mississippi to enable the army to bypass the Vicksburg batteries and

Right: *Union troops assault Rebel positions at Vicksburg. On May 22, 1863, Grant ordered an attack all along the line on the Rebel entrenchments that resulted in a bloody repulse.*

land south of the town. The difficulty of trying to construct engineering works on the muddy flood plain of the Mississippi defeated these plans.

Meanwhile, Grant had developed a daring scheme of his own. The first step was to destroy the Confederate gunboats that patrolled the river between Vicksburg and Port Hudson, Louisiana. Farragut's big ships accomplished this feat on March 14, sailing up from New Orleans. Two weeks later, Grant's army began marching a circuitous route through the woods inland

Mississippi

commanded by Brigadier General Benjamin Grierson began a sixteen-day trek through the state of Mississippi. His objective was the supply lines of Pemberton's army, and Grierson's troopers successfully disrupted Rebel railroads and telegraph lines before arriving at Union lines at Baton Rouge, having won several skirmishes against enemy troops for the loss of some fifty casualties.

Grierson's Raid had drawn Rebel infantry and cavalry away from the Mississippi as they attempted to catch him. Now was the time for Grant to push across the Mississippi to the south of Vicksburg. On April 30, the day before Grierson arrived at Baton Rouge, Grant crossed the Mississippi at Bruinsburg with two corps of his army. Grant's force first moved to Port Gibson, where they encountered a Rebel detachment of 8,500 men sent from Vicksburg. The Rebel forces were overwhelmed by the superior numbers of the Union army, and hastened back to Vicksburg. The following day, the Rebel garrison of Grand Gulf evacuated the town and Grant's troops occupied it on May 3. With Grand Gulf in his hands, Grant was able to summon Sherman's corps across the Mississippi. He now had 41,000 men south of Vicksburg, ready to attempt the capture of the city. The Rebels had Pemberton with 31,000 troops at Vicksburg, two divisions of which held a defensive position at the Big Black River, and 1,000 holding the railroad junction at Jackson. General Joseph E. Johnston was bringing 16,000 reinforcements from the direction of Tupelo. If Grant attacked Johnston, Pemberton could cut his line of supply and retreat. If he turned to face Pemberton, Johnston's army would be in his rear. If he allowed them to unite, they would outnumber him.

Grant now unleashed the most daring part of his plan. He loaded up his wagons with ammunition, slipped his line of supply, and left Grand Gulf on May 7. He allowed his troops to live off the land as they marched toward Jackson and the railroad line west to Vicksburg in three separate corps. On May 12, the left-

from the west bank and reached New Carthage, Louisiana, on April 6. Rear Admiral David Porter, with his fleet of gunboats, ran the batteries at Vicksburg in company with three transports and barges, on the night of April 16. The next day, a brigade of cavalry

hand corps, commanded by General James B. McPherson, arrived at Raymond and found a Rebel detachment there, which he sent reeling back to Jackson. On May 13, Johnston arrived at Jackson, but he was too late. McPherson's had already seized the railroad line at Clinton, blocking Johnston's fastest route to Pemberton.

Grant could now destroy the Rebel armies separately. On May 14, McPherson attacked Johnston's army at Jackson. With 25,000 to Johnston's 11,000, there was little chance for the Rebels to hold off the Union forces. Sherman's corps now entered Jackson and burned the town to the ground. Pemberton, meanwhile, attempted a half-hearted advance of his own, occupying Champion's Hill with 18,000 men. Johnston wanted him to abandon Vicksburg and join him at Canton, but Pemberton was determined to follow his orders and defend Vicksburg. Champion's Hill was a strong position, but Grant took McClernand's and McPherson's corps, some 29,000 men, and on May 18 attacked Pemberton. The fighting was hard and Union casualties exceeded Rebel ones, but in the end the Rebel position collapsed and Pemberton was forced into Vicksburg. On May 19, Grant had cut Vicksburg off. His men, confident of victory, were sent in a ferocious attack on the Rebel trenches, but this assault was beaten off. A second attempt was made on May 22. This was preceded by a heavy bombardment and was thrown back with nearly four times as many casualties.

The siege of Vicksburg lasted six weeks. The people of the city suffered as severely as in any of the great sieges of history, as food ran out and they were reduced toward the end to eating the vermin that previously ran relatively unmolested through gutters and cellars. Pemberton waited in futile hope that Johnston might

Right: *An oval belt buckle bearing the seal of the state of Mississippi.*

return with a larger army to raise the siege. Just as Johnston assembled reinforcements from all parts of the Confederate Department of the West, Grant received a steady flow of reinforcements until his army numbered 77,000, stronger than the combined forces of Pemberton and Johnston. At the end of June, Johnston marched to Jackson, where burned ruins had been christened "Chimneyville" by Union troops. Grant simply sent 30,000 troops under Sherman to block Johnston's advance. Facing too strong an army to overcome with his own forces, Johnston sent word to Pemberton to break out and abandon Vicksburg to Grant for the time being. A victory over Ulysses Grant in the field would enable the recovery of Vicksburg. But John Pemberton's troops were too weak from lack of food to sustain a campaign in the field. Pemberton asked for terms and surrendered Vicksburg to Grant's army on July 4, 1863. Grant had won his greatest victory.

Johnston remained at Jackson for a couple more weeks. Then a reinforced William Sherman started shelling his positions on July 16, and Johnston evacuated the city.

The war in Mississippi now became something of a minor theater. Rebel military forces used the region as a base for operations against Union railroad lines in Tennessee. In the spring of 1864, Sherman directed a column of 8,500 men, both cavalry and infantry, commanded by Brigadier General Samuel Sturgis into Mississippi from Memphis to search for Rebel General Nathan Bedford Forrest's cavalry command, which was the worst of the raiders against his supply lines. In June, Sturgis reached Brice's Cross Roads, near where Forrest was concentrating his forces. On June 10, in the afternoon, Forrest and 4,300 Rebel cavalry moved through the woods around Brice's Cross Roads to attack the Union column. When the Rebels threatened

the bridge across the Tishomingo Creek, the main line of retreat for the Union column, Sturgis ordered his troops to retire. A wagon on the bridge overturned, and as at other battles such as Bull Run, the possibility of being unable to escape caused panic. The Union withdrawal turned into a rout, and Forrest's men pursued the enemy for some twenty-five miles. The disparity in casualties illustrates the disorder into which Forrest had thrown Sturgis's command: 493 Rebel losses compared to 2,612 Union ones. It was one of the most brilliant small victories of the war.

The skill with which Forrest used his cavalry in this action reflected the battle-hardened nature of his command. The Rebel horsemen faked charges on the Union troops, retiring as they neared the Union lines and causing Union soldiers to use up their ammunition. In July 1864, Forrest found tougher opposition in a column commanded by General A. J. Smith. Smith's troops marched in a disciplined manner, giving Forrest far fewer opportunities for the hit-and-run tactics that he used with such success in the past. In a two-day fight near Harrisburg, Smith defeated Rebel attacks, before withdrawing to Tennessee to replenish his supplies.

Mississippi was the home of Jefferson Davis (1808–89). This statesmen was born in Kentucky, but opportunities provided by new settlement in the Deep South drew his family there. He received a congressional nomination to West Point and graduated in 1828. At West Point he became a close acquaintance of Albert Sidney Johnston and met a number of other future generals. Davis left the army in 1835 and retired to his plantation in Mississippi. Ten years later, Davis launched himself into public life with command of a regiment in the Mexican War of 1846–48, election to Congress, and service in the Franklin Pierce administration. Davis was one of the leading figures in the Democratic Party in the 1850s and a supporter of secession should Lincoln be elected.

Davis resigned from the Senate once Mississippi had seceded. When the Convention met at Montgomery,

Left: *Varina Howell Davis, the first lady of the Confederacy. Mrs. Davis was well educated and articulate and was a proper ornament to her husband's political life—as well as wielding some behind-the-scenes influence. However, in her own right she worked hard to relieve the distress of those impoverished or wounded by the war, and wrote an impressive memoir of her life. Something of a prisoner in her own time, she would have flourished more in today's South.*

Alabama, in February 1861, Davis waited patiently for word that he would receive an appointment as a general, based on both his military training and service in the Mexican War. To his surprise, and perhaps disappointment, he was elected provisional president.

Davis turned out to be a shrewd choice by the convention. He was an exceptionally hard worker, even if he complained about drowning in administrative tasks. No one could doubt his unwavering support for the Confederate cause, and he guided the war effort with determination and clarity. He established his guiding principles of strategy early on and never

Below: *The battle flag of the 7th Mississippi Infantry, carried in the Atlanta campaign. The regiment had already experienced some of the hardest fighting of the war at Stones River and Chickamauga.*

departed from them. The first objective was to wear out the patience of the people of the North, until they decided the price in blood and money to coerce the South back into the Union was too high. This meant that the highest priority was the survival of the Rebel armies as a fighting force. However, this sat somewhat uneasily with the location of industry in the South. This was largely concentrated in the states of Virginia and Tennessee, so it was important to defend the borders against Union invasion, which meant risking battle. Davis, partly thanks to the leadership of Robert E. Lee,

had considerably more success with this strategy in the East than in the West.

Davis also put a great deal of effort in the early stages of the war in securing recognition from the European powers of France and Britain. The attachment of the latter to the cause of the Confederacy was given a very high priority, since the Royal Navy might then intervene to break the blockade that would slowly strangle the South's war effort. France was more sympathetic to the Confederacy's cause if only because of ambitions of its own in Mexico, but would do nothing without

British support. The material difference of European recognition to Confederate chances is, however, open to debate if the European states refused to get involved in the conflict.

Davis's weaknesses did cause problems to the Confederate cause. He was not a charismatic man and did not inspire people to reach his level of determination and work. He was an obstinate man, and his stubbornness at times rendered him incapable of making the kind of political compromises that were a staple of his counterpart Abraham Lincoln's war-winning leadership. Consequently, he found it harder to rally public support for the hardships of the struggle, for instituting a draft, and for a war-winning financial strategy.

Davis was also less successful overall than Lincoln in handling his generals. Davis was both more intolerant of their political comments and less impatient with their military failures. He had a needless falling out with General P. G. T. Beauregard, who, while no military genius, proved both an energetic and adept defensive commander. On the other hand, he tolerated the inability of General Braxton Bragg to get along with his corps commanders for far too long. Davis's selection of General John Hood to command the Army of Tennessee in the summer of 1864 was an especially egregious error, as Hood destroyed the army over the next five months. It might be said that while Lincoln gradually improved the Union military leadership, under Davis's management Rebel military leadership deteriorated as the war wore on.

Davis never surrendered, although he was captured on May 10, 1865, by a cavalry unit. Although accused of treason, he never applied for a pardon. Instead he demanded a trial that the federal government in the end refused to grant him, thus weakening their case somewhat. Jefferson Davis wrote a memoir, *The Rise and Fall of the Confederate Government*, and died in 1889. Davis only had his citizenship restored posthumously in the 1970s.

Major General Earl Van Dorn (1820–63) was a native of Mississippi, but found his true home in the army. He graduated from West Point in 1842, served heroically in the Mexican War, and was content to chase Native Americans on the frontier in the 1850s. However, once Mississippi seceded, Van Dorn, without hesitation, resigned and offered his services to the Confederacy. Van Dorn had a good war at the outset, capturing Union ships in Texas and eventually being given command of the Trans-Mississippi Department, in January 1862. He tried a Lee-style tactical plan at the battle of Pea Ridge in March, dividing his army in the face of the enemy and sending part of it on a long flank march. However, Van Dorn's army was not as experienced as Lee's troops would be in August 1862 or May 1863, and poor communication between the two halves contributed to defeat. Van Dorn went on to command the defense of Vicksburg in the summer of 1862 and operations against Union troops in Mississippi in the autumn. He never did quite well enough nor quite badly enough, although court–of-inquiry proceedings were instituted against him after his failure in the second battle of Corinth in October 1862. He was moved sideways to a cavalry command. He survived war but this handsome man drank too much and also had an eye for the ladies, which resulted in his being shot by a jealous husband in March 1863.

Left: *Jacob Thompson had been secretary of the Interior in the antebellum Buchanan administration and during the Civil War was sent to Canada to organize espionage activities on the part of the Rebels. Here he liaised with the Copperhead political movement in the lower Midwest, which opposed the war, and plotted various schemes to capture gunboats on the Great Lakes or rescue prisoners.*

MISSOURI

"Rather than concede to the State of Missouri [the right to dictate to my Government] I will see you...and every man, woman, and child in the State of Missouri dead and buried!"

—General Nathaniel Lyon, during negotiations with pro-Rebel Missouri leaders, July 1861

The state of Missouri was acquired as part of the Louisiana Purchase of 1803. Its journey to statehood was straightforward. Missouri Territory was organized in 1812, after the admission of Louisiana. In 1821, a portion of Missouri Territory was admitted as the state of Missouri. The state experienced the tensions that tore the nation apart in the secession crisis. The Compromise of 1820, which limited slavery within the territory acquired by the Louisiana Purchase of 1803 to lands south of latitude 36° 30', was also known as the Missouri Compromise. It was the only territory north of this boundary that was allowed to retain the institution of slavery. In 1860 Missouri voted for Northern Democrat Stephen Douglas.

The inhabitants of Missouri in 1860 were drawn from two main streams. People from the South settled much of the countryside, especially in the southern half of the state. German immigrants and Americans of German descent predominated in the city of St. Louis and the land north of the Missouri River. Northeast of the state was something of an exception to this pattern, being known as "Little Dixie" from its southern flavor.

In the crisis over "Bleeding Kansas" of the late 1850s, David Atchison, a Missouri senator in Washington, rallied Missouri slaveowners to oppose, by force if

Above: Colonel Hugh Garland, commanding officer of the 1st Missouri Infantry, of the Confederate army.

Left: A monument at Vicksburg to Missouri's regiments, built at a point where Missouri units of the Rebel army faced their Union counterparts. Missouri was a state divided badly by the war, sending large numbers of soldiers to fight for both sides, as well as being the setting for an ugly partisan conflict within its own borders.

necessary, any attempt to prevent Kansas from entering as a slave state. "We will shoot, burn & hang, but the thing will soon be over," he wrote Mississippi senator Jefferson Davis. Bands of "border ruffians," armed gangs drawn from proslavery Missourians, put these words into effect. Atchison even led by example, crossing into Kansas at the head of a band himself.

Missouri, however, was not united behind Atchison's militant strategy. Thomas Hart Benton led a Missouri faction opposed to slavery in Kansas. Although a longstanding Democrat, he even gave strong support to his son-in-law, John C. Frémont, who in 1856 was the first Republican candidate for the presidency.

When the Secession Crisis came in the spring of 1861, the heads of these two factions were now represented by the newly inaugurated state governor, Claiborne Fox Jackson, who had been one of Atchison's border ruffians, and Congressman Francis P. Blair Jr., who numbered relatives among the leading members of Lincoln's administration.

At his inauguration, Jackson's speech embraced the cause of secession, and the strength of his fellow Democrats in the legislature made passage of a secession resolution dangerously plausible. The ace in the hand of the state's unionists, however, was the

Connecticut-born abolitionist Army Officer Nathaniel Lyon. Blair had secured his appointment to command of the garrison of the St. Louis arsenal. This was strengthened when the state convention summoned to consider secession turned out to be unionist.

As in other border states, the aftermath of the attack on Fort Sumter heated a simmering pan into a boiling cauldron. Jackson denounced Lincoln's call for volunteers and summoned the state militia to take charge within Missouri. Since the militia in St. Louis was solidly pro-Union and largely German, Jackson had to bring in proslavery militiamen from elsewhere. Lyon, backed by a vigilante Committee of Public Safety, made a reconnaissance of Jackson's camp in Lindell Grove dressed as a woman. He returned a few days later, on May 10, 1861, and compelled the surrender of the secessionist militia. While marching them back to the arsenal, a shot was fired from a crowd of onlookers and Lyon's soldiers returned it with several volleys. Two soldiers and twenty-eight civilians were killed.

The state was now divided, and Unionists opposed to coercion of the seceding states joined the ranks of

secessionists. Jackson appointed Sterling Price, a veteran of the Mexican War, to command of the Confederate militia. Lyon, however, acted promptly and drove up the Missouri River, occupying the state capital at Jefferson City and chasing Price to the state's isolated southwestern corner. Unionist representatives to the Secession Convention declared the state offices vacant on July 22, 1861. Three days later, however, Lyon's forces were beaten at Wilson's Creek by a considerably larger but less well equipped army commanded by Price and General Ben McCulloch. Lyon was killed and Union forces retreated, allowing the Rebels to reach the Missouri River at Lexington. The Union commander, General Frémont, eventually drove Price back to the southwest of the state with a much larger army than Lyon had deployed.

In November, Jackson summoned those members of the legislature who were loyal to the Southern cause, and they voted to secede from the Union. Missouri was admitted to the Confederacy on November 28, 1861, but this would remain a symbolic gesture as the Union military victory ensured Northern control of the state.

"Control" in Missouri was a relative term. While the North was able to mobilize the manpower and economic resources of the state to their advantage, the bitter enmity between the two factions created an

unpleasant guerrilla war, one similar to the years of "Bleeding Kansas." The border ruffians turned into "bushwhackers" and subjected Union communities and military bases to a savage war of ambush, murder, and raiding. The Union forces turned to the ancient rivals of the border ruffians and sent Kansas volunteer regiments to chase the Confederate guerrillas. Where the bushwhackers burned and pillaged out of revenge and a need for supplies, the Jayhawkers adopted the traditional strategy of those opposing guerrillas by destroying the homes and crops of those likely to offer support to the irregular fighters.

The names of the leaders of these forces include some of the most infamous of the entire war: William Quantrill, "Bloody Bill" Anderson, and Charles Jennison. This was an environment that also spawned the first romantic robbers of US history, the James brothers and the Younger brothers, men whose mythic status shrouded violent, lawless natures in a way that Hollywood has glamorized.

In September 1864, the Rebels made one last attempt to secure a foothold in Missouri. Ostensibly, the objective of the attack was St. Louis. However, General Price took an entirely mounted force on the raid with limited artillery, so any such intention rested on hopes that the garrison would be small and the fortifications basic. There was also thought that thousands of Missourians would rise up and join Price. While thousands did, Price did not have the armament for them and needed victories to supply them with captured armaments.

Sterling Price's command left its camp in Camden, Arkansas, on September 19, moving in the direction of Fredericktown. On the 27th, an attack on a small Union fort at Pilot Knob was repulsed.

Soon after, Sterling Price concluded from his scouts reports that there were too many Union troops at St. Louis to make an attack likely to succeed and redirected the objective of his advance toward Jefferson City. On October 7, Sterling Price reached the same

Left: *General Franz Sigel had emigrated from Germany and ended up settling in St. Louis. Sigel was not a successful commander in the war, and General Henry Halleck once said "It is but little better than murder" to give a command to Sigel.*

conclusion about Jefferson City and shifted his target once again, this time to Independence. At Boonville, Sterling Price and his men receive heroes' welcomes, and over a thousand volunteers. Sedalia was captured on October 14. Four days later, a heavily outnumbered band of Kansas, Colorado, and Missouri Union soldiers were driven off, opening the way to Independence. By this time, several Union columns were closing in on Sterling Price. There was fighting around Independence and Westport.

At this stage, Sterling Price had already turned his route southward, heading back for Arkansas. It was just as well. While in the vicinity of the Little Osage on October 25, Union troops caught the rear of Price's column and the fighting ended disastrously with several generals and cannon captured. On November 1, Price's column was back in Arkansas, the last Confederate offensive in Missouri.

Eng^d by Geo. E. Perine.

NEBRASKA

"The number of troops now stationed [on] the frontier...is much larger than in time of peace."

—Major General Henry Halleck, 1863

In 1803 the Territory of Nebraska was added to the United States as part of the Louisiana Purchase. However, it remained an unorganized territory until in 1854 Kansas and Nebraska territories were created by the Kansas-Nebraska Act. While Kansas was opened to slavery, Nebraska remained a free territory as its location above the Missouri Compromise line of 36° 30'N required. The population of Nebraska in 1860 was about 30,000. The boundaries of the territory underwent a number of changes during the course of the war. Originally, in 1860, it encompassed the bulk of the present states of Wyoming and Montana, plus parts of North and South Dakota and Colorado. In 1861, the territorial boundaries of the West were reorganized by Congress, and Nebraska was limited to the area of the present state plus the portion of Wyoming that previously was a part of Nebraska.

The settlements in Nebraska in 1860 were largely restricted to the counties along the Missouri and Platte rivers. There were no railroads, and transportation was either by foot, horse, or riverboat. Isolated as it was from the battlefields and with a small population, Nebraska's role in the war was limited. Even so, some 3,300 volunteers responded to Lincoln's call, including two companies of Indian scouts. In 1860, a number of army forts dotted the plains of Nebraska, protecting the settlers from the Indians (and, at times at this stage of

Above: *Hovey's Approach at Vicksburg stood before Fort Garrott, and consists of two trenches dug in traditional siege-work style toward the enemy position.*

Left: *John Milton Thayer was born in Massachusetts, and moved to Nebraska in 1854. When the war began, Thayer had already gained some military experience in campaigns against the Native Americans, and he became colonel of the 1st Nebraska Infantry. Thayer fought at the battles of Fort Donelson and Shiloh. He also commanded a brigade during the Vicksburg campaign.*

the Plains settlement, the Native Americans from the settlers). Fort Kearny and Fort Randall were the largest posts, but in the context of the national emergency, the garrisons of these places were withdrawn, as had also been done in Indian Territory to the south. Hence, when a regiment was mustered at Omaha, many thought that the troops would be used to garrison the forts. Instead, the 1st Nebraska Volunteers were sent east to St. Joseph, Missouri. After some service in the partisan war in Missouri, the 1st Nebraska went on to join General Ulysses Grant's army besieging Fort Donelson in February 1862. The regiment fought at Shiloh as part of General Lew Wallace's division.

After Shiloh, the 1st Nebraska returned to the Trans-Mississippi region. The fighting here was more of a guerrilla war than a fight between formed armies, and so in 1863 the 1st Nebraska was changed from an infantry regiment into a cavalry one. In 1864, following an Indian uprising in Nebraska, the 1st Nebraska, which had returned home for a furlough, did not return to the east, but remained at Fort Kearny to offer protection to stage coach routes and ranches.

Other Nebraska units that were formed in the war included four companies that served with the 5th Iowa Cavalry, and a cavalry regiment that fought against the Sioux in the Dakota Territory.

NEVADA

"I joined the army as a boy and left as a man."

—John Jennings of Nevada, Union army infantryman

By the terms of the Treaty of Guadalupe Hidalgo signed in 1848, bringing an end to the Mexican-American War of 1846–48, Nevada became a part of the United States. In 1850, most of Nevada was incorporated into Utah Territory, with the southern corner becoming part of New Mexico Territory. In 1861, the portion of Utah Territory that is today within the boundaries of the state became Nevada Territory. The southern corner was added later from New Mexico Territory.

Nevada's importance in the Civil War came about because two miners named Pat McLaughlin and Peter O'Reilly discovered some gold in Six-Mile Canyon in 1859. A third miner, Henry Comstock, claimed that they had found gold on his property. Even more gold was found further up the canyon and attracted even more miners. Working the gold required shovelling through some blue-grey mud that clung to every tool used. Finally, someone had the bright idea of assaying the mud and it turned out to be silver ore, and the mining town of Virginia City afterward began to attract get-rich-quick miners eager to get their share of that mud.

The name Virginia City suggests the presence of potential Confederate sympathizers, and the immense value realized in Nevada contributed to its being given separate territorial status. President Abraham Lincoln appointed James Warren Nye (1814–76) as governor of the newly created Nevada Territory in 1861. James W. Nye had been the first president of the Metropolitan Board of Police in New York City, serving from 1857 to 1860. On July 4, 1861, James Nye gave a speech in San Francisco in which he made it very clear that no public display of sympathy for the insurrection would be allowed, and even neutrality would be frowned upon.

The former law enforcement officer of one of the roughest cities in the United States found little trouble in putting down any manifestations in support of the Confederacy. There was one instance of a Confederate flag being flown in Virginia City. The gold and silver of Nevada Territory became a vital resource in ensuring that the value of the United States' currency and confidence in their investment bonds could be maintained.

As in most Western territories, regular troops were withdrawn from Nevada, requiring their replacement by volunteer units. The few recruits from Nevada were at first incorporated in California regiments that patrolled the Overland Mail route across the Great Basin between the Rocky Mountains and the Sierra Nevada. In 1863, Nevada's own volunteer cavalry and infantry units were raised and stationed in Utah Territory. Fort Churchill was the main mustering point for these cavalry and infantry units, as well as being a supply depot for the Nevada Military District. This fort on the Carson River had been built in 1860–61 to provide protection for early settlers, the Overland Mail, and other mail routes.

On March 21, 1864, Congress approved an act that enabled statehood for Nevada, even though the population of Nevada was below the threshold required by law. Whether this move was because of the great wealth of the Comstock Lode or because President Abraham Lincoln wanted the possible three electoral votes that the newly created state of Nevada would bring in the potentially close presidential election of 1864 is open to question. But on October 31, 1864, Nevada officially entered the Union. Following the admission of Nevada as a state into the Union, James Nye was elected as a Republican to the United States Senate.

Left: Virginia City grew up around one of the richest strikes of precious metal in the history of the United States, the fabled Comstock Lode. Although the people of Virginia City were divided, just like the country, the riches extracted here went exclusively into the coffers of the Union government, and helped avoid a currency collapse.

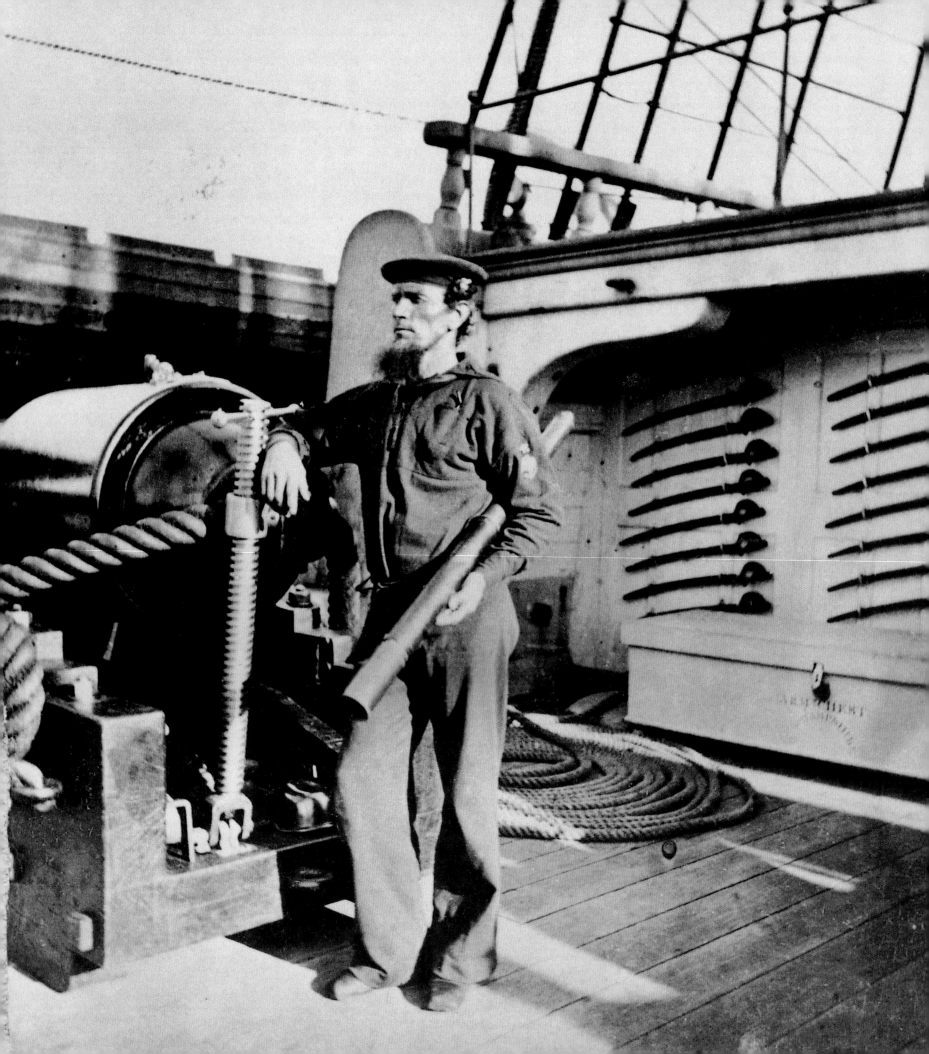

NEW HAMPSHIRE

"The lying reports of our general and reporters beat
anything that ever existed among the rebels."

—Henry Pearson, September 5, 1862

The first permanent English settlement in New Hampshire was established in 1623. New Hampshire was one of the original thirteen colonies that declared independence from Britain in 1776, it then became the 9th state of the United States in June 1788. In the 1860 presidential election, New Hampshire voted for Lincoln.

The state was the birthplace of Thaddeus Lowe (1832–1913), whose contribution to the Union war effort was one of the many examples of the ways the Civil War foreshadowed the conflicts of the twentieth century. Lowe was, in his own time, an aeronaut. On April 19, 1861, Lowe made a balloon flight from Cincinnati, Ohio, to Unionville, South Carolina. Of peaceable intent, Lowe almost found himself shot as a spy. Eventually, he convinced Rebel authorities that his flight was simply an innocent trip, and he was allowed to return to Cincinnati to collect his apparatus.

Thaddeus Lowe then received an invitation to the city of Washington and was soon working for the Union war department. He spent two years using balloons to gather information about Confederate troop deployments, most notably during the Peninsular campaign of spring 1862. As more money was spent, Lowe's equipment became more sophisticated, although this never overcame some of the inherent problems in the technology.

Balloons could be shot down easily, and if they fell behind enemy lines their crew and the intelligence gathered would fall into enemy hands. Also, the lack of control over balloon flight meant that the information arrived tardily. In the end, the expense of the program led to General Joseph Hooker, soon after his appointment as commander of the Army of the Potomac, sharply curtailing its work. After 1863, both sides made little use of ballooning.

Left: A quartermaster of the US Navy stands on the deck of the USS New Hampshire. His forearm leans on the elevating screw of a thirty-two-pounder smoothbore gun. The USS New Hampshire was used as a receiving ship throughout the war.

Among the regiments raised in New Hampshire, the 5th New Hampshire holds the dubious record of having suffered the greatest losses of any Union infantry regiment. The 5th New Hampshire was originally raised as a ninety-day unit in April, 1861, and in October was reraised for three years.

The 5th New Hampshire's first major engagement was in the battle of Fair Oaks on June 1, 1862, and it also saw some fighting along Blood Lane at Antietam on September 17, 1862. At Fredericksburg, on December 13, 1862, the 5th had to attack the stone wall under Marye's Heights. On marching out to battle the regiment numbered 258 men. The next day, at the call of the roll, there were only seventy left, and all the officers had been killed or wounded. Numbers only rose with the return of wounded soldiers and with some new recruits, and the next major battle for the 5th New Hampshire was Gettysburg. The 5th New Hampshire was a part of a division of II Corps sent to fill the gap torn in the Union lines by the defeat of Sickles III Corps in the Peach Orchard, the Wheatfield, and Devil's Den. In three hours of fighting, the regiment once again suffered hundreds of casualties and again its strength fell below a hundred combatants.

The regimental commanding officer since its formation, Colonel Edward Cross, was mortally wounded, leading the brigade containing the 5th New Hampshire into action. Worse was to come. The regiment returned to the Army of the Potomac for the Overland campaign of 1864 and suffered its heaviest losses of the war at Cold Harbor on June 3, when 202 of 577 fell in this futile assault on a strong Rebel position. The 5th New Hampshire strength was once again rebuilt, and served in the trenches around Petersburg, but Cold Harbor was the last major battle it fought.

NEW JERSEY

"Had it not been for slavery, we would have had no war!"

—John S. Rock, January 23, 1862

Dutch and Swedish communities were established in New Jersey (known as New Netherland) from 1638 and the English then seized the colony in 1664. In 1776 New Jersey declared independence and became part of the United States in November, 1778. Of all the Northern states, New Jersey was probably the least Free-Soil in sentiment, and even as late as 1850, seventy-five slaves were recorded in the census of the state's population. In the 1860 presidential election, New Jersey's electoral votes were divided between Lincoln and Northern Democrat Stephen Douglas.

The best-known Civil War figure associated with New Jersey is George Brinton McClellan (1826–85). This Union general, although born across the river in Philadelphia, settled in New Jersey after the war and even served a term as governor of the state.

George McClellan is one of the most controversial figures of the Civil War and a worthy candidate for the questionable accolade of being the most incompetent general of the Union side. Ironically, this hardly would have seemed a likely conclusion of a man generally regarded as a superb soldier in the prewar army.

McClellan graduated from West Point in 1846 and served in the Mexican War of 1846–48. Such was his regard in the army that he was given the prestigious job as the army's observer of operations in the Crimean War of 1854–56. He left the army in 1857 and took a job with the influential Illinois Central Railroad (which also retained Abraham Lincoln). Just before the outbreak of war, he moved to the Ohio & Mississippi Railroad, from which he returned to the army in 1861.

His first campaign, launched from Ohio into the western Virginia counties, provided a welcome success after defeat at Bull Run, and contributed to his appointment as General Irvin McDowell's replacement in July 1861. McClellan proved a superb organizer of an army of amateurs. The men were carefully drilled over the winter and fed and clothed properly. However, the point of an army is to put those well fed, neatly dressed soldiers in a place where they can kill the enemy at the risk of their own lives, and throughout the war McClellan showed a reluctance that seemed inappropriate in a general to take that step.

His constant excuse was that he faced 100,000 of the enemy, a number that remained constant whether he was facing Rebels across the Potomac, in the Peninsula, or at Antietam. The fact that the Confederate forces never had more than three-quarters this number, and then for only a few weeks, suggests that this number reflected some unconscious fear in his own mind rather than an assessment based on evidence.

If not wanting to fight conclusively indicates incompetence in a general, one can add that in his finest hour, George McClellan still could not capitalize on his luck to deliver a decisive blow to the enemy. In Lee's September 1862 campaign in Maryland, McClellan fortunately came into possession of Lee's order of march. McClellan should have moved quickly with all he had and smashed some part of the Rebel army. But he moved slowly, and gave Lee the chance to gather his army. For once McClellan fought, and even won, but so much more could have been accomplished with fewer deaths.

McClellan left the army, and became the Democratic candidate for president in 1864, where he lost again. He stands as a classic example of someone who tasted success and admiration too young, without being tested ever by adversity and consequently was promoted beyond his abilities.

***Left:** Major General George B. McClellan with his staff. McClellan's reputation as a good organizer and strategist has been questioned since it was established during the Civil War Centennial of the 1960s. His surprise at his downfall in the absence of decisive battlefield victories seems itself surprising.*

NEW MEXICO

"We had no clothing, blankets, and no place to draw from. Had no artillery and were only armed with shot guns."

—John T. Poe, Texan serving in New Mexico

At the end of the Mexican-American War of 1846–48, the United States acquired part of New Mexico from Mexico under the terms of the Treaty of Guadalupe Hidalgo. The southernmost portion, the little square on the map, was added as part of the Gadsden Purchase from Mexico in 1854. The whole area was initially incorporated in the Territory of New Mexico in 1850, administered from Santa Fe in the Rio Grande Valley. However, there was little felt in common between the largely Anglo settlers from Texas who lived to the northwest of El Paso and in the Gila River Valley, and the Hispanic residents of the Rio Grande Valley. The cultural background of the Anglos made them sympathetic to secession. It was, consequently, not much of a surprise when a secession convention was held at Mesilla in March 1861 and voted to separate from the United States.

The Union departmental commander, Colonel Edward R. S. Canby, had few troops at his disposal to suppress the rebellion, and in July 1861 a battalion of Texans commanded by former scout and Native American agent John Baylor arrived from Fort Bliss, Texas, to Mesilla, giving military force to the territorial government. He captured the garrison of nearby Fort Fillmore, but could not take on Canby's troops.

Baylor created a new Confederate Territory of Arizona on August 1. This would consist of all New Mexico Territory south of the 34th parallel. He established its capital at Mesilla. Baylor created a judicial apparatus, imposed marital law, and began a recruitment effort among secessionist sympathizers. At this time Brigadier General Henry Sibley was raising another force of Rebels in San Antonio. In December, these troops arrived at Fort Bliss and formed the Rebel army of New Mexico by joining with Baylor at Mesilla. Sibley left Baylor as territorial governor in Mesilla and marched up the Rio Grande

Left: *Fort Marcy, outside Santa Fe, was the seat of the Union military forces at the capital of New Mexico Territory. It was occupied by the Rebels when they took Santa Fe in March 1862. The Rebel interlude was a short one, lasting less than a month.*

Valley to Fort Craig, where Canby had located his headquarters. Once at Fort Craig, Sibley could not get Canby's surrender. Reluctantly, fearing leaving a Union force in a fort in his rear, Sibley started to bypass Fort Craig when Canby's men came out to prevent Rebel access to a spring at Valverde. A battle on February 21, 1862, there ended in a Rebel victory. Canby retired into Fort Craig again. Sibley resumed an advance northward.

While Sibley was advancing on Santa Fe, Baylor launched a punitive raid against the Apaches. The Apache chiefs Cochies and Mangas Coloradas had raided the Rebel horse herds. In response Baylor called out a militia and pursued the Apaches. Baylor's men captured some Native Americans and executed all the adults before returning to Mesilla. Mangas Coloradas attempted to negotiate with Baylor, but he made it plain that any hostile Native American group would be exterminated. This was, in fact, contrary to official policy, which saw Native Americans as potential allies against a common enemy. Baylor resigned when this difference of opinion became known and returned to Texas with some men whose enlistments were about to expire to launch a new recruiting drive. By March 10, the Rebels had occupied Albuquerque and Santa Fe, but were now aware that a large force was coming to relieve Fort Craig. On March 28, the Union column clashed with the Rebels at the battle of Glorieta Pass. The late arrival of the Union flanking column caught the Rebels unprepared and destroyed their reserve ammunition. Having been poorly supplied to begin with, the Rebels had no choice but to withdraw. Canby emerged from Fort Craig to add to the strength of the pursuers. On April 15, an artillery duel at Peralta used up further ammunition, and Sibley abandoned New Mexico to the Union forces for the rest of the war.

NEW YORK

"Forward to Richmond!"

—*New York Tribune*, June 1861

The Dutch West India Company began to settle the New York area in 1614. King Charles II decided to reclaim the territory between Virginia and New England in 1664. It declared independence from Britain in 1776 and became part of the United States in July 1778. New York was a divided state, and therefore more like a Midwestern state than its New England neighbors, in the growing crisis over slavery. Upstate New York was strongly Free-Soil, especially along the Mohawk Valley and the Finger lakes and western Long Island, regions that were settled heavily by transplanted New Englanders. However, the Lower Hudson Valley and New York City were more like New Jersey in their character, unsympathetic toward the plight of African American slaves. In the 1860 presidential election, Abraham Lincoln carried New York State thanks to his large upstate majorities.

New York State was both the manufacturing and financial heart of the nation. New York was the largest port in the country. The stock exchange and banks were the wealthiest. Factory towns scattered upstate supplied important supplies to the Union's armed forces. The Remington company of Ilion, for example, produced small arms for the US Navy. The Burden Iron Works of Troy, later the American Machine and Foundry Co., produced most of the Union army's horseshoes. The Watertown Arsenal, in the Adirondacks, supplied cartridges and converted flintlock muskets to Union forces. Furthermore, Brooklyn was an important shipbuilding location, and the USS *Monitor* was built at the Green Point Yard there.

The Brooklyn Navy Yard was the main center for converting purchased civilian vessels into warships and also played a significant role in repairing and refitting ships from the blockading squadrons of the Union navy. The stone dry dock there was considered a

Left: Grave markers for unknown soldiers stand in ranks beneath the New York Memorial at the Gettysburg National Cemetery, Pennsylvania. Over 19,000 New Yorkers were killed during the Civil War. The cemetery is the final resting place for US soldiers from all of the country's major wars.

particular marvel, and New York, as much as any state, deserves the title of the "Workshop of the Union."

In this context, therefore, it is surprising perhaps to learn that New York was also a major center for antiwar sentiment on the part of the financial establishment, which might otherwise have expected to do well out of the spending of government money. However, from the outset of the war, New York City's enthusiasm for the struggle was tepid. In January 1861 the mayor, Fernando Wood, proposed to the city council that the city itself take the opportunity to leave the Union and become a free city. These sentiments echoed in a newspaper editorial that suggested that the port would benefit from breaking free of the protective tariff imposed to aid industry upstate and New England. Horatio Seymour, the Democratic state governor, was another opponent of Lincoln and Republican policies.

With such feelings, it was hardly surprising that New York City was the setting for the worst riots in American history that occured in response to the introduction of a draft. At the beginning of 1863, the Union armies experienced a manpower shortage that was unlikely to be filled by volunteers alone.

All male citizens between the ages of twenty and forty-five were therefore required to enroll with provost marshals. Even immigrants who had filed for naturalization were required to put their names forward. However, the law provided for the purchase of substitutes by those who could afford the prices charged or the payment of a $300 commutation fee. Because of this, the draft intrinsically guaranteed that the slogan "a rich man's war, a poor man's fight" could be applied.

The first draft was held in July 1863, just as the casualty lists from Gettysburg were being published in

Above: *Captain Otis and his company of the 22nd New York Infantry on the Maryland Heights near Harpers Ferry, Virginia. The men of the 22nd New York were originally drawn from upstate and mustered in at Troy.*

newspapers. The names drawn in the first lottery, some 1,200 in all, were published on June 12. This was the trigger for mobs to assemble and protest the unfair legislation and its consequences.

The rioting lasted four days and required the bombardment of New York by naval vessels and the deployment of regiments of troops from the Army of the Potomac to suppress it. Draft offices and other federal buildings, plus police attempting to restore order, were the initial target of the mob, but the violence also targeted the large African American community in the city. Lynchings and beatings were commonplace, while a church and an orphanage were burned to the ground. Rioters even took the pro-Republican newspaper offices, such as the *Tribune*. Over a hundred people died and the damage to property has been estimated as totaling $1.5 million.

In spite of this record of hostility to the war, the schizophrenic nature of New York State is illustrated by the fact that the state supplied the largest number of men, in absolute numbers, and the highest number of casualties of any in the Union. Almost 450,000 New

Yorkers served in the Union army and nearly 20,000 of them were killed. Over 25,000 died from disease or other causes, a little over 10 percent. New York troops were also among the first and best-drilled to rally to Lincoln's call to arms on April 15, 1861.

Even in this era of American history, New York was already a "melting pot" of different ethnic communities, captured by regiments that focused their recruitment on specific ethnic groups. The 69th New York Regiment, which suffered heavily at Fredericksburg in 1862, was drawn from men of Irish origin. The 79th New York Regiment, the "Highlanders," had a uniform that resembled that of Highland Regiments in the British army and drew from the Scots and Scots-Irish communities. The 39th New York Infantry, known as the "Garibaldi Guard," borrowed elements of dress from the Italian army.

New York regiments repeatedly appeared in the war at crucial moments. On April 25, the arrival of the 7th New York Militia offered hope to Lincoln, who was feeling isolated in Washington.

This regiment, the "old graybacks" from their gray uniform, drew on the cream of New York society and consequently its members could afford to devote time to drill, making them one of the better militia units in the nation. While the 7th Militia was only in federal

Below left: An officer of the 39th New York Infantry, the "Garibaldi Guard," a regiment of Italian Americans. Many of the soldiers in this regiment had already fought in Italy to unify the separate states of the peninsula of the time.

Below: A color guard of the 7th New York State Militia. Not to be confused with the 7th New York Infantry, the 7th State Militia were mustered on three occasions for short-term service (ninety or thirty days).

Below: *A private of the 69th New York Infantry, the "Fighting 69th." Many of the soldiers in this regiment were of Irish origin, and it was one of the constituent units of the fabled "Irish Brigade" that suffered some of the heaviest casualties of any brigade in the war.*

Right: *Brigadier General Marsena R. Patrick (1811–88), outside his tent in Virginia in September 1863. He was provost marshal of the Army of the Potomac, a job he held until the end of the war. He was a native of Jefferson County, New York.*

service for short terms, men drawn from its ranks served in the other volunteer regiments recruited in New York and frequently as commissioned officers thanks to their experience of drill.

The New York regiment that suffered most heavily in the Civil War was the "Fighting 69th." The 69th New York Volunteer Infantry regiment began as a militia regiment drawn from citizens of Irish descent living in New York City. It was the second unit to depart the city for Washington following Lincoln's call for troops on April 15, 1861. At the first battle of Bull Run the following July, the regiment helped to cover the panicky retreat of the Union army, although its commanding officer was captured.

After Bull Run, the regiment was joined by two other regiments that recruited from those of Irish descent, the 63rd New York and the 88th New York, who formed the nucleus of the Irish Brigade of the Army of the Potomac.

The Irish Brigade first campaigned as a unit in the Peninsula campaign of spring 1862. At the battles of Antietam, Fredericksburg, and Gettysburg, the 69th fought in some of the worst sectors of the battlefields. At Antietam, it launched an assault on the Rebel troops defending the Sunken Road, also known as Bloody Lane. At Fredericksburg, it marched across the open fields between the town and the stone wall beneath Marye's Heights. At Gettysburg, it charged into the Wheatfield to block the Rebel attack that threatened to open a potentially fatal gap in the Union line. By the time the war ended, the 69th New York had participated in all the major campaigns in the East, from Bull Run to Appomattox.

Where the 69th New York had been among the first troops to respond to Lincoln's call, the 121st New York Regiment was part of a third wave of volunteers that Lincoln appealed for in the summer of 1862. The 121st New York drew its recruits from Otsego and Herkimer counties upstate and left for Washington City at the end of August. It was eventually assigned to the VI corps of the Army of the Potomac. On September 25, Colonel Emory Upton took command of the regiment and set about the hard work of transforming it into an elite unit. He set his men to drill twice a day and gave the officers night courses in tactics. He also applied a ferocious discipline and reduced the incidence of sickness in the regiment. For the first year and a half of its existence, the regiment saw little action, missing out on Fredericksburg, Chancellorsville, and Gettysburg. However, in the Overland campaign of 1864, the 121st participated in the ferocious fighting in the Wilderness and at Spotsylvania Court House. The 121st also took part in Sheridan's Shenandoah campaign of the summer of 1864. In spite of playing a minor role until 1864, the 121st still managed to suffer the second-most casualties of all New York regiments.

The most controversial of officers in the Union army was quite possibly New Yorker Daniel Sickles (1825–1914). Sickles started his professional life as a printer's apprentice, but turned to law, where eventually he became a corporate attorney. Success in the legal field drew him into politics as a Democrat, and the party's dominance of US politics in the 1850s led to him being sent as a diplomat to London. At the war's outbreak, Sickles was a congressman. He'd already had an encounter with controversy, when he shot and killed the son of Francis Scott Key (who wrote the words for *The Star-Spangled Banner*) for having an affair with his wife at the time. Sickles chose as his defense attorney the rising city of Washington lawyer Edwin Stanton (later Secretary of War in the Lincoln administration). Stanton made the first plea in legal history of temporary insanity, which got Sickles off.

Sickles went back to New York at the outbreak of war with the authorization to raise a regiment, but instead raised a whole brigade, known as the Excelsior Brigade.

Above: *The drum corps of the 93rd New York Infantry at Bealton, Virginia, in August 1863. The regiment was serving as a provost guard regiment for the Army of the Potomac at the time. Provost was a thankless task, as those who performed the job sternly were regarded with dislike, while the more lenient were thought to be corrupt.*

Right: *Castle William on Governors Island in New York Harbor was used as a prison for Confederate soldiers during the war.*

Right: *A shako worn by the 7th New York State Militia. This regiment did not fight any battles, but helped preserve order during the draft riots of July 1863.*

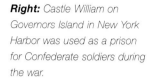

He led the brigade in the Seven Days' battles, and by the time of the battle of Fredericksburg, he was in command of a division. When Hooker took over the Army of the Potomac in early 1863, he was given command of the III Corps, and spent most of the battle of Chancellorsville marching instead of fighting. When Meade replaced Hooker in June 1863, Sickles's days may have been numbered. He drank too much, and there was too much scandal associated with his name. Lee's advance into Pennsylvania postponed Sickles' fate and perhaps encouraged him to seek some kind of redemption on the battlefield. Taking the initiative, he advanced his corps out of its assigned position on July 2 to what appeared to be higher, more easily defensible ground. However, it left both of his flanks hanging in the air and the corps suffered heavily in the ensuing Rebel attack. Sickles himself was badly wounded, losing a leg. After the war he returned to political appointments as a diplomat and a

congressman. Of course, controversy still pursued him—he was alleged to have fathered one of the queen of Spain's children while he served as minister to that country, which is why he was recalled.

New York is also the home of the famous United States Military Academy at West Point. The contribution of this institution to the command of armies—on both sides in the conflict—is well known. However, the military academy continued to train officers for regular army service throughout the war. It graduated two classes in June 1861, among whose ranks was Emory Upton, the commanding officer of the 121st New York and later a brigadier general.

There was an attempt to expand the number of cadets studying at West Point, but by the end of the war only 159 had graduated in spite of hopes that numbers could be increased to five hundred. However, the extra appropriations granted to the academy were wisely spent nevertheless, on practicalities such as books and buildings, and the standing of the academy was much higher among politicians and citizens in June 1865 than it had been in June 1861.

Below: *A color guard of the 118th New York Infantry in 1865. They are armed with Spencer repeating carbines, which gradually came to equip more regiments of the Union army toward the end of the war. The regiment was mustered into service at Plattsburg in August 1865 and saw most of its service in Virginia along the James river, including the May 1864 battle of Drewry's Bluff.*

NORTH CAROLINA

"Tell General Hancock that I know I did my country a great wrong when I took up arms against her, for which I am sorry, but for which I cannot live to atone."

—General Lew Armistead, July 3, 1863

In the 1580s the English established two colonies in North Carolina, both of which failed. In the 1600s permanent settlers from Virginia arrived and the area became part of the colony known as "Carolina." It declared independence from Britain in 1776 and became part of the United States in July 1778. North Carolina was not among the original states to secede from the Union and left after Lincoln's call for militia to suppress the revolt. The ordinance of secession was passed quickly. First the legislature called for elections to a convention on May 1, the elections were held on May 13, and the convention met on May 20 to pass the ordinance unanimously.

North Carolina's geographical position made it an unlikely place for much combat in the early stages of the war, since it was bordered on three sides by seceded states. However, the coast of North Carolina was vulnerable to invasion from the sea, although the treacherous waters around Cape Hatteras and the low-lying islands off the mainland made it difficult for any landing there to be an effective invasion.

The first move against North Carolina came in August 1861, when a Union squadron commanded by Flag Officer Silas Stringham, carrying nine hundred troops commanded by Major General Benjamin Butler, arrived off the coast of Hatteras Inlet. On the night of

Above: *A Rebel battle flag, captured by Union troops at Chancellorsville, that may be the colors of the 4th North Carolina Infantry.*

Left: *Braxton Bragg was probably the most unpopular commander on either side during the war. Yet President Davis persevered with him in part because he was willing to fight battles, something many generals during the war proved reluctant to do.*

August 28–29, 1861, the naval vessels began a prolonged bombardment of two forts guarding the entrance to the inlet. The rifled guns of the Union vessels outranged the smoothbore pieces that armed the Rebel forts, and it was an easy task to bombard the forts into submission. Butler's troops landed on August 29 and occupied the forts. It was a small victory, but a welcome one for a Union public still recovering from the disappointment of Bull Run.

Success at Hatteras Inlet stimulated imitation. Brigadier General Ambrose Burnside approached his friend Major General George McClellan with the idea of mounting a similar sort of operation against Albemarle Sound. Burnside's project was approved, and having assembled a small force of troops and some eighty ships, he set sail for the Carolina coast on January 11, 1862. Bad weather and the lack of correct information about the depth of the channel delayed Burnside's attack on Rebel forts on Roanoke Island until February 7. The Rebel position fell without much difficulty and Albemarle Sound became something of a Union lake.

A month later, Burnside seized the town of New Berne, which was an important railroad terminus for shipping goods brought into the North Carolina ports to the rest of the Confederacy. This also put a Union

force close to the only railroad connecting Richmond to the rest of the South, and a small Rebel force had to be assembled to challenge any possible Union attacks on this key supply line.

With all but the entrance to the port of Wilmington in Union hands by the spring of 1862, North Carolina became something of a quiet sideshow for over two-and-a-half years. In the last months of 1864, however, Union attention turned to Fort Fisher, which guarded access to Wilmington, probably the most important Rebel port.

On the model of the previous successes earlier in the war, a joint army-navy force was collected. Rear Admiral David Porter would command the ships, while the soldiers would be under General Butler, who was at least familiar with the type of operation and the terrain.

Butler and Porter, however, were already acquainted from operations in Louisiana and along the Mississippi in 1862, where they had antagonized one another. Fort Fisher contained forty-seven guns, placed in low bastions made of wood and sand that would be difficult to shell effectively. There were also primitive land mines arranged to protect the approaches to the fort from likely landing areas.

Butler came up with the madcap idea of filling an old hulk with gunpowder and exploding it near the fort. The resultant explosion would kill or disorient the garrison long enough to give Union troops a good chance of carrying an assault. Porter set the bomb ship off a day too early, on December 23, 1864, and placed more confidence in the effect of bombardment by his ship's guns. However, neither had any effect and the

Below: *The ruined gun battery at Fort Fisher after the fall of the Rebel bastion in January 1865. The fall of the fort opened the way to one of the most important Rebel ports during the war, Wilmington.*

Davis appointed the winning partnership of the first Bull Run: Joseph E. Johnston in command, with G. T. Beauregard as the second in command. Johnston directed the force to assemble at Smithville.

Starting February 14, 1865, a debate among Confederate commanders took place over what needed to be done in just this case. Lieutenant General James Longstreet suggested that Rebel forces in Virginia and North Carolina needed to link up in order to prevent Sherman and Grant from joining forces. On the 23rd, he offered to go to North Carolina himself. He thought that combing Virginia for men might provide enough troops to relieve his corps in the Petersburg entrenchments so that he could join Johnston. He renewed the offer on the 25th. Lee finally responded on March 9, saying that he could do nothing to help. On March 11, Lee requested that Johnston do all in his power to hold Raleigh, otherwise the Petersburg position would become impossible to supply. That same day, Johnston warned that his army was not good enough to stand up to Sherman and requested help. Lee finally decided that an assault from Petersburg might force Grant to shorten his line of entrenchments, which would enable Lee to hold him off with fewer men. On March 14, Sherman's forces crossed the Cape Fear River and began what they believed to be the final stage of the journey they had started at Atlanta in November. Their destination was a junction with Grant's army for some final battle with Lee in front of Richmond. The Confederate forces in front of them withdrew before the greater numbers of Union men. They made a brief stand at Averysboro, on March 16, but the line of their entrenchments was turned by a

troops refused to press home their assault on December 25. This first attack was a fiasco.

Benjamin Butler was removed from command. Brigadier General Alfred Terry replaced him and launched a carefully planned operation. Using traditional methods of isolating the fort from reinforcement, targeting its gun positions, and attacking it from more than one direction resulted in Fort Fisher's fall on January 15, 1865.

The land war came to North Carolina in early March, when Sherman's army crossed the border from South Carolina. A Rebel army was being assembled in the state from Hardee's Savannah garrison, the garrison of Charleston, and two divisions of the Army of Tennessee. Given the name Army of Tennessee, President Jefferson

Left: Two privates of a North Carolina infantry regiment. The North Carolinans were among the best dressed of all Rebel units in the sense of being able to maintain a uniform. These men wear gray coats and gray pants, with black shoulder panels and pants trim indicating their arm of service, the infantry. The large number of textile mills in North Carolina made this possible.

Left: A North Carolina twenty-dollar bill, issued in 1862.

Right: *A forage cap, worn by Colonel W. J. Clark, a North Carolina officer.*

Union brigade and forced the Rebel retreat. The Union advance resumed in the direction of Goldsboro.

The Rebels made their stand in front of the Neuse River on March 18, near the hamlet of Bentonville. The Army of Tennessee's cavalry, under Wade Hampton, had informed Johnston that this was a good position from which to attack the leading Union corps, XIV, which was somewhat isolated from the rest. Johnston headed at once for the position directing Hampton to hold it if possible. Hampton moved out on the morning of the 18th and skirmished with them all day.

The Union commander of the Army of Georgia, General Slocum, at first believed he faced only a cavalry screen, but Johnston arrived with the bulk of his army that night. The Rebels entrenched, and when Slocum renewed the combat on the 19th, he found a larger force. Slocum's attack was repulsed, but the Rebels failed to follow up this success. Slocum put his advanced troops on the defensive. The Confederates would either have to attack or Slocum could just wait until the remainder of Sherman's army would arrive and overwhelm the smaller Rebel force. Slocum sent word to Sherman, who dispatched a division to reinforce the Army of Georgia.

The Rebel counterattack was delayed until late in the afternoon. The fighting was sharp. The Rebels took the first two lines of Union entrenchments in the center, but the Union forces rallied in the woods. On the left,

however, the Rebels could not penetrate the Union lines, and any advantage was lost. Johnston withdrew his troops to their original positions.

The division Sherman had set in motion arrived that night, and on the 20th a series of attacks were made on the Rebel left, but all failed. The Rebel position was a good one to attack from, but a weak one to defend against an enemy with a considerable superiority in numbers. Sherman probed the left of the position again on the 21st and nearly achieved a breakthrough, but for a desperate attack by a Georgian brigade and the 8th Texas Cavalry. That night, Johnston withdrew, and the battle of Bentonville came to an end.

Sherman's troops reached Goldsboro on March 23 and paused once again. Events in Virginia now nailed shut the possibility of Johnston's army linking up with Lee's. On April 5, 1865 Lee surrendered to Grant at Appomattox Court House. Sherman resumed his march on April 6 and entered Raleigh on the 13th, the same day that President Davis arrived in Greensboro to meet with Johnston and Beauregard. Davis had found relations with these two men difficult throughout the war, and in their discussions he once again found himself arguing. Where Davis wanted to fight, Johnston believed the struggle was over. Davis allowed Johnston to contact Sherman, and Johnston sent word from his headquarters at Hillsboro to Sherman in Raleigh. The two met at James Bennett's farm house, about five miles

Right: *A Confederate officer's sword made by Louis Froelich, in Kenansville.*

south of Hillsboro, and negotiated a memorandum of surrender. Johnston's force formally surrendered on April 26, 1865, bringing the Civil War in North Carolina to an end.

Sadly for North Carolina, the one general of the Rebel army born in the state was Braxton Bragg (1817–76). Bragg had the worst reputation of any of them, although it is perhaps not entirely deserved. He graduated from West Point in 1837 and had a successful army career in which he gained a reputation as a stickler for the rules. Bragg was put in charge initially of the Gulf Coast, where he assembled, drilled, and provisioned a sizable force. Having displayed his aptitude for this vital part of military life, he asked to fight with General Albert Sidney Johnston, and his request was approved. Bragg saw action at Shiloh and eventually succeeded to Johnston's post of commander of the Army of Tennessee in July 1862. He carried out a masterful strategic redeployment from Tupelo, Mississippi, to Chattanooga, and from there invaded Kentucky. Braxton Bragg remained in command of the army until after the defeat at Chattanooga in November 1863, when his resignation was accepted and he became a military adviser to President Davis.

Historians' hostility to Braxton Bragg rests on his inability to get along with his subordinates. It is fair to say that there was no general in the Confederate armies more hated by the other general officers. On the other hand, he was highly regarded by his men and opposed corrupt practices in the requisitioning and allocation of provisions. Unfortunately, Braxton Bragg was also responsible for the needless attack on January 2, 1863, at the battle of Murfreesboro. Many other Civil War generals, including Grant and Lee, have similar actions on their resumes, but Braxton Bragg can add to this the route from Missionary Ridge at Chattanooga in November 1863. At best, it could be said that Braxton Bragg was a fighter, unafraid of battle, where many other generals in the Civil War were not.

Left: *A soldier of the 42nd North Carolina Infantry serving as a prison camp guard at the Salisbury Prison Camp in North Carolina. In the Confederacy, this duty fell either to convalescents, or to units that were seriously understrength and intended to be amalgamated with another understrength unit, as was the case here.*

OHIO

"Watch your language. Remember, the first bullet may send you to your grave."

—William S. Rosecrans, December 31, 1862

Ohio was the first of the states to be created out of the land north of the Ohio River that had been organized as the Northwest Territory in 1787. The Northwest Territory originally embraced all the land of the modern states of Ohio, Indiana, Michigan, Illinois, Wisconsin, and a part of Minnesota. In 1800, it was divided into two: Ohio and part of Michigan retained the old name; the rest became Indiana Territory. In 1803, Ohio was admitted to the Union. In 1860 it voted for Abraham Lincoln in the presidential election.

Ohio's first settlers in the 1780s came predominantly from Virginia. Large numbers of Pennsylvanians and New Englanders, however, began to arrive soon after. The competition between New England and the upper South to settle the state led to some residual enthusiasm for Southern rights during the Civil War. The nation's leading Peace Democrat, or "Copperhead," was the former Ohio Congressman Clement Vallandigham (1820–71), who lost his seat in Congress only because Ohio's Republican administration reapportioned it in such a way as to give it a Republican majority for the 1862 midterm canvass. The Copperheads held the view that the war was being fought not to preserve the Union but to free the slaves.

Above: *Boy drummers photographed by an Ohio infantry officer in 1861.*

Left: *William T. Sherman was relieved of his command after being driven into depression by his enormous challenges and the poor quality of the Union troops. Only the support of his wife and his political connections revived his career.*

Since they were not interested in freeing the slaves, there was no point to the cost in blood and treasure. The Copperhead rhetoric became increasingly inflammatory, and in May 1863 General Ambrose Burnside, then commanding the Department of the Ohio, placed Vallandigham under military arrest.

Vallandigham was convicted of "disloyal sentiments and opinions," and taken to the Confederate army at Murfreesboro to spend the rest of the war in exile. Vallandigham left the Confederacy and went to Windsor, Canada, across the river from Detroit, Michigan. From here he ran for governor of Ohio, which he lost, and spent the next two years advocating a peaceful settlement of the conflict. He returned to Ohio after the end of the Civil War.

The only significant military action to take place in Ohio during the war began on July 13, 1863, when the column of cavalry raiders, numbering some 2,000 men, commanded by Rebel General John Hunt Morgan, crossed the Indiana border near Hiarrisonville. Morgan's intent appears to have been to bypass Cincinnati and then recross the Ohio River at Buffington Island to make his way back across Kentucky to his base in Tennessee. Union commanders, however,

Below: *The 73rd Ohio on the main street of Chillicothe before parading through town during their veteran fulough in the winter of 1863–4. They had already fought at the second battle of Bull Run, at Chancellorsville, Gettysburg, and at Chattanooga. At the end of this furlough, they fought in the Atlanta campaign, on the March to the Sea, and finally at Bentonville.*

pursued him vigorously, including sending gunboats up the Ohio River to guard likely crossing points as far as these vessels' draft would allow. Heavy summer rains both helped the gunboats and harmed Morgan's chances by raising the river, making it too high for Morgan to cross easily and deep enough for the gunboats to travel further upstream than normal. Two had been positioned in the vicinity of Buffington Island, where there was also a small earthwork occupied by a few hundred men and a couple of cannon. In a dramatic

night march, Morgan's troopers edged their way around the suburbs of Cincinnati and continued on to Buffington Island, which they reached at nightfall on July 18. The earthwork was found abandoned, but Union troops were close. There was skirmishing around Pomeroy and Chester between Morgan's men and both Ohio militia and volunteers of the 23rd Ohio. As dawn rose on July 19, a thick fog covered the area, including the crossing of part of Morgan's command. However, as the fog began to lift, the two columns of pursuing Union

Left: *USS* Indianola *runs past the Rebel batteries at Vicksburg, Mississippi, in the night of February 13, 1863. The Cincinnati-built ship was sent south of Vicksbug to disrupt Rebel transfers of men and supplies along the only part of the river they still held, between Port Hudson and Vicksburg.*

Below: *An example of a prewar militia uniform worn by the Guthrie Grays of Cincinnati. This gray led to confusion on the battlefields of 1861.*

troops arrived and engaged the part of Morgan's force that still remained on the Ohio side of the river. Before long, the gunboats were also able to begin a bombardment of the Rebel positions. Morgan chose to remain with his men and they attempted to evade the two pursuing Union columns. However, the bulk of the Rebels were captured, leaving Morgan with about five hundred men.

Morgan continued to make his way in a northeastward direction, hoping for some kind of lucky break that would enable him to escape his tenacious pursuers. They crossed the Muskingum River near Rokeby Lock on July 23 and headed in the general direction of Salineville. Near this town, on July 26, Morgan finally accepted that escape was impossible, and surrendered to Union forces. Morgan was imprisoned in a civilian maximum-security prison in

Columbus. The Union troops did not hold him long, though, as he and six comrades tunneled their way out using an air vent under the floor. On November 27, 1863, Morgan made his escape, exchanging his Rebel uniform for civilian clothes and taking the train south out of Columbus, sitting next to a Union officer.

Ohio produced a galaxy of generals who fought for the Union cause. At the head of the list stands Sherman who was a member of a prominent Ohio family. His brother was a US senator from the state, and quite possibly his Civil War military career would have been nowhere near as memorable without this political influence. Sherman graduated from West Point in 1840. He saw service in the Mexican War of 1846–48 and left the army in

Below: *A commissary sergeant of the 30th Ohio Infantry. Commissary troops distributed food among the soldiers of the regiment. The 30th Infantry's commander at one time was Sherman's brother-in-law Hugh Ewing. The regiment served in West Virginia, was in the Army of the Potomac for Antietam, and then spent the rest of the war in the West.*

1853. His civilian career had the stability of Ulysses S. Grant's, which is saying a lot. At first he tried to run a bank in California, but this enterprise failed in the Panic of 1857. Then he tried to practice law in Leavenworth, Kansas. Eventually he took the job of superintendent of the Louisiana Military Academy (today's Louisiana State University), but resigned when he saw the likely political course for the state. Instead, he took a job running a St. Louis streetcar company in 1861. While living here he witnessed the capture of secessionist Camp Jackson by Union soldiers on May 10, 1861. (Coincidentally, Grant was visiting St. Louis that same day.)

When the war came, Sherman offered his services and commanded a brigade at the first battle of Bull Run. His troops performed creditably in a losing cause and secured him promotion to brigadier general and the command of the Department of the Ohio. Unfortunately, Sherman's failure to aid pro-Union movements in east Tennessee and an inability to cultivate good press relations led to his replacement by Don Carlos Buell in November 1861. He returned to command in charge of a division in Grant's army in March 1862, and Grant became a loyal patron of the Ohioan.

Sherman's career now proceeded without a faltering step in spite of some difficult moments. He was almost blamed for the surprise of the Union army at Shiloh, Tennessee, on April 6, 1862, and his attempted assault against Chickasaw Bluffs, Mississippi, in December 1862 resulted in heavy casualties. However, he proved an adept student of Grant's style and consequently both a capable subordinate and a man who could be entrusted with independent command.

Sherman succeeded Grant to command of the main Union army in the West in December 1863, and his campaign to take Atlanta presents an interesting contrast to Grant's Overland campaign in the same period. Where Grant consistently was compelled to attack, Sherman relied on maneuver to force his Rebel opponents out of their positions. Sherman is held in infamy in the South for his legendary March to the Sea in December 1864, during which his army created a path of devastation across the state of Georgia. Less famous, but equally destructive, was his march across South Carolina in February and March 1865. After the

Murfreesboro, Tennessee. When Grant headed east for the 1864 campaigns, he took Sheridan with him and gave him command of the cavalry corps. Sheridan's natural pugnacity and organizing ability soon gave his men, for the first time in the war, an ascendancy over their Rebel counterparts. His campaign in the Shenandoah valley in August 1864, however, was a catalog of unfinished business. His energetic pursuit of Lee once the Rebel general had abandoned Richmond in April 1865 did much to secure an end to the war.

Left: A detail of the Ohio Monument at Vicksburg. Twenty-four regiments of Ohio infantry served in the campaign.

Quincy A. Gillmore (1825-88)

This commander is not numbered among the famous Civil War generals, but his career encompassed some of the most important strategic events of the war. Gillmore was born in Black River, Lorain County, and attended the US Military Academy as part of the class of 1849. He first made his mark as an engineer, part of the Port Royal Expedition that seized Port Royal, Hilton Head, and Fort Pulaski. Then he led the Union forces at Charleston, South Carolina, in the summer of 1863. He ordered the attacks on Fort Wagner that included the famous assault by the 54th Massachusetts Regiment of African American troops and masterminded the siege that eventually led to that fort's capture. In 1864 he went with his troops to Virginia, where he participated in the fighting of the Army of the James in May and June around Bermuda Hundred and Petersburg. His conduct in a reconnaissance of the Petersburg attention brought him the unfavorable notice of Major General Benjamin Butler, and he was moved to the forces defending Washington. His war came to a premature end in a riding accident, when he was seriously injured. He died in Brooklyn and is buried at West Point.

war, Sherman remained a soldier, eventually becoming commander in chief of the army.

One of Grant's more inspired moves was to bring another Ohioan east with him and put him in charge of the Army of the Potomac's cavalry. Philip Sheridan (1831–88) was born in New York, but grew up in Ohio. He graduated from West Point in 1853. As a junior officer in the regular army at the war's outbreak, it took a while for Sheridan to gain promotion. Ironically for a man renowned for his capacity to conduct a battle, Sheridan spent the first months of the war as a quartermaster and commissary. He then commanded the 2nd Michigan Cavalry and an infantry division in the Army of Ohio. His division served with some prominence at the battles of Perryville, Kentucky, and

OREGON

"Ten good soldiers are required to wage successful war against one Indian."

—J. W. P. Huntington, superintendent of Indian Affairs, Oregon

Oregon's journey to statehood was possibly more tortuous than any other state at the time of the Civil War. The United States claimed the territory during the Washington administration when a fur trader sailed up the Columbia River. Britain also had strong claims, based in part by the visits of the explorer Vancouver around the same time, when there was nearly naval conflict with Spanish ships in the area. Spain ceded its "discovery rights" to the United States by treaty in 1819, and Russian claims were removed by a treaty with the United States in 1824. The settlement of the region by Americans following trails across the Great Plains and over the Rocky Mountains helped resolve the matter finally in 1846, when Britain and the United States defined their boundary along the 49th parallel by treaty.

In 1843 these settlers formed a provisional government for themselves, under the Stars and Stripes. Formal territorial government from Washington City came in 1848. The provisional legislature had defined Oregon to be a Free-Soil territory in 1843, and the legislation instituting territorial government extended the provisions of the Northwest Ordinance of 1787, which had banned slavery, to the Oregon Territory. Thus there was never any possibility of the territory entering the United States as anything other than a free state. In 1853, the northern and western portions of Oregon Territory were separated by Congress and established as Washington Territory. In 1857, Oregonians voted to hold a constitutional convention as the first step toward statehood, and in 1859 President Buchanan signed legislation admitting Oregon to the United States.

Oregon's Pacific Coast location left it outside of the conflict. The main effect was the standard one in the West, with the withdrawal of federal troops from the forts that protected settlements from the Indians.

Some pro-secession feeling erupted in Oregon in Jacksonville. According to rumor, another group contemplated seizing Fort Vancouver. Late in the day in May 1865, a minor scuffle occurred in Eugene when a citizen went around proclaiming his enthusiasm for Jefferson Davis. He was arrested and spent three months in jail. Afterward, he won a small legal settlement for false arrest.

Four new posts were founded in Oregon during the war: Fort Klamath, in the southwest of the state near Klamath Lake; Camp Alvord, in the southeastern corner; and Camps Watson and Logan, southwest of the Oregon Trail in the northeastern quadrant. The whole area was troubled not by any organized Native American raids, but by individual groups of Klamaths and Modocs, who joined with the more warlike Northern Paiutes (also known as Snakes). These normally picked out isolated groups of miners, stealing horses and equipment and killing the men.

There was little that organized military campaigns could do to help the miners, since the raiding parties were too small to pursue effectively with large bodies of soldiers. At the war's end, there was still no real peace in this region, and the volunteer units handed the problem over to the regular forces who returned once the war in the East had ended.

Left: *Philip Sheridan was one of the trio of leading Union generals who before the war had minor roles, and came to prominence only slowly. A captain in the regular army at the war's beginning, Sheridan was stationed in Oregon, having been there for several years engaged in helping settlers fend off Indian attacks.*

Two volunteer units were raised in Oregon during the war. The 1st Oregon Volunteer Cavalry and the 1st Oregon Cavalry filled in for the absent U.S. Army troops. Other troops in Oregon during the war years were supplied by the California volunteers. The 1st Oregon Cavalry fought a few skirmishes against Indians around Fort Klamath (which had been founded in 1863) during 1864–65. Otherwise, it was a very quiet war for the state of Oregon.

PENNSYLVANIA

"The world will little note, nor long remember, what we say here,
but it can never forget what they did here."

—Abraham Lincoln, November 19, 1863

King Charles II signed the Charter of Pennsylvania in 1681. It was granted to William Penn, a Quaker, in return for debts owed to him by the king. Pennsylvania then declared independence in 1776, and became part of the United States on July 22, 1778. The state's traditionally turbulent political history contributed toward strong indifference in some areas as to whether the Southern states stayed in the Union or not. Abolitionist sentiment was strongest in the north and west and weakest in Philadelphia and the Lower Susquehanna Valley. The last antebellum president, James Buchanan, was sometimes suspected of proslavery attitudes. However, Abraham Lincoln carried the state by a majority in the 1860 presidential election.

Pennsylvania was one of the most important states to the Northern war effort. The immense quantity of coal available in its land and the location of Pittsburgh near Lake Erie, along which iron ore could be brought from the mines in Minnesota, helped Pittsburgh on its way to being a steelmaking center. The Allegheny Arsenal, an ammunition factory also at Pittsburgh, was the scene of the worst industrial accident of the war, when powder at the factory accidentally ignited, causing a massive explosion. Coincidentally, this occurred on the same day as the battle of Antietam, September 17, 1862, and killed seventy-five workers,

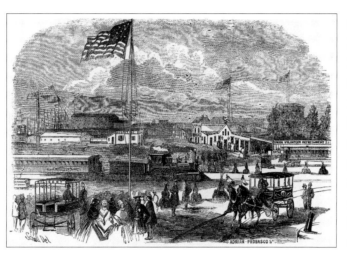

Above: *A refreshment saloon for Union soldiers at Philadelphia. Philadelphia was on the route used by troops traveling to Washington from New York and New England.*

Left: *State regimental flag presented to the 138th Pennsylvania Infantry by the citizens of Bridgeport and Morristown in 1864, while the regiment was in the trenches before Petersburg.*

the majority of them women. The Frankford Arsenal, on the Delaware River near Philadelphia, was another important source for ammunition. Philadelphia was also the home of an important naval yard and the Cramp shipbuilding yards, both of which produced a number of ships for the Union navy during the war, including the USS *New Ironsides*, the largest ironclad vessel to serve in the navy during the war.

The first action in Pennsylvania during the war occurred on October 10, 1862, near Chambersburg, when that town was made the target of a Rebel cavalry brigade. Some supplies were taken and a storehouse was burned before the Rebel cavalry left the town.

Pennsylvania was put into the front line of the war by Robert E. Lee's invasion of the North in 1863. After Chancellorsville, Lee chose to repeat his strategy of autumn 1862, when he crossed the Potomac. This time he moved his army up through the Shenandoah Valley, which enabled his cavalry to better mask its movements. General Joseph Hooker, still in charge of the Army of the Potomac, in spite of his defeat, sent his own cavalry toward Culpeper Court House to see what Lee's army was up to. The consequence was probably the largest cavalry fight in American history, the battle of Brandy Station on June 9, 1863. The Union cavalry of

the Army of the Potomac for once gave a good account of themselves, although the battle itself could be characterized as a draw.

Lee's army crossed the Potomac June 23–25, and moved so rapidly that he reached Frederick before Hooker guessed that he was heading north. Hooker immediately sent three corps on the march, and readied the rest of his army to move out. By this time, Hooker had lost the confidence of a number of his generals, and in the overtly political manner that had developed in the Army of the Potomac, a cabal had already formed to suggest General George Meade as his replacement. On June 27, Hooker offered his resignation to President Lincoln. Abraham Lincoln had pondered replacing Hooker already and now he took the opportunity and appointed Meade in his place. Hooker's replacement, from the outset, made it clear that it was not his intention to attack Lee. He instead sought to position the Army of the Potomac in such a way that Lee would be forced to attack him. Meade studied the map carefully. Two corps were at Chambersburg and a third was between Carlisle and York. In the center of this was the town of Gettysburg, an important road junction. Meade selected good defensive terrain at Pipe Creek in Maryland. This would position him behind Lee's army. Just to be on the safe side, however, he ordered a move on Gettysburg by some of his forces in case he could catch part of Lee's army.

Above: *A jacket as worn by a sergeant of the 6th Pennsylvania Cavalry, also known as "Rush's Lancers." They were initially issued with the same equipment as other regiments, but then were given lances, as used in many European armies, but these were found impractical.*

One division of Robert E. Lee's army, commanded by General Henry Heth, was looking for shoes in Gettysburg on June 30 when some Union cavalry arrived on the outskirts. Heth withdrew his command, but asked permission to return the next day. Meanwhile, the Union cavalry, part of General John Buford's brigade, took possession of the town and summoned the rest of their comrades. In the morning of July 1, 1863, Heth's troops approached Gettysburg again, but this time encountered more cavalry, who occupied McPherson's Ridge to the west of the town along the Chambersburg Pike.

Firing broke out and Buford sent word to the nearest Union corps commander, General John F. Reynolds, a native of Lancaster, to come quickly. John

Reynolds arrived ahead of his I Corps to scout out the ground so that a defensive line could be established rapidly. As Reynolds directed regiments into the fray, Reynolds was shot by a Confederate sharpshooter. General Abner Doubleday, who later in life would be declared the inventor of baseball, now took command of Reynolds' troops.

Heth, meanwhile, realized that more than a few cavalry pickets were blocking his hunt for supplies and sent word to his own corps commander, General A. P. Hill, that Union forces seemed to be massing at Gettysburg. More and more troops arrived for each side. The Union General Oliver Howard's XI Corps arrived and deployed to the north of the town, while General William Pender's and General Robert Rodes's divisions reinforced Heth and deployed to the north as well, respectively.

In the afternoon, General Jubal Early's division arrived and hit XI Corps' right flank. The Union line gave way, rippling from the northeast to the west. In places the retreat approached a rout, but it never got that bad, and the fleeing troops did not go any further than the heights to the south of Gettysburg—Cemetery Hill and Cemetery Ridge. General Winfield Hancock and the lead elements of his

Left: *Major General John F. Reynolds was offered the command of the Army of the Potomac before the campaign at Gettysburg, but declined. Consequently, he was in the front line on July 1, 1863, organizing the defense of McPherson's Ridge by his I Corps, when he was shot dead.*

Left: *Cavalrymen of Company I, 6th Pennsylvania Cavalry, in Virginia in May 1863. Also known as "Rush's Lancers," after their commander Richard Rush, they were issued with the lances on the order of General McClellan. Their equipment was changed from lances to carbines in May 1863. Their war service included Brandy Station, the biggest cavalry battle of the war.*

Right: The Pennsylvania Memorial at Gettysburg, an enormous neoclassical design, is the largest on the battlefield. Each of the bronze plaques along the base is dedicated to one of the Pennsylvania regiments that fought at the battle.

II Corps were now arriving and he laid out the defensive position that the Union army would occupy. One end was fixed on Culp's Hill, to the southeast of the town. The line then ran to Cemetery Hill, along Cemetery Ridge and ended on some lower ground below two other hills, named Little Round Top and Big Round Top.

Robert E. Lee had beaten George Meade to the field, and as dusk approached he sent a request to corps commander General Richard Ewell to push "those people" (as he always called Union troops) off Cemetery Hill. As it was a request and not an order, Ewell assessed the tactical situation and chose not to risk envelopment from Culp's Hill of his troops who had been disorganized already by the battle. This was the first of the controversial decisions of the battle that has provided historians plenty to debate in the years since.

Both armies assembled themselves for what they believed to be the decisive day of battle, July 2. Meade had General Henry Slocum's XII Corps on Culp's Hill, Howard's XI Corps on Cemetery Hill, Hancock's II Corps on Cemetery Ridge, with General Daniel Sickles's III Corps extending the line southward. General Doubleday's I Corps was positioned between Slocum and Howard. Two more corps, General George Sykes' V Corps and General John Sedgwick's VI Corps, were on their way.

Left: A cavalry officer's hat worn by Captain Alexander H. McHenry, Company G, 13th Pennsylvania Cavalry.

Below: Zouaves of the 114th Pennsylvania Infantry outside Petersburg, Virginia, in 1864. Unusually so late in the war, they maintain their characteristic Zouave uniform.

suggested that the Rebels disengage. Lee preferred to fight here and gave Longstreet his instructions at 9 a.m. Six hours later, Longstreet still had not attacked. Whether he was dragging his feet on purpose or whether his troops genuinely needed that much time has been a second controversial point about the battle.

When Longstreet's assault finally began at 4 p.m., Meade was horrified to discover that Sickles had abandoned his position in the line and moved forward to some higher ground. Sickles thought the position was stronger, until Meade pointed out to him that both his flanks were in the air. Meade rode off to organize the necessary reinforcements, while Sickles and his men were forced to buy Meade time with their lives.

The Peach Orchard, the Wheatfield, Devil's Den, Little Round Top—the names of these points on the battlefield have entered into American history, along with Bloody Lane of Antietam and the Stone Wall of Fredericksburg. Little Round Top was the idyllic setting for the most dramatic fighting of the day. Both sides raced troops to capture this picturesque, rocky, wooded hill, better suited to picnics than bloodshed. The Union troops attained the summit first and drove back every attempt by the Rebels to take it. The Peach Orchard, the Wheatfield, and Devil's Den were mileposts on the road to the destruction of III Corps. The outnumbered Union soldiers fought hard and long, but in the end they gave way and retreated. The III

Lee now had a night to study the lay of the land and likely Union positions. He chose to make his main effort against the Union left, beneath the two Round Tops. Lee's army, however, was slower to concentrate, as at Antietam. In the morning of July 2, the last divisions of General James Longstreet's corps, which were to strike at the Round Tops, were only just arriving. Longstreet did not like the look of the Union position and

Corps suffered so many losses that it was disbanded after the battle.

As night fell on July 2, the Confederate forces could only wonder how they had not achieved a victory. Hancock had skillfully managed to fill the gap created in his line by the defeat of Sickles with troops of his own corps and of V Corps.

Robert E. Lee now made the third controversial decision of the battle. On July 3, he massed 15,000 men, with the all-Virginia division of General George Pickett at the front and sent them across the fields between Seminary Ridge and Cemetery Ridge to attack the Union center.

A lengthy artillery barrage had little effect on Union guns and the Confederate infantry were under fire the whole way. Yet they still managed to ascend the ridge, and one man, General Lew Armistead, managed to reach a stone wall just in front of a coppice of trees that Lee had identified as the point where the Union line must be breached.

This moment in the action has been sanctioned by tradition as the Confederacy's high watermark: Armistead and a handful of his soldiers crossed the wall in the teeth of a storm of Union shot. He was mortally wounded, and the Confederate infantry tide ebbed back to Seminary Ridge to be greeted by a tearful Lee saying, "It is all my fault." On July 4, in a rainstorm, the Confederate forces began to retreat back to Virginia. General George Meade had done something five other Union commanders had failed to do: he had defeated Robert E. Lee.

On November 19, 1863, President Abraham Lincoln gave a speech at Cemetery Hill in a ceremony commemorating the soldiers who had been killed in the battle of Gettysbury. President Lincoln's Gettysburg Address has become one of the great speeches of American history.

The last major military event in of the Civil War in Pennsylvania occurred as a by-product of General Early's raid into Maryland in July 1864. Chambersburg, which had hosted Rebel invaders twice before in the war, was occupied by two cavalry brigades who demanded a larger ransom. The people of Chambersburg refused to pay, and the Rebels burned the town on July 20.

GEORGE MEADE (1815–72)

The victor of Gettysburg was a native of Pennsylvania, although he was born in Cadiz, Spain, where his parents were living at the time. Meade graduated from West Point in 1835, resigned from the army a year later, and then rejoined in 1842. He was an engineer by training, and his preference for defensive warfare reflected the consequent good eye he had developed for examining the lie of the land. Meade was commanding V Corps of the Army of the Potomac when he received command of the army. Lincoln was angered by Meade's failure to launch a counterattack on Lee on July 4, and again at Williamsport, Maryland, where the Confederate army had its backs to the Potomac as it waited for a new pontoon bridge to be built. Major General Meade was effectively supplanted by Ulysses Grant in the spring of 1864, although he was officially left in command of the Army of the Potomac until the end of the war, thereby becoming the longest serving and most successful general to occupy that post.

RHODE ISLAND

"Now I lay me down to sleep/ In mud that's many fathoms deep;/ If I'm not here when you awake,/ Just hunt me up with an oyster rake."

—Satirical prayer during Burnside's Mud March, January 1863

The first permanent settlement of Rode Island and Providence Plantations (to give it its full original name) was established in 1636 and the religious freedom which prevailed there made it a refuge for several persecuted sects. Rhode Island officially became part of the United States on July 9, 1778, when its delegates to the Continental Congress signed the Articles of Confederation. Like the rest of New England, Rhode Island voted for Abraham Lincoln in the presidential election of 1860.

Rhode Island, being a small state, did not raise a large contingent for service in the war. However, Rhode Island did raise some of the best artillery batteries that served in the Army of the Potomac. Unlike the infantry regiments raised by states, artillery units were distributed around the armies not by regiments but by batteries. The different experiences of Rhode Island's Battery B and Battery F of the 1st Rhode Island Light Artillery Regiment illustrate this well.

Battery B was mustered on August 13, 1861, and was assigned to the 2d division of II Corps of the Army of the Potomac. It first fought at the disastrous affair of Ball's Bluff in October 1861. At Fredericksburg, they worked their guns within two hundred yards of the Rebel line behind the Stone Wall at Marye's Heights. It was also

Above: *General Ambrose Burnside, born in Ohio, had resided in Rhode Island for several years before the outbreak of the war. He is mostly associated with military catastrophes. However, he did secure some important victories along the North Carolina coast in 1862 and in eastern Tennessee in 1863.*

Left: *A midshipman of the US Naval Academy and a cadet of the US Military Academy.*

involved in the fighting during the battle of Reams Station on August 25, 1864, the battery was nearly captured in the fighting.

Battery F was mustered on October 29, 1861, and left for Washington in November. Its guns consisted of four ten-pounder Parrott rifles and two howitzers. In December, Battery F was assigned to an expedition to North Carolina to capture Roanoke Island. After a difficult sea voyage, the battery arrived at Hatteras Inlet on January 21, 1862, and landed ashore. Battery F then remained in North Carolina for nearly two years until at the end of 1863 it was transferred to Fortress Monroe and became part of the Army of the James until the end of the war. The battery saw little action during the war, unlike Battery B, even though they were of the same regiment.

Of the infantry regiments raised in Rhode Island, the 1st Rhode Island infantry, a ninety-day regiment raised in response to the call for militia issued by Lincoln on April 15, 1861, attracted considerable attention in the city of Washington's high society thanks to its colonel being the extremely wealthy Governor William Sprague. This man, however, showed a certain courage in combat. At the first battle of Bull Run, Sprague was brave enough to have two horses shot out from under

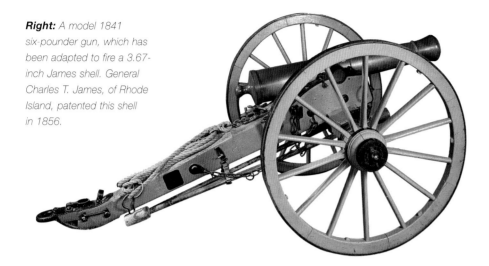

Right: A model 1841 six-pounder gun, which has been adapted to fire a 3.67-inch James shell. General Charles T. James, of Rhode Island, patented this shell in 1856.

company into the largest calico printing textile mill in the world. In 1860, Sprague secured election as Rhode Island governor and at the time was the youngest governor in the United States. Sprague was active during the secession crisis in preparing to raise troops to send to the defense of the city of Washington, and three days after the first call for troops dispatched a "Flying Artillery" battery from Rhode Island. After his experience at Bull Run, Sprague sought to become a general, but was informed that he could only be a general if he stopped being a governor. Sprague preferred the political life and returned to Rhode Island. In 1863 he became US senator from the state and later married Kate Chase, the daughter of the Secretary of the Treasury.

him, not something that happened to officer skulking in the rear ranks.

Sprague (1830–1915) was the son of a textile mill owner who was murdered in 1843, at which point his education was abandoned and he was put to work in the family firm, A&W Sprague Manufacturing. Sprague became an active managing partner in 1856, and by the time of the Civil War had converted his father's

The highest-ranking Rhode Islander of the war was Major General Ambrose Burnside (1824–81), who was in fact born in Indiana. Burnside graduated from West Point in 1847 and resigned his commission soon after his marriage to a Rhode Island woman in 1852. He made the state his home thereafter and tried to develop

Right: A bayonet charge by the 34th Rhode Island Infantry in an action on James Island on June 16, 1862.

a breech-loading rifle to sell to the US Army, but the government wasn't interested and his business failed. Burnside then took a job at the Illinois Central Railroad's New York office, in order to help meet his debts. The war therefore came as something of a relief, as Burnside was able to join the US Volunteers, in which he received promotion to brigadier general. His friendship with General George McClellan secured support for Burnside's idea to take an expedition to the North Carolina coast and seize Roanoke Island. He accomplished the capture both of the island and of the important railroad terminus of New Bern by the end of March 1862. After this promising start, Burnside's reputation rapidly went downhill. Commanding the IX Corps of the Army of the Potomac at the battle of Antietam in September 1862, Burnside's inability to control his sector of the battle once fighting began cost McClellan the chance of a decisive victory over Lee's Rebel army, and his job. Had Burnside attacked along a wider front, he might have beaten the much-smaller Rebel force in front of him. But Burnside was cautious and slow. Consequently, Burnside replaced his friend McClellan over his own objections of unsuitability for command of the Army of the Potomac. Once again, Burnside started well, surprising Lee by getting to undefended Fredericksburg, Virginia, in order to cross the Rappahannock river unopposed. But as soon as things began to go wrong—the pontoons for his bridge failed to arrive in time—he became slow. In the end he commanded an attack against a too strong position, and his plans ended in the slaughter below Marye's Heights. Burnside was replaced in early 1862 as commander of the Army of the Potomac and was sent to command the Department of the Ohio. Here, he was able to achieve a longstanding goal of President Lincoln's by leading an army into eastern Tennessee and capturing Knoxville. This act restored him to favor and led to his return to the Army of the Potomac as a corps commander.

Burnside led his corps throughout the Overland campaign of 1864. During the siege of Petersburg, Burnside set in motion a plan to blow up part of the Rebel trenches. The battle of the Crater on July 30, 1864, was a disaster, although only partly through Burnside's fault. It was the end of his luck, though, as he was removed from command of IX Corps and he was sent on leave of absence for the rest of the war.

Left: *A 1st lieutenant of the 2nd Rhode Island infantry in the Rhode Island militia uniform of 1861. The pleated blouse of this uniform required a lot more care than would be possible under field conditions during the war, and the uniform was little seen after 1861.*

SOUTH CAROLINA

"Captain Carpenter…said 'Boys I am killed, but you press on,'
then yielded up his spirit to the cause."

—Micah Jenkins, June 1862

A permanent English settlement was established in South Carolina in 1670. The colony of Carolina was divided in 1710. South Carolina declared independence from Britain in 1776 and became part of the United States on July 9, 1778, when the colony's delegates signed the Articles of Confederation. South Carolina's presidential electors voted for John C. Breckinridge, the proslavery Democratic candidate, in the 1860 presidential election. This state was the first to rebel, voting to secede from the Union on December 20, 1860. The fact that the Palmetto state would take a lead in these matters had been apparent in April 1860, when the Democratic national convention was held in Charleston. Delegates saw for themselves how strong the sentiment for pushing the national crisis to some kind of resolution, secession, or submission was among Charleston's citizens.

South Carolina responded to Lincoln's victory by voting to hold a convention to consider a motion of secession. This was passed, and the union was dissolved as far as South Carolinians were concerned. One item of business left unfinished by the mere passage of a motion by a parliamentary assembly was the presence of a number of federal fortifications and other installations across the state. From a military point of

Union Prisoners
Castle Pinckney

Above: *Union prisoners at Castle Pinckney. This old fort was militarily useless for warfare in the 1860s, but served well enough as a prisoner camp.*

Left: *The interior of Fort Sumter today. Most of the visible damage done to the fort was not by the Rebel bombardment of April 1861, but by Union naval action later in the war. The fort remained a bastion protecting the harbor until Charleston was evacuated by Rebel troops in 1865.*

view, the most important were the forts surrounding Charleston harbor. This was an important deep-water port, and large sums of money had been invested in protecting it. Hundreds of thousands of dollars had been spent on building one particular structure, which stood on an artificial island in the center of the harbor—Fort Sumter.

On December 20, 1860, Sumter stood unoccupied by any military force. Charleston was garrisoned by some seventy-odd federal troops, based at Fort Moultrie. This was a fabled fort that dated back to the Revolution, but was not really designed to face an attack from land. The US commander, Major Robert Anderson of Kentucky, chose to move from Moultrie to Sumter, which would be an easier position to defend.

Anderson's action outraged South Carolinians, who regarded it as a dishonorable move unworthy of a Southern gentleman. On orders from South Carolina's governor, Francis Pickens, the next day state militia seized all federal installations that they could, including Castle Pinckney and Fort Moultrie. The construction of batteries around the harbor and its entrance began. One of these batteries, on Morris Island, fired the first shot at the steamer *Star of the West*, which carried supplies for the Union garrison. The steamer turned

back after being hit by rounds fired from Fort Moultrie.

After New Year's Day, 1861, South Carolina was joined by six more states in rapid succession. On February 4, delegates from these seven states assembled at Montgomery, Alabama, and in six days created a provisional government for a Confederate States of America, headed by Jefferson Davis. President Davis inherited the crisis over Fort Sumter. Recognizing the nature of the military problem, on March 1 Davis appointed former US Army Officer Pierre Gustave Toutant Beauregard to command operations against the Union-held fort, with the rank of brigadier general. Beauregard had been an excellent student of artillery at the US Military Academy, ironically under Robert Anderson, who taught the course at that time.

Beauregard arrived and surveyed his resources. He had some 9,000 militia, but few of them had any military experience. Several new batteries had been constructed that could bombard either the Union-held fort or any attempt to relieve it. However, he hoped that this would not be necessary, since sooner or later the Union garrison would run out of supplies. One of Beauregard's first acts on taking command was to ban the sale of food to the garrison of Sumter.

On April 8, a messenger arrived in Charleston from President Lincoln for Governor Pickens. It informed the South Carolinan governor that there would be an attempt made to provision the garrison at Sumter. Pickens reported the content of this message to Beauregard and Davis. On April 9, the Confederate cabinet endorsed an order to Beauregard instructing him to secure the evacuation of Sumter by negotiation or bombardment before the arrival of the Union provisions. On April 11, Beauregard requested the surrender of the fort. Anderson declined to do so, but reported that he would soon be out of food. Beauregard chose not to wait, and a bombardment of

Above: *An 1862 ten-cent note indicates how short of coinage Rebel states were during the war.*

Fort Sumter began at 4.30 a.m. on April 12, 1861. The shelling lasted some thirty-three hours, and Fort Sumter officially surrendered on April 14. The fort now became a vital component of the Confederate defenses of Charleston harbor.

From the start, the Union plan to overcome the Southern states' rebellion had been based on imposing a blockade of the Rebel ports. The Commission of Conference, also known as the Blockade Strategy Board, met to outline what needed to be done. They identified Port Royal Sound as a good place to establish a naval base that would give ships blockading the South Atlantic coast of the Confederacy a place to rest and repair. On October 19, 1861 a squadron of ships under Flag Officer Samuel DuPont, departed New York for Hampton Roads, where it rendezvoused with a large fleet of troop transports. This force would occupy Port Royal sound, establishing a base on Hilton Head Island. It sailed from Hampton Roads on October 29, 1861, and arrived off Port Royal on November 3.

The Confederate secretary of war, Judah P. Benjamin, was aware of the likely destination of the Union fleet on November 1 when he alerted the governor of South Carolina of its approach. President Davis took action by establishing a new Department of South Carolina, Georgia, and East Florida, and appointed a surprised Robert E. Lee to command it. Lee received word of his appointment on November 5 and left the following day.

At Port Royal, the Confederate forces had made a show of force in the evening of November 4, when three small river steamers opened fire on some Union gun boats. They came out again on the next day, as Union vessels came close inshore to conduct a survey of the two Rebel forts guarding the mouth of the sound. The Rebels withdrew as more Union ships rushed to engage, and the opportunity of the two Rebel batteries to open fire arose. The gunfire was to no effect, except to reveal to observers on the Union ships the strength of the Rebel defenses. On November 7, around 9 a.m., the Union fleet formed up in close order, and the

action commenced with the firing of Rebel guns about half an hour later. The Union fleet concentrated fire on the Rebel fort on Hilton Head Island, Fort Walker. The smaller Union warships occupied a flanking position to block any intervention by Tattnall's flotilla. The rest of the fleet steamed on an elliptical course, firing on each fort in turn. Tattnall's flotilla did come out but retreated

up Scull Creek. This enabled a couple of the smaller Union warships to set up an enfilading fire on Fort Walker. After a four-hour cannonade, the Rebel defenders of the earthwork evacuated their post. A naval officer went ashore to investigate and hoisted the Stars and Stripes. Some Marines came ashore to provide a small garrison. Eventually the fort was

Above: *The USS* Catskill, *a monitor of the Passaic class, in Charleston harbor in 1865. The ship was one of the monitors used in the bombardment of Charleston harbor in April 1863, which was repelled by the Rebel defenses of this port.*

handed over to the Union army. A reconnaissance during the night suggested that Fort Beauregard, on the opposite point, might also have been abandoned. In the morning, this was confirmed, and at noon this fort too was taken over by the Union army.

On November 8, a Union vessel established that the town of Beaufort had been abandoned, and this was also added to the military administration being established around Port Royal Sound. Control of Port Royal gave the Union one of the best harbors on the Atlantic coast. It was developed into a base for future operations, serving as a coaling station, with workshops and supply depots to support the blockade. Old hulks were lashed together to provide floating accommodation for work and storage.

For Robert E. Lee, the fall of this important installation on the very day that he arrived to take command of a newly formed department was a severe blow. At this point the Union forces could easily have

disrupted the railroad between Charleston and Savannah, if they had not lost a significant part of their ammunition supplies during a gale off Cape Hatteras on the voyage south.

Lee was not disheartened. He established the basic principles that would govern the defense of South Carolina's coast during the civil war.

Recognizing that the Union naval supremacy enabled them to add the artillery aboard to any accompanying a military force, he sited his strongpoints upriver, where the ships would be unable to deploy their guns effectively. At Charleston Lee ordered the obstruction of the rivers and kept up the strength of the principal forts in case of an attack.

On September 24, 1862, a hero of Charleston returned to the city after spending over a year away from the place that had made him famous. General Pierre Gustave Toutant Beauregard was appointed by President Davis as commander of the Department of South Carolina, Georgia, and Florida, and located his headquarters in Charleston.

Charleston had taken on a totemic significance for the Union forces. This city was perceived as "the cradle of secession." It was also a key port for the blockade runners, especially those carrying luxury goods. Its seizure would be both politically popular in the North and would eliminate one of the three major ports used to break the blockade.

Charleston was, however, a very well protected place. It had experience of assault from the sea as long ago as 1776, during the American Revolution, when the guns of Fort Sullivan (later renamed Fort Moultrie) repelled a British fleet. A second attempt in 1780 to run the guns of Fort Moultrie, prior to the capture of the city, had been successful.

In addition to the original three forts defending Charleston, a number of batteries had been built

around the harbor entrance, originally to bombard Fort Sumter. Sullivan's Island had added Battery Bee and Fort Moultrie had Battery Beauregard. Morris Island had the Cumming's Point Battery, or Battery Gregg. Battery Wagner, also on Morris Island, protected the approaches to the harbor's mouth.

In addition, there was a small Confederate naval squadron at Charleston. Commodore Duncan M. Ingraham was in command and had organized it from almost nothing. When Beauregard took command of the department, it included some small wooden gunboats, together with two larger ironclads, the *Chicora* and the *Palmetto State*, being built at that time. These were both completed in November. Beauregard was not impressed with them. They were sorely underpowered and could barely travel against the tides. Beauregard lent his support to an apparently promising idea conceived by Captain Francis Lee of using small armored boats armed with spar torpedoes that could be directed against the undersides of the blockading vessels.

As a result of Beauregard's interfering with naval matters, Confederate Secretary of the Navy Stephen Mallory put Ingraham under pressure to do something about attacking the blockading squadron with his ironclads. In January 1863 some monitors had joined the Union South Atlantic Blockading Squadron, but were not actually present off Charleston. Ingraham chose to strike before they arrived. He sailed out on the night of January 30–31, in a period of calm weather. The ensuing engagement pitted the two Confederate ironclads against two Union gunboats, the *Mercedita* and the *Keystone State*. The *Palmetto State* battered the *Mercedita* into submission, while the *Chicora* put to flight the *Keystone State*. Other Union ships attempted to intervene, but largely kept out of range. The *Chicora* and *Palmetto State* returned to the cheers of the Charleston populace.

From January 1863, Flag Officer Samuel F. DuPont, commander of the Union squadron, had come under

increasing pressure from the city of Washington to take his ships into Charleston harbor. Secretary of the Navy Gideon Welles dispatched five monitors of the Passaic class for him to use. DuPont had displayed some reluctance to undertake the mission. Beauregard had

Below: *A banded gun on a turntable mounting at Fort Moultrie. Fire from Moultrie helped repel the Union attack of April 1863.*

placed all kinds of obstacles—pilings, nets, and electrically detonated mines, among others—in the various channels of Charleston harbor, in addition to buoys that would assist the ranging of guns from the batteries in Sumter and the other harbor fortifications. In addition, there were some seventy heavy guns defending Charleston, and most were sited to enable a crossfire of either channel passing Fort Sumter.

DuPont attacked on April 7, 1863, using all seven ironclads at his disposal. Apart from the monitors, he also had the large broadside ironclad *New Ironsides* and an ugly armored-casemate ship named the *Keokuk*. The Union squadron sailed into the main ship channel, which carried them between Sullivan's Island (with Fort Moultrie) and Fort Sumter. They would take up a position, an imaginary line drawn between Moultrie and Sumter, that would enable them to bombard the northwestern wall of Moultrie. The lead monitor, the USS *Weehawken*, pushed a raft that would be used to sweep aside any torpedo mines. When the *Weehawken* neared the bombardment position, lookouts spotted a very dangerous obstacle, consisting of nets and cables studded with torpedo mines. The *Weehawken* halted, and as the rest of the Union squadron caught up with the *Weehawken* and halted, the Confederate batteries opened fire.

The guns blazed away for about an hour, firing some forty shots a minute. ninety-three projectiles struck the *New Ironsides*, ninety struck the *Keokuk*. The monitors, with their substantially lower freeboard, were luckier and were struck about half as many times. However, two had their turrets damaged, and two more had guns disabled. The effect of this damage was to severely restrict Union counterfire. While the Confederate barrage numbered in the thousands of shot and shells, the Union ships managed to fire off only 139 projectiles and only one broadside from the big *New Ironsides*. The *Keokuk* had to pull out of the action after firing but three shots, and was so badly damaged that she sank the next day. After about an hour, the rest of the Union squadron pulled out. Partly as a consequence of this engagement, DuPont was removed from command in August 1863 and naval ordnance expert John Dahlgren appointed in his place.

The failure of a purely naval assault on Charleston prompted the use of army troops against the secessionist city. A force commanded by Major General Quincy Gillmore began operations in July, when a two-pronged operation was put in motion. The objective was to place troops on Morris Island, in order to assault the batteries there. On July 10, 1863, a bombardment of the Rebel fortifications on Morris Island by ships of the blockading squadron covered the landing of troops. An assault on Fort Wagner the following day was repulsed. Troops had also landed on James Island as a diversion to prevent the Confederates from reinforcing Morris Island. On July 16th, the Rebels launched an attack on the brigade at Gimball's Landing, but this failed. Two days later, the famous attack by the 54th Massachusetts against Fort Wagner was bloodily repulsed. General Gillmore believed that a third assault would similarly end in failure, and the Union forces sat back to think again.

Admiral Dahlgren had to contend with a new kind of warfare, one that was enthusiastically embraced by Beauregard. A small boat with a crew of six and armed with a torpedo was sent against the gunboat USS *Powhatan*. This initial attempt failed, but the little boat manage to reach its target before the attack was abandoned. Having achieved that with a makeshift craft encouraged more ambitious projects. Captain Francis Lee, an army officer, had already promoted the idea of a partially submerged craft armed with a spar torpedo. The idea had taken real shape, but the navy was in no

Left: *The Sumter light guards stand to attention for the camera. They were typical of the militia companies that, as in the North, were gathered together to form regiments in the army.*

hurry to finish the craft until after the attempt on the USS *Powhatan*.

The Confederates finally launched Lee's ram and took it into action on August 20. Problems with the engine and misunderstood steering commands caused the failure of this attack on *New Ironsides*, but once again the little torpedo boat got close enough—actually alongside—to offer continuing encouragement to the notion, particularly if it was only a matter of a few technical problems. The Union operations on Morris Island, in particular against Fort Wagner, were conducted as a siege. In order to keep the fort under fire, a number of batteries were constructed. The siege works were of the classic variety, with a succession of parallels being constructed closer to the breastworks of Fort Wagner. Although the fort was the objective of these works, the location of batteries on Morris Island enabled the application of pressure on another target. On August 17, these land guns and guns aboard ships began a sustained bombardment of Fort Sumter. The bombardment's aim was to make a breach in the comprehensive defenses of the harbor's mouth. The attack knocked down the brick walls but left the island still capable of mounting guns to defend the entrance.

A second, two-day bombardment of Fort Sumter began on August 29, 1863. On September 5, the Union

troops completed the siege works around Fort Wagner. Whereas the first two assaults had been made across open ground, this time the attacking Union troops would be largely under cover except for a short space of a hundred yards from their trenches to the ditch around Fort Wagner. Since the Union troops had entered the fort during the July 18 assault, even though they were eventually driven out again, the likelihood of success was high. During the night of September 6–7, the Confederates abandoned Fort Wagner and Battery Gregg on Cummings' Point.

The Union commanders followed up their success by putting more pressure on the fortifications guarding the harbor's mouth. Fort Sumter was bombarded by *New Ironsides* and accompanying monitors on

Above: *A US government slaughterhouse at Hilton Head. Union forces occupied this part of the state in November 1861.*

September 7. Just after midnight on September 9, a daring operation was attempted to capture the fort. Some four hundred troops (including a hundred marines) in twenty barges were towed in the direction of the fort. Only seven boats actually reached the beach at the fort. The rebels defending the fort used a

locomotive headlamp to illuminate the beach and opened a heavy fire of rifles and hand grenades at the troops who disembarked. They expected to find a slope upward to the fort but instead found a vertical wall. Gunfire from the batteries on Sullivan's Island and the CSS *Chicora* hit the retreating barges heavily. The whole affair was a total failure, and the Rebels took a hundred prisoners.

Private industry offered a third chance of sending a torpedo ram against the Union blockading squadron. The Southern Torpedo Company constructed a small torpedo ram named the *David*. On October 5, 1863, Lieutenant Glassel took the *David* out against *New Ironsides*. The commander of *New Ironsides* moored the ship in the same place every night, off Morris Island. Glassel had no trouble locating the Union flagship and waited for the turn of the tide before making his attack. The craft worked up a full head of steam and then sped across the water. About three hundred yards from the target, the lookouts on the *New Ironsides* spotted the *David*. Glassel shot the man who was raising the alarm, the torpedo struck the Union vessel and exploded, and the *David* was drenched with water. The water swamped the vessel, and put out the fires of her engine's boiler. Glassel and his three-man crew abandoned ship, but when the *David* failed to sink, a couple of the crew returned and sailed her back to Fort Sumter. Glassel and another sailor were captured.

At first, it was thought the *New Ironsides* had survived the attack fairly lightly. Later, work in the coal bunkers revealed more serious damage that required the vessel to be taken first to Port Royal and later to Philadelphia for repairs. One final attempt to use torpedoes against the Union blockaders of Charleston was made. On February 17, 1864, the *H. L. Hunley*, a submarine, left the harbor. A crew of eight men propelled her by turning cranks within the vessel's hull that rotated a screw propellor in the stern.

The submarine *Hunley* was armed with a spar torpedo extending from her bow. Several accidents

occurred during trials with this vessel. These accidents claimed the lives of some thirty men, including the submarine's inventor, Horace Hunley.

The experimental Union vessel targeted the USS *Housatonic*, a wooden screw sloop, and when the torpedo struck, it may have hit the magazine near the mizzenmast. The explosion was terrific. Water flooded into the stern of the USS *Housatonic*, and she sank so quickly that she dragged the submarine *Hunley* down with her. Once again, the *Hunley* turned into a coffin for her crew, but she had finally taken an enemy vessel with her. The submarine *Hunley*, a historic ship, was raised in August 2000 and, at the time of writing, is being conserved for eventual display within the Charleston Museum.

The civil war finally came to inland South Carolina with William T. Sherman's army in early 1865. Sherman's army spent about six weeks in Savannah replenishing its supplies after its March to the Sea, before embarking on a new march in similar vein on February 1, 1865.

This time the target of its depredations was the state of South Carolina. The Union soldiers who made up the army, from their commander down to the rank and file were determined to inflict a severe lesson on the land and people of South Carolina, whom they held primarily responsible for the last four years of national crisis and bloodletting.

As through Georgia, the army advanced in two wings. The armies intended to reunite at Columbia in the interior of South Carolina. The two wings finally reached Columbia on February 17. That night considerable parts of the city burned to the ground, the flames fanned by strong winds, although the responsibility for this act remains unclear. Confederate forces evacuated Charleston on February 18.

Heavy rains in the wettest winter for twenty years caused muddy ground and rivers in torrent, leading to some delay for William T. Sherman's army. The army's wagons required the construction of corduroy roads—

chopping trees down to lay along the roadway to prevent wagon wheels from sinking in mud. From Columbia the army then moved toward Fayetteville in North Carolina, arriving there on March 10. The civil war campaigns in the state of South Carolina were finally at an end.

Above: *Harriet Tubman (c.1821–1913) was an escaped slave who spent much of the war at Beaufort helping slaves to escape and aiding those who already had.*

TENNESSEE

"Tell Mr. Alford I am getting tired of the army and would like to help him fish this summer, but fear I will have other fish to fry."

—James Hamner, April 11, 1863

When Tennessee became a part of the United States under the Treaty of Paris in 1783, there were already colonial settlers in the state. In 1789, the US Congress created the Territory of the United States South of the Ohio River, often called the Southwest Territory, in order to give it a government. In 1796, after a referendum showed a three-to-one majority in favor of joining the Union, Tennessee was admitted to statehood.

In the presidential election of 1860, Tennessee voted for the Constitutional Union candidate John Bell. The state delayed its secession until after Lincoln called for troops to suppress the insurrection by the seceding states. The Tennessee legislature then passed a declaration of independence, which it submitted to the voters on June 8, 1861. In the voting, the eastern portion of the state was decidedly opposed, while the center and west gave independence a landslide victory.

Tennessee was in the front line of the Confederacy at the start of the war. Important posts were established at Island No. 10 on the Mississippi River, at Fort Henry on the Tennessee River, and at Fort Donelson on the Cumberland River. Unfortunately, these last two were not particularly strong. When General Ulysses Grant launched the Union advance into Tennessee in February 1862, his first target was Fort Henry. This fort was so badly sited that it fell to a gunboat attack alone on February 6. Grant now turned his attention to Fort

Above: A one-dollar bill issued by the Bank of Ocoee, Cleveland.

Left: A captain in Arthur M. Rutledge's Light Artillery. The unit was raised in Davidson County and fought at Shiloh. It was then amalgamated with McClung's Battery.

Donelson. An attempt to take it with the gunboats on February 14 appeared to have failed, but that same day the Rebel commander, General John B. Floyd, decided his force was too small to hold the fort. The next day he attempted to break the Union siege lines with an attack in order to escape from Grant's encircling army. After the failure of this attack, the fort was surrendered to Grant on February 16, although many of the garrison, including a cavalry commander named Nathan Bedford Forrest, escaped during the night before.

The fall of the two forts compelled the retreat of the Rebel army in Kentucky, which opened central Tennessee to the Union armies. On February 25, 1862, Union troops of Buell's Army of Ohio entered the Tennessee capital, Nashville. One of the more important cities of the Confederacy had fallen without a shot fired. Combined with the fall of forts Henry and Donelson, a dangerous breach had been opened in the Confederate defensive line in the West.

From Nashville, a Union army could turn either west toward the Mississippi and Memphis or east toward Chattanooga and Atlanta. More dangerously, two large Union armies now stood between two smaller Confederate ones. The larger one, under General Albert Sidney Johnston, hovered around Murfreesboro in Tennessee, while a smaller one, under Major General Leonidas Polk, occupied Columbus, Kentucky.

On March 17, 1862, the victor of Sumter and Bull Run, General Beauregard, was appointed second in command to Johnston in the Department of the Mississippi and arrived at Jackson, Tennessee. Johnston ordered Polk to fall back on Jackson, and then on Corinth, Mississippi. Johnston then marched in that direction himself. He also brought up forces from the Gulf Coast commanded by Major General Braxton Bragg. On March 23, the concentration of Rebel forces there was complete, with the Army of Mississippi divided into four corps.

Major General Henry Halleck was the mastermind behind the Union strategy in the West at this phase of the war. Like Johnston, and as that commander feared, he sought to unite his considerable forces. His objective was Corinth, where the Rebel army had concentrated, which was a vital junction in the railroad network across the South. In mid-March, the first two divisions of the Army of Tennessee reached Pittsburg Landing and by March 17, all six were located between Shiloh Church and Crump's Landing. Grant was in command. Here they awaited the approach of Buell's army and Halleck's orders to advance. Buell, however, was proving very slow. This was in part on account of the muddy terrain and flooding rivers, but Buell was also overcautious, worried that Johnston would maneuver around his flank and cut him off from his base.

Buell's moves were not far from Johnston's mind, but not the way Buell believed. Grant was closer to the Rebel base at Corinth, perhaps twenty-five miles away, and Johnston's fear was that Buell would reinforce Grant's smaller army before the Rebel army of the Mississippi was able to strike. Therefore, on April 1, Johnston announced to his officers that the advance on Grant would begin on the 3rd.

The Rebel order of march and plan of attack was drawn up by Beauregard. The victor of Bull Run had an aggressive temperament, but his aptitude for staff work was poor. This weakness was intensified by the amateur nature of the armies at this stage in the war. None of the general officers in the field on either side had any experience of controlling the movements of armies tens of thousands strong. This combined with the muddy roads to slow the advance of the Rebels. They were anticipated to reach Pittsburg Landing in time to attack on April 5, but in the event they were a day late in assembling. Only one Rebel corps had reached its position in time.

Beauregard and Bragg had an attack of nerves, believing that the element of surprise was totally lost. There was no way that the Union forces could be unaware of such a large army a mere two miles away, especially with one corps having arrived so far in advance of the rest. They advocated the planned attack be abandoned. Johnston curtly declared that the attack would take place on the 6th.

Johnston had read the mentality of his opponent better than his subordinates. If Beauregard's weakness lay in staff work, Grant's weakness lay in not worrying excessively about what his opponent intended to do. Grant had placed his headquarters at Savannah, Tennessee, where he waited for Buell. Some eight miles away his five advanced divisions were camped between the flooded Owl Creek and the Tennessee River.

The battle started slowly. The Union commanders at first believed that the Confederate forces had launched a large reconnaissance in force. However, as the shooting intensified they came to realize that this was a full-scale assault. The wooded terrain prevented Union pickets from catching sight of what was coming until suddenly a long line of soldiers in Rebel gray emerged from the tree line.

At 6 a.m. the Rebels struck first at the division commanded by Brigadier General Benjamin Prentiss. Prentiss's troops were largely inexperienced, and most of his regiments failed to stand against the Rebel onslaught. Sherman's division was next to feel the burn of the Rebel attack. However, Sherman's troops had fought at Fort Donelson and were able to halt the first wave of the Rebel attack. Moving across country disrupted the advance of the second wave, and it hit the Union line piecemeal. The remnants of Prentiss's

Below: *A contemporary engraving of the battle of Shiloh from the Union side. This battle came as a shock to both sides, as neither had experienced fighting of such intensity before.*

THE BATTLE OF SHILOH.
Charge and taking of a New Orleans Battery by the 14th Regt. Wisconsin Volunteers Monday, April 7, 1862.

Right: *The visitors center and museum at Shiloh Battlefield Park. The preservation of Civil War battlefields started in 1899, and over the next fifteen years many states and citizens' groups began to spend considerable sums of money to dedicate memorials on these sites. The preservation got a second wind in the 1960s, with the centennial. The last ten years has seen increasing encroachment on the battlefields by suburban developments, especially in areas such as Atlanta, Chattanooga, and northern Virginia. Organizations dedicated to the preservation of our Civil War heritage have sprung up to defend these places, and information can easily be found via the Internet or at public libraries for those who wish to join in these efforts.*

division gave way, and the pressure on Sherman's troops increased. Both Prentiss and Sherman were selling the lives of their men in order to buy time for the rest of the Union army to rush reinforcements forward. As Sherman's division looked to be flanked on its left by the rebels, and its line of retreat cut off, the first reinforcements began to arrive. These were thrown into the maelstrom on Sherman's left and suffered the same fate as Prentiss' men. Sherman's line finally gave way around 11 a.m.

Union reinforcements were now arriving from McClernand's, Hurlbut's, and W. H. L. Wallace's divisions, and a new line intermingling these reinforcements with the remnants of Sherman's and Prentiss's divisions was established that was based on a peach orchard and a sunken road. Likewise, the Confederates brought up their own reinforcements, preparing for an attack on this new line.

When the assaults came, the Union forces were better organized than they had been in the morning. The sunken road offered some protection, and the gunfire from both sides was ferocious. Four times the Rebels went forward, and four times they were repulsed with heavy casualties. The whizz of bullets reminded soldiers of the buzzing of hornet's, and the area around the sunken road was known ever after as the Hornet's Nest. Around 2 p.m., fresh rebel troops hurled themselves in a bayonet charge against the Union line and finally found some purchase. They reached the edge of the Peach Orchard, where heavy gunfire again brought them to a halt, but this time they had turned the Northerners' right flank, although they had not realized it yet. Unfortunately for the Confederates, this same attack saw Johnston hit by four bullets. Three of them caused only bruises, but the fourth struck him behind the knee, severing an artery. Had Johnston realized his predicament, his life might have been saved by prompt medical attention. Unfortunately, no one saw the blood flowing from his leg, and when he toppled from his horse because of loss of blood, it took some

time for them to find his wound. Within half an hour of being shot, Johnston was dead.

It took the Confederate high command some time to reorganize itself, as Beauregard was in the rear, but the battle was so advanced that the Rebel troops knew what was expected of them. Another assault was made on Hornet's Nest, and this one may not have broken into the nest itself, but swept around and surrounded it. Around 5:30 p.m., Brigadier General Prentiss waved the white flag and surrendered 2,200 exhausted men.

The Rebels paused briefly and then pushed on. But Grant had been hard at work to the rear of his position, making use of the valuable time that had been bought by the resistance of his men, especially those of Prentiss. He had gathered together the skulkers who were sheltering in terror under the bluff at the Tennessee River, and his troops that had not yet been committed to action. He established a final line of defense along the heights above Pittsburg Landing.

The Rebels pushed forward once more, but this time they were repelled by the best-organized line of defense they encountered that day. Beauregard believed that the battle was more or less won, and to keep pushing his disorganized army onward would cost the possibility of a decisive victory. He ordered the army to halt for the night and prepare for a renewed assault the next day.

Beauregard's optimism was misplaced. Buell was close at hand, and his troops would cross the Tennessee River that night and reinforce the left of Grant's army. Grant's Sixth Division, commanded by Brigadier General Lew Wallace, finally arrived, having gotten lost on the way from Crump's Landing. Grant was as optimistic as Beauregard and with better reason. He had doubled the size of his army, with fresh troops.

A heavy rain fell that night. The following morning, Buell launched an attack from the Union left that threatened the Rebel line. Beauregard ordered a counterattack that was stopped cold and pushed back by fresh troops from Buell's army. Beauregard kept trying to halt the Union advance with counterattacks of

his own, but without success. At 1 p.m., Beauregard began preparing to withdraw. His troops did manage a sustained attack on the right of the Union line, but this too was halted and broken up by artillery fire. Buell renewed his attacks from the left, and Beauregard took to the front line himself to spur his troops on to counterattack and stop the Union assault. At 3:30 p.m., Beauregard ordered his men to retire from the field.

Ulysses Grant did not pursue the Confederates with any great vigor. His army had suffered heavily, and even his fresher troops had been marching all night and fighting all day. This was the first experience of combat for many of these soldiers, and the shock of the noise and the gore and the horrific cries of badly wounded soldiers would have left many of them mentally exhausted and disoriented. The battle of Shiloh came to a subdued end.

On the same day as Shiloh, a Union army under General John Pope captured Island No. 10 without a fight, after Union gunboats eliminated the Rebel shore batteries that controlled the approaches to the fort by troops. Fort Pillow was abandoned after the fall of Corinth, Mississippi, on May 30, and Memphis was occupied by Union troops on June 6.

At the end of 1862, the newly appointed commander of the Army of the Cumberland (formerly Buell's Army of Ohio), Major General William S. Rosecrans, came under considerable pressure from Washington to attack Bragg's Army of Tennessee before the Rebel leader could do something that would threaten the Union position in the West. Bragg was at Murfreesboro, an important road junction south of Nashville. He was well placed to attempt to recover Nashville for the Confederacy or to threaten Grant's army at Memphis. Rosecrans waited until after Christmas, then on December 26, 1862, he led his army out of Nashville against Bragg.

Bragg believed he held a strong position, since he could maneuver to either flank of the enemy. But now he found that the Union forces could do the same to

him. He was uncertain from which direction the main push would come and waited until Union movements made him confident that their target was indeed Murfreesboro. This town stood near the Stones River, and Bragg decided that it would be better to meet Rosecrans advance on the far side, away from the town. On December 27, the Army of Tennessee crossed the Stones River and deployed with his army in a battle line.

On December 29, when the first Union corps neared the Rebel position, a small action occurred on Wayne's Hill, which overlooked the position of the Rebel corps

commanded by Major General John C. Breckinridge. Union troops tried to take Wayne's Hill, which was only occupied by an advanced battery, but the Kentucky Orphan Brigade pushed them off.

There was a pause until December 31, as Rosecrans waited for his entire army to come up. The day before, Bragg believed he detected a weakness in the Union army's right flank and arranged for a two-division assault to be made against it. This, along with a general

Left: Union commander Don Carlos Buell. On February 25, 1862, troops from Buell's Army of Ohio entered Nashville, the Tennessee capital. Buell succeeded in securing of the Confederacy's major centers without any bloodshed.

Above: A detail from the Confederate monument at Shiloh show two tired faces of Rebel soldiers. They went to bed on April 6 thinking they had won, but the next morning were overwhelmed by the Union counterattack.

advance all along the line and a sweeping cavalry flank march to the Union rear would bring victory. Unfortunately, Bragg forgot to allow for the broken nature of the terrain, which was heavily wooded and would disrupt his advance.

Rosecrans, meanwhile, was devising a scheme for a decisive battle of his own. The attempt to take Wayne's Hill had drawn the Union commanders attention to this part of the field, where an important piece of high ground appeared to be weakly held. A strong thrust here ought to bend the Confederate line back, and if followed by another powerful assault on the Rebel center, it offered the prospect of crushing the men in gray in a vice of blue.

New Year's Eve 1862 opened with a charge of the men in gray, which prevented the creation of a vice of blue. Bragg's men got into formation more quickly and hit the Union right around 6:20 a.m. A Union brigade

was swallowed up by the gray tide, and a second one collapsed as a consequence. Rosecrans's right flank was in ruins some forty minutes after the battle opened. Had the Rebel troops been disciplined enough to perform a complex wheeling maneuver on the battlefield, the Union disaster envisaged by Bragg may have resulted. Unfortunately, the victorious lead Rebel division pursued the routing Union brigades, while the second Rebel division wheeled only to find the friendly troops to its front that it expected had somehow turned into a fresh Union brigade. However, being badly outnumbered, it served only to slow, not to halt, and the gray columns pushed it into a new Union line that was attempting to form out of two more Union brigades. This did not hold for long either. At 8 a.m., five Union brigades on Rosecrans' right wing were routing.

This near-perfect picture on the Confederate left, however, turned less pleasing in the center. The Rebel

Right: The United States' Military Prison at Chattanooga was where the Provost Guard sent those who it had arrested and seen convicted of crimes against the military code. After the defeat of the Rebel besiegers of Chattanooga in November 1863, the Tennessee town became an important part of the supply network that sustained Union armies in the field.

troops here were slow in getting into action, and instead of assaulting in divisional strength, they probed in the shape of brigades. These half-hearted attacks were easily beaten off, but an additional Rebel assault, this time one that was better coordinated, nearly surrounded this division commanded by Brigadier General Philip Sheridan. In spite of receiving reinforcements, Philip Sheridan's right rested on a Confederate division, and he pulled back to a new line.

Rosecrans had at first focused on his own plans, but the noise of firing to his left finally made him realize his army was in trouble. He energetically set about forming a new defensive line where the retreating brigades could make a stand, bucked up with reinforcements. The important part was to delay the Rebels in the center.

The focus of the combat here was an area known as the Round Forest, held by a brigade of Union troops. One Confederate brigade, commanded by Brigadier General James Chalmers, had already suffered heavy casualties in a prolonged firefight with the Union troops who had erected rudimentary breastworks using the trees of the forest. The fighting here continued on until 1 p.m., when Bragg finally drew on his unengaged left wing, brought up a fresh division, and hurled that into the Round Forest. And that blow was stopped, too. However, the Rebel right at this stage finally pushed back the Union division that had eventually blocked their wheeling maneuver, and the Union forces had to withdraw from the Round Forest. The Rebels, who had fought all day, were almost too tired to notice. Bragg

Above: *Union cavalrymen, possibly of the 9th Pennsylvania Cavalry, on the summit of Lookout Mountain. The summit of this handsome mountain was a popular vista for Union troops after the battle of Chattanooga had ended.*

believed he had won a great victory, but New Year's Day 1863 dawned with Union troops still on the battlefield, now preparing entrenchments. Bragg did nothing.

On January 2, having surveyed the scene and recognizing how he had achieved success on his left and center on New Year's Eve, Bragg announced that the Rebel attack would be launched from the right. His commanders were outraged. This was one of the stronger parts of the line. Bragg insisted and being commander got his way.

Late in the afternoon the assault, led by the Kentucky Orphan Brigade, stormed out of the Confederate lines. The little success they achieved was undone by cannonades from massed Union guns, and

in the end the Rebel troops were forced to retire back to their own lines.

Bragg had fought Rosecrans to a standstill. But Rosecrans refused to believe he was beaten and was even receiving reinforcements. So Bragg decided that though in his mind he had won, he would leave the field to the Union forces. The Army of Tennessee withdrew to Duck River and went into winter quarters.

There was little fighting in Tennessee during the first half of 1863. On August 16, however, two separate Union armies launched a coordinated offensive. General Ambrose Burnside led a force from Kentucky that captured Knoxville on September 3. The important railroad junction of Chattanooga fell to Rosecrans' troops five days later. Rosecrans pushed on into

Georgia, where he was defeated at Chickamauga. His routing troops did not stop until they reached Chattanooga, where the Rebel victor of Chickamauga, Braxton Bragg, laid siege to them. Rather than assaulting the Union position, Bragg hoped to starve them out. He nearly succeeded. But Lincoln called on Grant to retrieve the situation. Grant arrived in Chattanooga on October 23, 1863. He opened a line of supply, and then in a two-day battle on November 24–25, he delivered a crushing defeat on Bragg's army. The battle was capped by the advance of the veterans of Chickamauga on Missionary Ridge. The whole Rebel force seemed to be seized with fright at the sight of those blue lines of troops marching out of the town and across the intervening fields with flags flying and

bayonets fixed. In spite of the best efforts of Braxton Bragg to rally his troops, they fled as the Union troops closed up on their positions. "Chickamauga, Chickamauga!" taunted the Union soldiers at the retreating Rebels.

Tennessee was now largely Union territory for the rest of the war. General Forrest led many raids into the state that achieved considerable disruption of Union supply lines, but could establish no lasting presence. During one of his raids, he attacked Fort Pillow, now occupied by Union troops, many of them African Americans. The fort fell on April 12, 1864, and the African American soldiers were murdered in cold blood.

There was one more attempt to restore Rebel fortunes in Tennessee. After the fall of Atlanta, General John B. Hood, commander of the Army of Tennessee, came up with an extraordinary plan that he believed would alter the scales of balance in the West. He presented the idea to President Jefferson Davis, who embraced it enthusiastically. The project envisaged a march into central Tennessee, away from the Union army under Sherman at Atlanta. The objective was Nashville. The aim was to destroy Union forces in Tennessee. The concept was predicated on the fact that Sherman's army was running low on supplies, owing to attacks on the railroads and a lack of wagons. Long-term, Hood believed that thousands of new soldiers would flock to Confederate standards from newly liberated Tennessee, enabling him to advance into both Kentucky and across the Ohio river, before turning east to fall on the rear of Grant's army.

This scheme was set in motion when Hood departed Gadsden, Alabama, on October 22, 1864. He arrived at Tuscumbia, Alabama, to wait for supplies, at the end of the month. He discussed his plans with General Beauregard, who had been appointed commander of the Military Division of the West, encompassing western Georgia, Tennessee, Alabama, Mississippi, and eastern Louisiana, in September 1864. Beauregard expected Hood to leave Tuscumbia on November 9 and to strike for Lawrenceburg, Tennessee. However, on November 17, Hood was still at Tuscumbia, and Beauregard reminded him of the need for urgency. But it was still another four days before Hood moved.

The Union forces were scattered across Tennessee. The largest concentration was under the command of General John Schofield and consisted of the Union 4th and 23rd Corps at Pulaski, Tennessee, numbering about 30,000. The other large concentration, under General Thomas, in command of all Union forces in Tennessee, was at Nashville. It numbered about 16,000, but grew every day as reinforcements were pulled in from around the state and elsewhere.

Hood's line of march aimed to put his army of 40,000 in between the two Union armies. Schofield detected Hood's movement and withdrew his army from Pulaski to Columbia, beating the Rebels who had chose the same target. Hood tried to action the same maneuver that had failed, pulling away from Columbia and then swinging his army around aiming it for Spring Hill, between Columbia and Nashville. Schofield again detected the maneuver, and the race was on. This time, the Army of Tennessee had better luck, reaching Spring Hill on November 29 after the initial Union forces, but in much greater numbers. Unfortunately, the Rebel attack was not pressed with much vigor and ground to a halt before it had accomplished much. The failure of the Rebel attack gave Schofield time to bring up the remainder of his army.

Hood's two attempts at gaining a strategic advantage had failed, and he now had no choice but to follow behind Schofield. On November 30 Schofield offered Hood battle outside the town of Franklin. Schofield's men had withdrawn from Spring Hill during the night and dug themselves in during the morning. Hood ordered his men to attack that afternoon. His commanders protested, arguing that the Union forces were in a position of their choosing and that all the Rebel artillery had not come up yet. Hood was adamant. His attack swept forward and was bloodily repulsed. Among the dead was Major General Patrick Cleburne, the "Stonewall of the West" and perhaps the general most in sympathy with Hood's approach to warfare. He too had opposed the attack.

Schofield withdrew from his position that night. Hood's army was too battered to hinder the retreat, and Schofield marched into Nashville on the following day. Hood's army established itself outside the city on December 2nd.

Grant, in overall command of the Union armies, was puzzled by Thomas's strategic approach. He had allowed Hood to "bottle him up" in Nashville, in the same way that Beauregard had trapped Butler at Bermuda Hundred during the Overland campaign of spring 1864. Grant feared that Hood might slip around Nashville and north of the Cumberland River, which could conceivably demand the reinforcement of Union forces in the West with troops from the East. Beauregard was similarly shocked by the conduct of Hood after the battle of Franklin. He recognized there was no chance of Hood taking Nashville, since it was occupied by an army of equal size behind entrenchments. With a far better force, he thought to turn against a much smaller Union force at Murfreesboro, which could have easily been destroyed,

Below: Major General John M. Schofield had a successful career as a professor in the prewar army at West Point and gradually emerged as an important Union commander in the last two years of the war. He defeated John Hood and the Army of Tennessee when the Rebel commander hurled his troops over the protests of his subordinates at Schofield's lines at the battle of Franklin in November 1864.

followed by a retirement to winter quarters. The existence of Hood's large army might have compelled the Union forces to withdraw from Chattanooga and possibly allowed the shifting of troops from Hood to South Carolina, where Sherman's march to the sea threatened to wreak havoc.

Both Thomas and Hood followed their own instincts. Ironically, these were in reverse of their characters. Hood had fought his army to a standstill at Franklin. Many of his men were without shoes in bleak December weather of winter storms and cold. He could do little except keep them behind entrenchments and hope that they could treat any Union assault in the manner of Fredericksburg or Cold Harbor. Thomas reckoned he could not only defeat the Army of Tennessee, but destroy it, provided he could assemble enough cavalry to exploit any breakthrough. Thomas stood stolidly, this time not in the face of a Rebel assault but absorbing the brunt of Ulysses Grant's demands that he move.

On December 15 Thomas reckoned the time had come. It was a foggy day, as warm weather had arrived, thawing the frozen ground. He planned his attacks on both flanks. On the Union left, Major General James Steedman took a reinforced division, including a number of African American soldiers, into an attack that would serve as a diversion to the main blow, coming from the Union right.

Steedman's attacks went in all morning, before he slackened the pressure off. Hood had not been deceived. He suspected the main blow would fall on his left and stuck to his gut feeling. The strength of the Union assault, however, was too much.

The cavalry on the Confederate left were too outnumbered to do more than delay the advanced of their Union counterparts. When the Union infantry launched their attacks just after noon, a methodical approach of artillery barrage followed by infantry assault took Rebel redoubts one after another. Even a Rebel division holding behind a stone wall was driven off by

the combination of artillery and infantry. Hood's line was pushed back, and he withdrew to a second position between the Frankline and Hillsboro pikes.

John Bell Hood might have been better off at this stage if he pulled his army away from Nashville altogether. Hood gambled that he could get one more day's fight out of his men. He had shortened the line they had to defend and shifted fresh troops to the left of his line, taking the fought-out veterans of the December 15 fighting out of the likely pressure point of his attack. But the weight of Union numbers would now tell, as Thomas redeployed his own army in such a way as to overlap both Confederate flanks.

In the morning of December 16, Thomas set his army in motion, but again counselling methodical approach work. All morning the Union guns boomed,

while the infantry threatened their assaults. Thomas was waiting for the point when he would deliver a knockout punch. When an attack on the Confederate right pulled some troops out of line on their left, Thomas recognized his chance.

Schofield's corps and the Union cavalry were hurled against the Rebel right, another corps against their center. With Union troops threatening their line of retreat, the Rebels here thought discretion the better part of valor, and the line gave way.

What started as a flight in small groups soon turned into a rout of disastrous proportions, as a ripple effect ran along the Confederate army and the gray tide ebbed southward. General Thomas's dream of trapping the Army of Tennessee with his cavalry failed when the outnumbered Confederate cavalry managed to hold

their Union counterparts off long enough to allow the army to evade the encircling movement that would have spelled the end of a Rebel force in the West.

The Army of Tennessee retreated toward Columbia. The Union cavalry harassed the retreat effectively, with saber charges penetrating the Confederate lines. John Bell Hood hoped to remain in Tennessee at the Duck River. After arriving at Columbia, however, he abandoned this plan, given the state of his troops. Another blow by General Thomas in these circumstances would prove fatal.

They started crossing the Tennessee on Christmas Day. Thomas's men followed as far as Pulaski, Tennessee, before he halted the pursuit. Hood led his troops to Tupelo, Mississippi, where, at his own request, he was relieved of his command.

TEXAS

"I am so sick of war that I don't want to hear it any more till old Abe's time is out and then let a man say war to me and I will choke him."

—W. M. Moss, December 28, 1863

The territory of Texas was originally a part of Spain's colony of New Granada and following independence, a part of Mexico. However, from 1821, settlers from the United States received permission to take up land there. There was tension between Mexican settlers and Anglo settlers from the United States. Mexico had abolished slavery in 1829, while the Americans from the South brought their slaves with them. These two were just some of the grievances that led to Anglo Texans declaring independence from Mexico in 1836. For nine years, an independent Republic of Texas maintained its autonomy against repeated attempts by Mexico to recover these lands. However, in 1845 the dream of most Texans to be accepted as a state was finally realized when the Polk administration secured passage of a bill of annexation through Congress. The ensuing Mexican War of 1846–1848 was a result of the United States recognizing the boundaries claimed by Texas, and not those respected by Mexico. Texas had claimed the Rio Grande as its border, and after the end of the war it still claimed the Rio Grande although the United States had now acquired New Mexico, and the residents of that area of the Rio Grande Valley were unenthusiastic about rule from Texas. Eventually, as part

Above: *The flag of the Van Dorn Guards, although there were two units that carried this name: Coy A, 8th Texas Infantry and the 4th Battalion, Texas Artillery.*

Left: *A sergeant and color bearer of the 8th Texas Cavalry, "Terry's Texas Rangers."*

of the Compromise of 1850, the current boundaries of Texas were established. Texas voted for John Breckinridge, the proslavery Democrat, in the 1860 presidential election.

Texas's secession was the most scandalous of any state's. A convention of delegates met and passed on ordinance of secession on February 1, 1861. The commander of federal troops in Texas, General David Twiggs, a Georgian who had declared his intention of following his state if it seceded, had been asking the War Department what to do.

The War Department sent him a letter in the mail, which took three weeks to reach him, ordering him to hand over command to another officer. By the time the letter reached Twiggs, he had already surrendered all US installations to state authorities. This step shocked public opinion in the North, which felt that Twiggs had betrayed his honor.

There were few battles fought in Texas during the war. The first Union action against Texas occurred on July 2, 1861, when the USS *South Carolina* imposed the blockade on Galveston. In the following month there was an exchange of shots between a Rebel battery and the South Carolinans.

Right: *The Texas Monument at the Railroad Redoubt, Vicksburg, Tennessee. Like the other Western states of the Confederacy, a large number of Texans were captured at the fall of Vicksburg.*

Below: *A captain of the 9th Texas Cavalry. He is armed with a shotgun and a Dance .44 revolver, a close copy of the Colt .44 dragoon revolver. The shotgun was a more popular weapon for close-quarters cavalry combat than the saber.*

In September 1862 the action at Sabine Pass provided a curiously small-scale version of the kind of actions that had occurred on the North Carolina coast in August 1861 and February 1862. The fight pitted two schooners, the USS *Rachel Seaman* and the USS *Henry James* (carrying a mortar) against a shore battery on September 24, 1862. Neither side fired accurately at first, then the Union vessels pushed more closely to shore and succeeded in damaging the battery where the Rebel forces still could not hit anything. At night, the Rebels abandoned the position, allowing Union forces to occupy an important base from which they were able to conduct raids into Texas.

The next battle in Texas was also a ship to shore engagement. On October 4, 1862, a Union squadron began an artillery duel with Fort Point, when the Confederate commander Colonel Joseph Cook sent word to negotiate with the Union commander, Commodore W. B. Renshaw. Eventually a settlement was agreed to allow women and children to evacuate the city, but Colonel Cook took his whole force out of the city as well and left the port for the Union navy to occupy. Union forces only held the city until January 1, 1863, when a larger Rebel army arrived and retook the city, capturing three Union vessels and causing the destruction of another.

The last battle in the Civil War occurred in Texas. A small Union column from Brazos Santiago attacked a Rebel camp at Palmito Ranch on May 12, 1865, and was in turn counterattacked on May 13 and driven off.

Texas supplied one of the most famous units of Lee's Army of Northern Virginia when it sent a brigade composed of the 1st, 4th, and 5th Texas infantry regiments to fight in the East. Two non-Texas regiments were added later, the 18th Georgia Infantry in November 1861 and the 3d Arkansas Infantry in November 1862, which replaced the 18th Georgia. The brigade made its name in the hard fighting of 1862, starting with the Seven Days' battles.

The Texas Brigade, with its dramatic charge in the evening that pierced the Union line at Gaines' Mill on June 27, 1862, gave Robert E. Lee his only outright victory on the battlefield during the whole campaign. The victory cemented the brigade's reputation as an elite unit of Lee's army on September 17 when it halted a Union advance that was grinding its way slowly but inexorably through the Wheatfield.

Other battle honors won by the Texas Brigade include Gettysburg and Chickamauga. In one of the

more touching incidents of the Civil War, on May 6, 1864, during the battle of the Wilderness. Robert E. Lee led the Texas Brigade in a desperate counterattack to halt a Union advance that threatened to breach the Rebel line. With cries of "Lee to the rear," the brigade refused to move until their beloved commander was out of harm's way. They then went forward and halted the Union attack. The Texas Brigade finally surrendered with the rest of the Army of Northern Virginia on April 10, 1865.

Two Rebel generals were associated with the Texas Brigade during the early stages of its career. Louis T. Wigfall (1816–74) was born in South Carolina but moved to Texas in the late 1840s and became active in state politics, eventually taking one of the state's seats in the US Senate until secession. Wigfall was an ardent secessionist and took the surrender of Fort Sumter on April 13, 1861, having been appointed to the staff of General P. G. T. Beauregard. He served for a time in the Confederate army before resigning and returning to politics as a senator in the Confederate Congress.

General John Bell Hood (1831–79) was born in Kentucky and graduated from West Point in 1853. Hood was a courageous and aggressive fighter, to the point of recklessness. One of President Jefferson Davis's most egregious errors during the Civil War was to appoint John Bell Hood to command of the Army of Tennessee in July 1864, during the Atlanta campaign. Hood

completely reversed the strategic direction of the campaign all at once and committed the Confederate army to a series of attacks that failed to achieve any shift at all in the direction of the campaign. He then threw the army completely away in a misguided assault at Franklin, Tennessee in December 1864.

Below left: *A Texas belt plate.*

Below: *Louis T. Wigfall was a strongly pro-secession politician before the war who served in the Rebel army for a time before entering the Confederate Congress.*

UTAH

"Leave their bodies exposed as an example of what evil-doers may expect while I command this district."

—Brigadier General Patrick Connor, autumn 1862, about the treatment of hostile Indians

Utah was part of the territory acquired from Mexico by the United States by the terms of the Treaty of Guadalupe Hidalgo signed in 1848, which brought an end to the Mexican-American War of 1846–48. In 1850, Utah Territory was created by Congress, encompassing not only the boundaries of the present state, but also large parts of Colorado and Nevada. In 1861, the creation of Nevada Territory and Colorado Territory reduced the boundaries of Utah to that of the current state.

This area could easily have been fertile ground for the Confederate ambitions in the West, except that it was too far north to be of use in constructing a railroad from New Orleans to California, the grand hope for many future Confederate politicians in the 1850s. However, Utah had been settled by the Mormons, as the Latter-day Saints were more commonly known, who had fled homes in the Midwest in order to find some peace to practice their faith and live their lives. However, when the Mormons arrived, the area around the Great Salt Lake was part of Mexico. In 1848 it became a part of the United States. Hence, the very country the Mormons had attempted to escape from had followed them.

In 1857, the determination of the US Government to control the situation led the administration of President James Buchanan to take severe measures to repress the growing rebellious nature of Utah. Soldiers were sent to enforce the authority of the Washington-appointed territorial governor. Meanwhile, militant Mormons massacred a wagon train of California-bound emigrants at Mountain Meadows. There were also accusations that Mormons were formenting trouble with the Native Americans. The biggest stumbling block to an alliance between the Mormons and the

Left: The building of the Mormon Tabernacle, Salt Lake City, began in 1853 and continued through the Civil War until its completion in 1893. The Mormons had originally planned their journey here when the area was a part of Mexico, in an attempt to escape hostility to their theology in the East and Midwest. In spite of their grievances against the federal government, they proved supportive to the Union cause, in part because of Lincoln's attitude of one war at a time.

Confederacy was the opposition of the Mormons to slavery. President Abraham Lincoln, however, adopted a policy of leaving the Mormons alone if they left him alone. Brigham Young (1801–77), president of the Church of Jesus Christ of Latter-day Saints from 1844 until his death, could live with that, and Utah experienced a largely peaceful war in a military sense.

The Mormons did not send men to fight in the army, nor did the Union invite them. Some residents of Utah did to fight at the front but this was on an individual basis. U.S. volunteer forces were stationed in Utah during the Civil War to protect the Overland Mail route and telegraph lines to California. This included the Nauvoo Legion, the local militia force, whose members performed short-term volunteer service during the civil war. Also a number of skirmishes occurred in Utah between Native Americans and Union soldiers.

One significant act of loyalty to the Union occurred when Brigham Young sent the first message from Salt Lake City on the new transcontinental telegraph stating Utah's commitment to the Constitution. The arrival of Colonel Patrick E. Connor, however, as commander of the Union forces in the territory opened a new front in the political sensitivities within Utah. Patrick Connor was firmly opposed to Mormons, with their doctrine of polygamy and preference for laws ordained in their scripture rather than by legal process. Even after the Civil War had ended, Colonel Patrick Connor remained in Utah to help organize the opposition of non-Mormons to the dominance of the territory by the Latter-day Saints. Consequently, the death of President Abraham Lincoln was genuinely mourned in Utah, with even the Tabernacle draped in black crepe.

VERMONT

"Glory to God, Glory to God! See the Vermonters go it!"

—General Abner Doubleday, July 3, 1863

Vermont's location between New York and New Hampshire ensured that when the Treaty of Paris ended the Revolutionary War in 1783 the land of Vermont would be included within the boundaries of the new republic. Vermont had long been claimed by its three neighboring states and this was only resolved permanently on the admission of the state of Vermont, previously regarded as the Republic of Vermont, to the Union in March 1791. Vermont gave the highest percentage of its popular vote to Abraham Lincoln in the presidential election of 1860.

As a percentage of those who served, Vermont suffered the heaviest losses of any state except Pennsylvania. The Vermont Brigade, comprised of the 2nd, 3rd, 4th, 5th, and 6th Vermont Infantry lost more soldiers than any other brigade in the Union army. These were all three-year regiments. The 1st Vermont Infantry was a ninety-day regiment raised under the April 15, 1861, call by Lincoln for 75,000 volunteers, and saw action at Big Bethel, a small battle in June 1861 in Virginia.

The Vermont Brigade saw action first in the Seven Days' battles in June 1862, at Antietam in September, and at Fredericksburg in December. Lastly it was part of the disastrous assault on the Rebel position at Marye's Heights. The Vermont Brigade also fought in all the battles of the Overland campaign of 1864 and suffered over 1,500 casualties in the engagements in the Wilderness and at Spotsylvania Court House, May 5–18, 1864, over half its strength in less than two weeks. It also served under General Phil Sheridan during the Shenandoah campaign of 1864.

Over four hundred members of the 4th and 11th Vermont Infantry were captured during the fighting around the Weldon Railroad outside Petersburg, Virginia, on June 23, 1864, after being surrounded by

Left: The 5th Vermont at an encampment, 1861. It's companies were organized at the following towns: Company A, St. Albans; B, Middlebury; C, Swanton; D, Hyde Park; E, Manchester; F, Cornwall; G, Rutland; H, Brandon; I, detachments from Burlington, Poultney and Tinmouth; and K, Richmond.

Rebel troops. The enlisted men were first moved to Libby Prison in Richmond, Virginia, and then sent to Andersonville Prison Camp in Georgia, where nearly 60 percent of them died. The second Vermont Brigade was composed of some nine-month regiments recruited in October 1862. Its moment of glory came on July 3, 1863, when it opened an enfilading fire from Cemetery Ridge on Pickett's Charge, which played a significant part in the repulse of this attack.

Vermont was the scene of one of the most audacious Rebel raids of the war. In 1863 a group of Rebel soldiers was sent to Canada to help organize prisoner-of-war escapes and other actions against Northern states. A raid on towns in Vermont was just one scheme hatched by this group. The commander of this raid, Bennett Young, was a Rebel who had escaped from a prison camp into Canada and was commissioned as a lieutenant in the Confederate army. In October 1864, Young crossed the border and went to St. Albans, where he collected information about the community. Over the next few days Young was joined by more men, and on October 19, 1864, they walked into the bank and drew revolvers on the bank teller. They announced their status as Rebel soldiers and demanded the money in the bank, acquiring over $70,000. Two other banks were also robbed, bringing the total to nearly $200,000.

Meanwhile, other members of the party rounded up the citizens of St. Albans and put them under guard. However, a former Union officer raised an alarm and after some shooting the Rebels fled.

The Rebels then escaped back to Canada. A number of them were arrested there at the request of Union authorities on October 20. A lengthy legal dispute then ensued, which ended in 1865 with the award of a belligerent status to the Rebel raiders, much to the disgust of Union authorities.

VIRGINIA

"I have not been able to make up my mind to raise my hand against my relatives,
my children, my home."

—Robert E. Lee, April 20, 1861

Virginia was one of the original thirteen colonies that declared independence in 1776 and officially became part of the United States of America when the state's delegates signed the Articles of Confederation on July 9, 1778. It boasted the largest population of any of the slaveholding states, the largest ironworks in the South, and a sizable industrial base. However, secessionist sentiment here was not strong enough to carry Virginia along with the Deep South states that voted to leave the Union in early 1861. Although Virginia had more slaves than any other state, slaves and slaveholders were a smaller proportion of the population. It took Lincoln's call on April 15 for a military force to suppress the rebellion to push Virginia into the Confederacy. The state authorities wasted no time in pushing secession through. On April 17, an ordinance of secession, passed by the legislature and providing for ratification by referendum, was signed by the governor.

Although the referendum was not scheduled until May 23, the state militia moved quickly to seize the armory at Harpers Ferry and the navy yard at Gosport. While the Harpers Ferry armory fell into Rebel hands only lightly damaged, several of the ships at the navy yard were scuttled, although the hull and engines of the steam frigate *Merrimac* survived to be put to use.

After the secession of Virginia and its admission to the Confederacy, the Virginia state government invited the Confederate government to make its capital at Richmond, which it agreed to on May 21, even before the referendum. The depth of support for Virginia leaving the Union was captured in the voting of the referendum: 128,884 to 32,134—four to one.

With the capital at Richmond within easy reach of the massing Union armies at the city of Washington, the

Confederate government began building up a strong army of its own in the rolling terrain of northeastern Virginia. On June 1, 1861, General P. G. T. Beauregard, the victor of Fort Sumter, was appointed to command the Rebel troops here. He saw his best line of defense was at Bull Run, but he advanced some of his brigades to Centreville. A second Rebel army was deployed in the Shenandoah Valley under General Joseph E. Johnston. The key to the Confederate position in Virginia lay at Manassas Junction. Control of the junction gave control of an important east-west railroad, which enabled the Rebel armies to be mutually supportive. An attack on one could be reinforced by moving troops from the other.

The commander of the Union Army of Northeastern Virginia, Irvin McDowell, planned a line of advance that would take him through Centreville and across Bull Run into Manassas Junction. Bull Run would be a difficult proposition to cross if its far bank was defended, so McDowell planned to turn the Rebel flank. He began his march from his camp outside Washington on July 16, 1861.

The Confederate commander Beauregard recognized that the federal forces would most likely make Manassas their target. He deployed his troops to guard the fords and bridges across Bull Run.

Once McDowell began his advance on Centreville, Beauregard began sending requests to President Jefferson in Richmond to be reinforced by Johnston's army. Johnston did not move until July 18, by which time he was convinced that the Union troops facing him were unlikely to make a move down the valley.

On the night of July 20, McDowell set in motion his planned flanking assault on Beauregard's position. Sending a division to make a diversionary attack on the stone bridge that brought the Warrenton turnpike

Left: *A detail of the Virginia State Monument on Seminary Ridge at Gettysburg Battlefield Park, showing the central rider figure at the base of the monument. An equestrian statue of Robert E. Lee tops the monument.*

across Bull Run, he also ordered two divisions to make a wide flanking advance toward Sudley Springs ford. Beauregard had planned an offensive of his own, but McDowell put his into operation first.

The Union plan might have achieved a success had the Rebel commander at the stone bridge, Nathan Evans, not recognized quickly that this was not the main attack. Evans shifted the bulk of his forces toward Matthews Hill, which blocked the Union advance from Sudley Springs. Beauregard rushed three brigades to Evans's support, and a fierce battle now erupted on Matthews Hill. The weight of Union numbers began to tell, and the Rebels withdrew first to a line along Young's Branch and then to Henry Hill. McDowell believed the battle was now won, but the Rebel line held, partly thanks to Stonewall Jackson's brigade of Virginians, who were reluctant to attack but resolute in defense. The Rebels were assisted by the failure of the Union forces to mount anything like a powerful assault.

Instead of a brigade-strength thrust that might have achieved a lasting foothold on the hill, Irwin McDowell's forces squandered their advantage in numbers by regimental-sized attacks that relied too much on artillery to blast the Confederate troops away.

While Irwin McDowell had no reinforcements, more and more Confederates were arriving from unthreatened parts of their line. Around 4 p.m., when the last of the brigades from the Shenandoah Valley joined the Confederate line, they found an exposed Union flank. Hitting it hard, a spectacular rout by one brigade turned into a pell-mell retreat by the whole army when Beauregard ordered the advance of his whole line. McDowell managed to organize some kind of resistance to cover the retreat, but a defensive line was only established around Centreville. Had the Confederates not been amateur soldiers as well, they might have destroyed the Union Army of Northeastern Virginia. However, both Beauregard and Johnston recognized their forces to be exhausted by the day's action and incapable of exploiting the victory properly.

After the failure of McDowell's attack, he was pushed sideways and replaced by George B. McClellan. The watchword for the Army of the Potomac, as the Union troops were renamed, was "all quiet along the Potomac tonight." A concerned Lincoln finally pushed McClellan into revealing a grandiose scheme for shifting 100,000 troops from in front of Washington to the mouth of the Rapahnnock River, which was to the east of Richmond. McClellan's argument was that this would turn the flank of the Rebel army at Manassas, forcing them to abandon a strong defensive position. Lincoln was not convinced, but believed doing something was better than doing nothing. And so, McClellan's army began making its way south on March 17, 1862.

Eight days earlier, a new era in naval history began with the first naval battle between ironclad warships. The Rebels had taken the hull and engines of the USS *Merrimac* and constructed an armored carapace on top. The vessel was renamed CSS *Virginia*. On March 8, the *Virginia* steamed out of Norfolk to break the blockade of the James River. Two wooden warships, the USS *Congress* and the USS *Cumberland*, were sunk, and a third, the USS *Minnesota*, run aground. The *Virginia* steamed back to Norfolk, intending to return to sink the *Minnesota* the next day. Meanwhile, the Union navy had been building an ironclad warship of its own. The USS *Monitor* was an unusual design with a very low freeboard and a turret mounting two guns. The US Navy knew that the *Virginia* would sooner or later attempt to break the blockade, and on March 6, the *Monitor* sailed for the James River. It was a timely move, for the vessel arrived on March 9, just in time to confront the Rebel ironclad. A four-hour battle between the two ships ended in a draw, although the *Minnesota* was saved and eventually refloated.

McClellan's grand plan might have succeeded if he moved quickly. However, he was frightened by Rebel fortifications along the Warwick River near Yorktown.

Above: *A painting of the duel between the USS* Monitor *and the CSS* Virginia, *March 1862. The first battle between ironclads was an inconclusive affair, although the* Monitor *achieved its mission of stopping the* Virginia *from doing further damage to the Union ships blockading the James River.*

Far right: *A bird's-eye view of Fair Oaks. The use of balloons during the Peninsula campaign gave such artist's impressions a degree of believability they might not have otherwise had.*

Believing he faced a force equal in numbers (in fact, the Rebel commander had 18,000 compared to the Union force of 55,000), McClellan cautiously began a siege of the Rebel lines. Consequently, Johnston was able to shift his army from northeastern Virginia to Richmond, defeating the whole object of McClellan's strategy.

Both presidents became increasingly annoyed with their generals in command. Lincoln kept prodding McClellan to advance, while McClellan did not. McClellan treated the whole operation as a siege, and heavy rains and flooding rivers hampered his troops from bringing up heavy artillery. Davis kept prodding Johnston to attack. Eventually the Rebel general struck part of McClellan's army near Fair Oaks on May 31. The attack failed and Johnston suffered a serious wound. Davis appointed General Robert E. Lee to replace the wounded Johnston. Lee went over to the attack. He reinforced his army by summoning Stonewall Jackson,

who had fought a masterful campaign in May 1862 in the Shenandoah Valley, defeating three separate Union armies. Jackson arrived on June 22. Lee had already gained valuable information from a sortie completely around the Union army by cavalry under General J. E. B. Stuart, June 12–16. Lee launched his campaign on June 26. During the next seven days, battles were fought at Mechanicsville, Gaines' Mill, White Oak Swamp, Savage Station, Glendale, and Malvern Hill. Lee's forces suffered heavy casualties—a quarter of his force—but pushed the Union armies away from Richmond.

Lincoln, who had performed his constitutional role as commander in chief directly in the spring of 1862, handed the job back to the military by bringing two generals from the West in the summer of 1862. General Henry Halleck was named commander in chief, while General John Pope was given command of the three armies beaten by Jackson in the Shenandoah. These

Right: *An engraving showing a view of the battle of Fair Oaks on May 31, 1862, when the Rebel army defending Richmond attacked the Union forces advancing up the James River peninsula. Union General George McClellan had foolishly divided his army in the face of the enemy, putting the smaller part of it across the Chickahominy River. Rebel General Joseph Johnston attacked and drove this force back. The timely intervention of a Union division that crossed the river over a barely floating pontoon bridge and hit the Rebels in the flank saved the battle from turning into a serious defeat. Johnston was wounded in the engagement, and replaced by General Robert E. Lee.*

BIRDS EYE VIEW
OF THE
SEAT OF WAR AROUND RICHMOND
SHOWING THE BATTLE ON CHICKAHOMINY RIVER JUNE 1862

John Bachmann, Publisher.

Above: *Wounded Union troops in 1864 outside a military hospital at Fredericksburg. They appear to have come from the leg-injury ward, with many on crutches, but none appear to have undergone the horror of an amputation.*

were renamed the Army of Virginia, and some of McClellan's troops were also given to Pope.

Lee shifted Jackson's corps back toward Manassas on July 13 and later brought the bulk of the army he commanded at Richmond. Pope adopted a defensive strategy, as his army and Lee's were in almost equal numbers now, although Pope would soon receive more reinforcements from McClellan's command. Lee couldn't wait and pushed up Rebel troops close to Pope. The two armies collided on August 28, near

Manassas Junction, scene of the first major battle of the war. John Pope's forces fought hard, but dissension in the Union command hampered his efforts to control the battle. The fighting was spread over two days, August 29–30, and at its end Pope was in retreat.

McClellan resumed command of the Union forces fighting in Virginia following Pope's interlude. However, his activity after the September battle of Antietam led to his removal and replacement by Ambrose Burnside. Burnside at first moved energetically, intending to cross

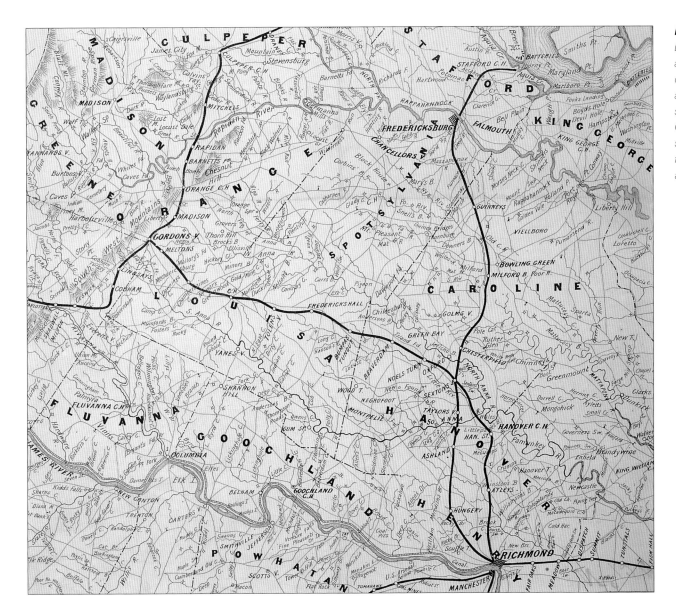

Left: *The seat of war in the East between October 1862 and June 1864 were the few counties between the Rapidan and the James. This map shows Fredericksburg, Chancellorsville, and all the sites of the major battles during the Overland campaign of 1864 appear here.*

the Rappahannock at Fredericksburg, which the army reached on November 17, before Lee had realized what was happening. But Burnside expected to find pontoons to make a bridge, and none had arrived. So he decided to wait, and Lee arrived, taking the high ground overlooking Fredericksburg. Burnside eventually had to settle on a direct attack against the entrenched Rebels. His men were butchered, losing three times as many casualties in the battle of Fredericksburg on December 13, 1862.

Burnside tried another offensive in January 1863, attempting to cross the Rappahannock by a ford above Fredericksburg—what he should have done in December. But heavy rain forced him to abandon the plan as his army literally got stuck in the mud. Burnside resigned and the intriguing, in both senses of the word, General Joseph Hooker replaced him. Hooker recognized the futility of trying to cross the Rappahannock around Fredericksburg in the face of Lee's army. In April 1863, Hooker left part of his army at

Fredericksburg and marched northwestward to cross further up the Rappahannock. Lee blocked him at Chancellorsville. In a daring maneuver on May 2, 1863, Jackson's corps was sent on a flanking march that caught Hooker's army in its left flank and routed it. Jackson, however, was mortally wounded by one of his own men. Lee's army would never fight as well as it had with Jackson.

The crushing blow inflicted by Lee on Hooker encouraged him to take the risk of leaving Virginia and invading the North. Defeat at Gettysburg saw all armies return to Virginia. Meade and Lee maneuvered to little

effect in December around Mine Run. Then, in the spring of 1864, Grant came to Virginia. Grant was commander in chief of all the Union armies and drafted a strategic plan for a general offensive across the seceded states. In Virginia, the Army of the Potomac would advance on Lee's army, while the Army of the James, commanded by Major General Benjamin F. Butler, and based at Fortress Monroe, pushed up the James River from City Point toward Richmond. Butler only had some 25,000 men, but aggressive use of them would either result in the capture of Richmond or the transfer of forces from Lee's army facing Grant to

Below: Fortress Monroe, in Hampton Roads, was never surrendered by Union forces after the secession of Virginia and served as a useful base for operations along the Atlantic coast of the Rebel state. After the war, it was used to imprison Jefferson Davis.

Left: *City Point was another important base for the Union campaigns against Lee's army in 1864–65, as the row of artillery caissons here suggests. The harbor was seized in May 1864 by General Benjamin Butler's Army of the James, and became the base of operations for Grant once he had crossed the Rappahannock River.*

defend the Rebel capital. Butler succeeded in securing City Point and Bermuda Hundred, which would be his base of operations, on May 5, 1864.

However, like another general who tried to enter Richmond through the back door, Butler now displayed a McClellan-like case of the "slows." He spent the first few days entrenching his position, then pushed forward in the direction of Drewry's Bluff.

The Confederate commander was General P. G. T. Beauregard, who had exchanged his command of the Department of South Carolina, Georgia, and Florida for that of North Carolina and Southern Virginia in April

1864. (Coincidentally, the Army of the James had been reinforced with Beauregard's old opponent from Charleston, Major General Quincy Gillmore, with some of his veterans of operations around there.) Beauregard's whole army was entrenched in front of Drewry's bluff.

Butler's army had already occupied the outermost line of the Rebel entrenchments and breastworks in the area. Beauregard's plan was to attack from his left, trying to turn the Union right back on its center, which would put Confederate troops between the Union army and its base at Bermuda Hundred. Beauregard's attack

Right: *A private of Company E, 23rd Virginia Infantry. This regiment saw heavy service throughout the war, including in the Shenandoah Valley in 1862 and 1864.*

Below: *Two officers, a colonel (standing) and a first lieutenant (seated) of the 16th Virginia Infantry.*

on Butler took place on May 16, 1864. The day dawned with a heavy fog, which caused some confusion to both sides as it hung around through the early morning. The attack on the left pushed the Union forces out of their position, paused to await reinforcements, and successfully repelled a counterattack.

The Confederate right advanced too, but had a tougher job because the Union line was bent, allowing some crossfire along its line of advance. Confederate troops held up well under a heavy fire and even captured some Union guns.

By now it was early afternoon, and the arrival of the troops from Petersburg was eagerly awaited. Unfortunately, these men never put in an appearance. Pierre Beauregard ordered a new attack, but a heavy rainstorm delayed the forming of the assault force, and darkness put an end to the day's fighting. Butler withdrew back to Bermuda Hundred. Beauregard followed him up and dug a line of entrenchments between the banks of the James and Appomattox Rivers, which secured the railroad south from Richmond. Benjamin Butler built his own line of entrenchments. It was a strong defensive position for the Union forces, but served Confederate purposes well. In the words of Union General John G. Barnard, whom Ulysses Grant had sent to review the situation, "the enemy had corked the bottle and with a small force could hold the cork in place."

Benjamin Butler's errors were mirrored in the other theater of operations in Virginia, the Shenandoah Valley. The smallest of the three Union armies involved, the Army of West Virginia under Major General Franz Sigel, advanced up the Shenandoah Valley, lush farming land that supplied vital foodstuffs to Lee's army.

Franz Sigel had about 6,000 men, operating supposedly in close coordination with a similar-sized force under General George Crook. Sigel encountered a slightly smaller force under the command of General Breckinridge, who had made his reputation in some of the great battles of the West. Breckinridge challenged Sigel at New Market and he failed the examination. He stood to receive the Rebel attack and found himself outflanked by cavalry in his original position. Sigel withdrew to a second line, half a mile behind his

original position. The battle was marked by a charge by teenage cadets of the Virginia Military Institute that helped drive Sigel's army from its first line. The second line fared little better. A cavalry attack on the advancing Rebels was broken up by Confederate artillery firing canister, and Breckinridge sent his troops forward once more to chase the Union forces away again. The battle ended with a long-range artillery duel. The battlefield is preserved today as a park.

Grant meanwhile had already begun his own attacks. On May 4, he pushed into the Wilderness, the scene of Lee's most masterful tactical victory. A ferocious two-day battle on May 5–6, 1864, ended with a disparity in casualties greater than at Fredericksburg. But Grant refused to accept he was beaten, disengaged, and marched around Lee's right flank. Lee abandoned his own entrenchments and the two armies met for a battle at Spotsylvania Court House that started on May 9 and

Left: *The battle flag of Courtney's Virginia High Constabulary, captured by Union forces at the battle Spotsylvania Court House in May 1864. The unit was part of Jackson's command in the Shenandoah Valley campaign of 1862.*

only ended on May 19. Afterward, Grant again disengaged and marched south for the North Anna River. Lee again beat him to it, and Grant abandoned the idea of attacking here after a few skirmishes. Again he disengaged and began moving south.

On June 1 Grant's army reached Cold Harbor to find that once again Lee had reached there quickly enough to establish a strong defensive position. Grant, however, believed that Lee's army was beaten in spirit. Furthermore, this would be the last chance to attack it outside of the strong entrenchments around Richmond. So he committed the Army of the Potomac to an attack all along the line that was bloodily repulsed. It was the worst mistake Grant made in the war.

After the failure of Robert E. Lee's army to give way at Cold Harbor, as Grant had believed was possible, the Union commander decided the time had come to implement the second phase of his plan, which was to lay siege to Richmond. He planned to shift his troops across the James using a pontoon bridge. Beauregard warned Richmond on June 7, 1864, that Petersburg was almost defenseless.

Two days later, Butler's forces poked their noses out of their bottle and sent a two-brigade force with cavalry against Petersburg. The effort was described as a "movement" with the intent of destroying railroad installations and supplies in Petersburg, but a more alert commander may have made more of what transpired.

The force pushed its way across the Appomattox and the local Rebel commander, General Henry A. Wise, had little more than an understrength brigade and the Petersburg militia of old men and boys armed with squirrel guns defending entrenchments that were incomplete. By early afternoon, the situation appeared desperate with Union forces occupying the front line of the Rebel entrenchments. The Union plan called for a cavalry brigade to enter the city from the south, but the Petersburg Home Guard delayed them long enough for fresh Rebel troops to arrive. However, had General Gillmore, commanding the infantry, pushed more

vigorously, he could well have occupied the Rebel entrenchments and possibly held them with the prospect of being reinforced from the rest of the Army of the James. The Union cavalry did not keep him informed of their movements and the opportunity to take Petersburg without a siege was lost.

A second opportunity to achieve the same end occurred five days later as Grant's army disengaged from its Cold Harbor position. One of the first corps to move was XVIII and Grant had ordered it to make an attempt on Petersburg. The Union commander, Major General William F. "Baldy" Smith, leading some 16,000 men, was fearful of the strength of the Rebel lines, based on the experience of Cold Harbor. Beauregard had barely 3,000 men. After an early success on June 15 by a division of African American troops, Smith merely reinforced the position they held, instead of continuing the attack. During the night, Beauregard assembled troops from the force watching Butler at Bermuda Hundred, while Grant and Meade arrived with two more army corps. The Rebels now had about 14,000 men; the Union had 48,000. A frontal assault by the Union forces carried another line of trenches, but the actual operation had been left until too late in the day. Lee was only now convinced by Beauregard's report of the prisoners he had taken that Grant had actually shifted his position.

Lee now moved his whole army toward Petersburg, while another corps joined the Union forces. A final Union assault on June 18 was repelled with heavy losses. (In total, these four days of attacks cost as many casualties as had been suffered at Cold Harbor.)

Meade was furious; Grant resigned himself to winning through a campaign of siege. Grant had worn his army out. Some 65,000 casualties had been suffered and the numbers stayed steady as inexperienced troops were added in place of the veterans who had been killed or wounded. Grant recognized that his men were tired and that the bloody Overland campaign had made them extremely cautious about risking their lives.

Lee, meanwhile, recognized the seriousness of his position. He had already declared at the outset of the campaign, that in the case of a siege, it would only be a matter of time. However, the vital railroads to Richmond were still in Rebel hands although vulnerable to Union raids. At this early stage of the siege of Petersburg, the Union forces had not cut off the western end of the city. The siegeworks were only gradually extended westward, and on June 22, 1864, a raid against two Union divisions advancing westward netted 1,600 prisoners.

The last weeks of June were hot and dry, and in the debilitating heat there was little action. But there was no loss of ingenuity. A strong Rebel redoubt attracted the attention of the commander of a regiment drawn from the coal-mining regions of Pennsylvania. He approached his corps commander, Major General Burnside, with an idea of digging a tunnel some five hundred yards long that would enable the placement of a large mine under the Rebel fort. Exploding the mine and attacking immediately afterward would theoretically lead to the fall of an important segment of the Confederate entrenchments. Burnside embraced the idea enthusiastically and Grant also believed it practical. Meade, however, was unconvinced. Burnside selected his one division of African American troops to carry out the attack and they received special training.

Toward the end of July, knowing that the mine was almost ready, Grant planned a second operation around the Confederate left. Lee's forces were somewhat overstretched, having to defend not only Petersburg, but also to keep Butler's Army of the James bottled up in Bermuda Hundred. The area just north of Bermuda Hundred, across the James River, was inviting, and Grant ordered II Corps, commanded by General Winfield Scott Hancock, to probe into it, at least with the hope of unleashing a cavalry raid. A cautious General Hancock did not move fast enough to prevent the Rebels strengthening this weakly held area and the opportunity slipped away on July 27th. An attempt to

Left: *Congressional Medal of Honor holder Sergeant Major Christian Fleetwood of the 5th Colored Troops received the award for bravery at Chaffin's Farm, near Richmond, in 1864.*

open a gap on the left of the Confederate line for the cavalry to pass through also was lost on the 28th. But this maneuver had pulled about half of the Rebel infantry from Petersburg, just in time for the attack using the mine.

Unfortunately, the mine attack had become increasingly controversial. Meade and Grant both told Burnside to change his choice to lead the attack with an African American division. Burnside, instead of actually choosing an alternative, left the matter up to a lottery. The winner was a division of converted cavalry and artillery, commanded by a known incompetent. The mine was set off early in the morning of July 30 and tore a huge hole in the Confederate line. The Union division entered the resulting crater, but did not get out, partly because the commanding general had remained in the

Right: *General Winfield Scott, born in Virginia, remained loyal to the United States, which he had served loyally in combat since the War of 1812. In spite of his age and battles with gout, the consequence of his taste for rich living, he retained a certain liveliness of mind that served the country well. His military strategy for defeating the rebellion, popularly known as the Anaconda Plan, was applied throughout the war, even though he was removed from his post as general in chief in the autumn of 1861.*

Union trenches, out of touch with the action. Also, the crater itself initially appeared to provide good cover against enemy rifle fire, and the steep sides made it difficult for the troops to get out. The supporting divisions achieved some success to the right and left, but again there was some confusion. The troops in the crater now became the target for crossfire from Rebel artillery and casualties were soon becoming heavy. Lee organized a prompt counterattack, shifting troops from other parts of the line. Burnside sent in his African American division. The Union plan had envisaged a push directly forward out of the crater toward Cemetery Hill, the last piece of high ground between the Rebel lines and Petersburg. A single attack made by the Union forces was beaten back. The Confederate counterattack was pressed with vigor and routed the Union forces out of the crater.

Two weeks after the crater failure, Grant resumed probing the Confederate line. Like a metronome, he swung his army now against the Confederate left, then against the Confederate right, edging a force around the Petersburg defenses toward the railroads that kept Lee's army supplied. A week of fighting around Globe Tavern cut the single railroad that directly connected Petersburg with the rest of the South. From now on Lee's supplies had to take a roundabout route to reach him. The noose Grant was throwing around Petersburg was growing tighter and tighter.

While Grant knotted this noose, developments were occurring in the Shenandoah Valley. Sigel's army was now commanded by General David Hunter and he had more success than the German American. On June 11, Hunter was only a couple of days' march from Lynchburg, through which ran Lee's main railroad connection to the West. Lee had no choice but to rush reinforcements there and did so in the shape of a corps commanded by General Jubal Early. He attacked Hunter on June 18, but found Hunter had already retired from his positions and was headed for the Allegheny Mountains of West Virginia. So Early kept marching up

the Shenandoah Valley until July 5, when he crossed the Potomac and threatened the city of Washington, then returning to Virginia on July 14 and retiring to Strasburg. On July 24, two days after reaching Strasburg, Early was on the move again, chasing Union troops out of Winchester and sending a raiding party of cavalry north again. This time Grant decided to deal with Early once and for all. General Phil Sheridan was put in charge of the newly created Army of the Shenandoah, of 50,000 men, where Early only had 18,000. Sheridan did not show his customary aggression at first, and Early was able to advance up the Shenandoah at the end of August

to ensure that the harvest was gathered in. Sheridan seemed unusually cautious and Grant had to make a personal visit on September 15 to get him to move.

Sheridan then fought four battles in rapid succession against Early that saw him drive the Rebel leader's army to the south of the valley. At Opequon Creek on September 19, Sheridan drove Early out of a strong position near Winchester.

On September 22, a flank attack pushed Early out of another good position at Fisher's Hill. Sheridan then turned his army's attention to devastating the Shenandoah Valley, while Early collected reinforcements. He then positioned his army at Cedar Creek, where Early struck at it on October 19. Early's army gained a tactical surprise, but it was Shiloh all over again. Sheridan, who had been on his way back from a conference in Washington, made an all-night ride from Winchester to rally his army and inflict a decisive defeat on Early. Both armies then went into winter quarters. Early was still available to be a nuisance, but the threat he posed with raids into Maryland and Pennsylvania was stopped for good.

Right: The ruins of Richmond in 1865. Confederate government archives and buildings of military value were set alight by the fleeing authorities, but the flame spread throughout the town destroying much of it.

For the Confederates in Virginia, the winter of 1864–65 was a desperate one. Lee's army in Petersburg ran low on supplies, while Grant continued to maintain steady pressure, switching attacks from the left and right on the Confederate lines. By March 1865, Lee recognized he must do something to break the siege or else he would be cut off from the rest of the Confederacy. Grant's forces were nearing the last railroad running out of Petersburg, the Southside Railroad. Lee decided the only way to recover the initiative was to attack. Lee concentrated one corps for

an attack on a relatively isolated Union position, Fort Stedman. The attack, on March 25, was initially successful. But a Union counterattack by a full division threw the Rebels out of Fort Stedman and even captured the Rebels' forward positions.

While Lee was planning the assault on Fort Stedman, Grant had been concocting his own March surprise. He sent the cavalry under Sheridan and two infantry corps against the Southside Railroad. Sheridan's troopers were the striking force, and Lee sent General George Pickett with two infantry divisions to aid the small Rebel cavalry force.

In fighting on March 29 and March 31, the Rebels gave vital ground in some places, but blocked the Union cavalry in others. With the battle in the balance, on April 1 at Five Forks, the Union V Corps attacked Pickett's troops in the late afternoon, turning their flank and moving into a gap between the Rebel Petersburg entrenchments and Pickett's positions. Thousands of Rebel soldiers were captured. When Grant heard of this, he ordered a general assault all along the line at Petersburg. The opinion he had held of Lee's army before the assault at Cold Harbor was valid now.

Left: *A flag of an unknown unit that was captured at Sayler's Creek on April 6, 1865. The last major action fought by the Army of Northern Virginia during the war.*

On Sunday, April 2, 1865, the Rebel defenders of Petersburg were driven out of their entrenchments. Lee sent word to Richmond, where President Davis received it while attending divine service. The Rebel head of state fled the capital, while Lee's troops, under the cover of night, abandoned Petersburg after an eight-month siege. On April 3, while Lee's army was trying to reassemble itself at Amelia Court House, President Abraham Lincoln made the first visit of his term in office to Richmond. He was greeted with great joy by a crowd of now-free slaves.

Lee's army attempted to flee, but were pursued closely by Grant's forces. At Sayler's Creek on April 6, the Army of Northern Virginia fought its last battle, and the part of it engaging the enemy was cut off and compelled to surrender. The fight had gone out of it. On April 9, 1865, Lee attempted to break through a cordon of Union cavalry, only to find two corps of Union infantry behind it. He was surrounded and surrendered to Grant at Appomattox Court House.

The most significant unit raised in Virginia during the war was the Stonewall Brigade of the Confederate army. Its official title was the 1st Virginia Infantry Brigade, and it comprised on its formation in June 1861 the 2nd, 4th, 5th, and 27th Virginia Volunteers, and the Rockbridge Artillery. In July, the 33rd Virginia Volunteers were added to it. The brigade's battle honors eventually included most of the major engagements of Lee's Army of Northern Virginia during the war. It particularly distinguished itself at the second battle of Bull Run in August 1862 and at the battle of Spotsylvania Court House in May 1864. The brigade made its reputation at the first battle of Bull Run, when it stood stolidly to repel Union attacks on Henry House Hill. It cemented it by rapidly marching up and down the Shenandoah Valley during Jackson's valley campaign in April and May 1862. In May 1864, the Stonewall Brigade was reduced to about two hundred men and was merged with two other brigades. It took part in Early's valley campaign of 1864, including the march that took his army close to the city of Washington and surrendered with the rest of Lee's army at Appomattox Court House.

Two generals, natives of Virginia, were among those who fought for the Union. Major General Winfield Scott

(1786–1866) has already been general in chief of the army for two decades when the war began. His main contribution was to outline in detail the grand strategy of the Union plan to defeat the rebellion by seizing the Mississippi River and blockading the coasts. At the age of seventy-five, weighing in at three-hundred pounds, and suffering from gout, Scott could only expect a staff role in the war. He received a lot of the blame for the poor initial showing of Union forces. After the defeat at Ball's Bluff in November 1861, when the field commander made a series of disastrous mistakes, Scott tendered his resignation, which was accepted by Lincoln.

George H. Thomas (1816–70) graduated from West Point in 1840. At the start of the war he served in the 2nd Cavalry Regiment of the regular army and then served briefly in command of a brigade in the Shenandoah Valley. In October he was transferred to the Department of Ohio and spent the rest of the war in the West. He slowly ascended the promotional ladder, making his reputation both as a commander of a small independent force operating in eastern Kentucky and as a solid subordinate commander of a corps and division. At Chickamauga in September 1863, he saved the Union army by his refusal to retreat in the face of strong Rebel attacks. The Rock of Chickamauga was never highly regarded by Grant, who considered him too slow, but he won the greatest Union victory of the war at Nashville in December 1864.

At the head of any list of Confederate commanders from Virginia must stand the paladin of the Confederacy, Robert E. Lee (1807–1870). Lee was a reluctant secessionist, but when the time came to make a choice, he identified with his state and resigned from the US Army. Lee graduated from West Point in 1829 and was a leading member of the antebellum army. Scott had even wanted him as commander of the US forces, but Lee refused to fight against his kin. Robert E. Lee's early war in no way foreshadowed the superiority he would later establish over his Union opponents. His first campaign, in West Virginia, ended in defeat, and he spent the winter of 1861 exiled to the Department of Georgia, South Carolina, and Florida. Lee was recalled in March 1862 and brought to Richmond to act as military adviser to President Jefferson Davis. The president and Rebel commander Joseph Johnston had argued over matters of rank, and Davis probably already had in mind to replace him with Lee. When Joseph was wounded, Robert E. Lee was on hand and closely familiar with the situation.

Left: A captain of the 11th Virginia Infantry, Company G, the Lynchburg Home Guard, in the regulation gray frock coat and trousers. The red sash was part of Confederate army regulation dress for officers below the rank of general.

Below: *Two soldiers of the 15th Virginia Infantry, a regiment formed in May 1861 at Richmond. Its first engagement was at Big Bethel. In 1862, it was reorganized, this time as an eight-company regiment, and was engaged at Fair Oaks, Malvern Hill, South Mountain, and Antietam. It spent much of the rest of the war away from the main theater of action in the East, serving in southeastern Virginia and North Carolina.*

Lee's approach to war belied the image he displayed of the ideal Southern gentleman—humane, educated, and religious. In war, he proved a consummate gambler, repeatedly dividing his smaller army in the face of the enemy to gain an advantage on the flank, as he did at the second battle of Bull Run and at Chancellorsville to gain his greatest victories. Nor can the comment he made as his troops shot down Union soldiers at Fredericksburg in December 1862 be entirely reconciled with the image: "It is well that war is so terrible—we should grow too fond of it." An early

enthusiasm for entrenchments was restored when he faced General Grant's attempt to force his way to Richmond in the Overland campaign of 1864. Lee compensated for his inferior numbers by repeatedly digging in. But the relentlessness of Grant was the undoing of Lee, and several times in 1864 Grant might well have outmaneuvered "Marse Robert" if his subordinates had read the battlefield situation better. Lee was loved by his men, although on more than one occasion, such as Pickett's Charge at Gettysburg, he was profligate with their lives.

Joseph E. Johnston (1807–91), by contrast, is probably the most controversial Confederate commander of the war. He graduated from West Point in 1829 and like Lee remained in the army until his state seceded. He was the victor at the first battle of Bull Run, and stymied McClellan's advance up the James River Peninsula on Richmond. However, he was annoyed in August 1861 when Davis appointed three other officers to full general ahead of him, including Robert E. Lee, whom he had outranked in the U.S. Army. This poisoned relations between him and the president throughout the war. Johnston, unlike Lee, was a cautious commander, preferring a defensive fight on the battlefield and campaigns of maneuver as opposed to defending cities. His greatest success came in his defense of Atlanta, but quite possibly he was removed from command too early to develop fully his strategic vision of Atlanta as a pivot. On the other hand, he did display an unwarranted reluctance to attack the enemy when the strategic situation required it. Grant regarded him highly.

Jubal Early (1816–94) graduated from West Point in 1837. Early did not stay long in the army, but instead took up law and politics for a time in the 1840s. He was what has been called a "conditional unionist," opposed to secession until Lincoln made clear his policy to suppress the rebellion with military force. At the first battle of Bull Run he commanded a brigade. He served with the Army of Northern Virginia until 1864, at times

displaying some talent for independent command, such as during the Chancellorsville campaign of 1863. When the Rebels needed a commander for a campaign in the Shenandoah Valley in 1864, Early was consequently the best choice from Lee's army. Heavily outnumbered, Early still managed to approach the gates of the city of Washington and avoid the total destruction of his army. He nearly pulled off a surprising victory at Cedar Creek, although he didn't have enough soldiers to exploit initial success.

Thomas Jonathan Jackson (1824–63) stands second to Lee among the pantheon of Confederate military leaders. He graduated from West Point in 1846, just in time to serve with distinction in the Mexican War of 1846–48. At the time of Virginia's secession, he served as a professor at the Virginia Military Institute, and had adopted a devout Presbyterian faith.

Jackson came to prominence in the first major battle of the war at Bull Run. Apart from an uncharacteristic lethargy during the Seven Days' campaign, he proved a brilliant commander. After Jackson's mortal wounding by one of his own soldiers at Chancellorsville, Lee said, "I have lost my right arm."

Ambrose Powell Hill (1825–65) graduated from West Point in 1847 and served in the army until he resigned during the 1861 secession crisis. Lee had a high opinion of Hill, and repeatedly gave his division some of the toughest assignments in battles during the Seven Days' campaign of 1862.

Hill's crucial arrival at Antietam after a forced march from Harpers Ferry probably saved Lee's army from defeat. Hill became a corps commander in time for Gettysburg, but his early war brilliance faded somewhat with larger command.

George Pickett's (1825–75) name will be forever associated with the battle of Gettysburg, and the forlorn charge on the third day. He was a notably poor student at West Point, from which he graduated in 1846. He was a career soldier until he resigned from the army in 1861. At the time of the fated charge, he didn't have a

J. E. B. Stuart (1833–64)

This officer commanded Lee's cavalry for most of the war. Lee had served as his commander in the 1st US Cavalry (pictured) before the war, after Stuart graduated from West Point in 1854. Lee regarded him highly, especially for his ability to dominate Union cavalry and give the Army of Northern Virginia a valuable advantage in reconnaissance. However, Stuart mismanaged his role during the Gettysburg campaign and contributed to the series of errors that led to defeat. He was mortally wounded in the battle of Yellow Tavern on May 11, 1864, after which Lee commented, "I have lost my left eye," thus equating him in value with Jackson.

particularly distinguished war record, and although he performed well under fire at Gettysburg, he did not have an especially notable record afterward. Most notoriously, he missed the crucial battle of Five Forks in April 1865 while attending a shad bake.

WEST VIRGINIA

"Citizens of West Virginia, your fate is mainly in your own hands."

—General William S. Rosecrans, August 20, 1861

West Virginia has a unique status among the states of the Union. It is the only state of the Union created from another state under the provision of the US Constitution.

Prior to 1861, its history is identical with that of Virginia. When the Old Commonwealth's legislators voted its ordnance of secession, they provided for a referendum to confirm the decision. The vote, on May 23, totaled 128,884 in favor of secession, with 32,134 voting against. However, by a substantial margin those who voted against came from the northwest of the state. Here the margin against secession was three to one.

This part of Virginia was remote from the tidewater aristocracy that dominated state politics and provided the bedrock of support for secession. The mountaineers north of the Kanawha had more in common with settlers in Ohio; the city of Wheeling was north of Baltimore and Cincinnati.

On June 11 representatives from thirty-five counties in this part of Virginia assembled at Wheeling to lay the foundations for creating a separate state. The legal position was clear. No state could have its boundaries adjusted except by its own permission, and theoretically there was a state government in Richmond that would oppose the loss of the

Above: The Big Supply Co. premises in Dorothy during the Civil War.

Left: Harpers Ferry, now in West Virginia, repeatedly featured in the campaigns of the first year of the war. This view was taken from the Maryland side of the river. The firehouse, the last remnant of the once-great armory, is in the lower left of the picture, next to the railroad.

northwestern portion of the state. However, since that state government had proclaimed its own independence from the United States, the Wheeling convention adopted the view that it had acted illegally. A new state government for Virginia was formed, and duly elected two senators and three representatives to Congress.

However, there were two views prevalent in the Wheeling convention. Some wanted to act as a kind of "government in exile" from Richmond. But a small majority wanted to end the continuing problems they had with living in a very different society to the tidewater region. West Virginia was a mountainous area that was divided into several separate valleys and farmed land in smaller plots mostly growing food for subsistence. This was very unlike the tidewater, where large plantations grew cash crops for export.

For this small majority, the only long-term solution would be secession or, using a less-inflammatory term in the times, dismemberment. The Wheeling convention voted on August 20, 1861, to separate thirty-five counties. The decision needed approval by a referendum due to be held on October 24, 1861, at which time the electors would also vote for delegates to a constitutional convention. As well as a political track toward dismemberment, there was also, in the nature

Left: *The ruins of Savory Mill in Harpers Ferry. The building was in use during the Civil War period. Throughout its history, Harpers Ferry has been the backdrop for remarkable events. It became part of the National Park System in 1944. The park covers over 2,300 acres in the states of West Virginia, Maryland, and Virginia.*

The commander of the Virginia state forces, General Robert E. Lee, sent 4,500 troops under General Robert S. Garnett. On July 11, 1861, at Rich Mountain, the Rebels were defeated, and Garnett was killed in a skirmish two days later. West Virginia was now in Unionist hands.

So, when the Wheeling convention met in August, its votes reflected a winning position on the field of battle. But the referendum date in October gave the Rebel authorities in Richmond a deadline of their own. If they could recover even just a substantial portion of western Virginia, they would embarrass the Unionist regime in Wheeling, and possibly nip dismemberment in the bud.

Robert E. Lee went personally to take command of the effort. However, bad weather and a tactical plan asking too much of an amateur army cost Lee the chance of surprise in an action at Cheat Mountain on September 10. Lee made a second attempt in early October, and was outmaneuvered by the Union commander, Brigadier General William S. Rosecrans. Lee went back to Richmond. The West Virginia referendum went forward, although not many participated in the vote.

The only region covered by dismemberment that showed secessionist sentiment was the Kanawha Valley. Here there was the kind of bushwhackers' war that occurred in other regions where large numbers of Unionists and Confederate sympathizers lived close by. This continued throughout the rest of the Civil War, but there was no further Confederate military campaigning.

The constitutional convention met at Wheeling in January 1862. The Unionist legislators endorsed the constitutional convention's work in May, and in December Congress finally approved the enabling legislation that would admit West Virginia to the Union. Slavery was gradually abolished, with all slaves born after July 4, 1863, being freed, and all others freed on their twenty-fifth birthday. West Virginia entered the Union on June 20, 1863.

of the times, a military track. The little tongue of Virginia that poked up between the borders of Ohio and Pennsylvania, and the part of Virginia between Martinsburg and Parkersburg, affected two important transportation routes for the Northern cause. The Baltimore & Ohio Railroad, which connected the city of Washington with Ohio and points west, ran through Martinsburg. The Ohio River linked the arsenal and factories of Pittsburgh, and the farmland of eastern Ohio and western Pennsylvania, with markets along the Ohio River Valley. Rebel troops were already in control of parts of the Baltimore & Ohio, at Harpers Ferry and Grafton respectively.

The first Union troops to enter West Virginia were Ohio and Indiana state troops sent by the governors, under the command of Brigadier General George McClellan. By the end of June 1861, McClellan had built up an army of 20,000 in the region and beaten a badly equipped and drilled Virginia force at Philippi.

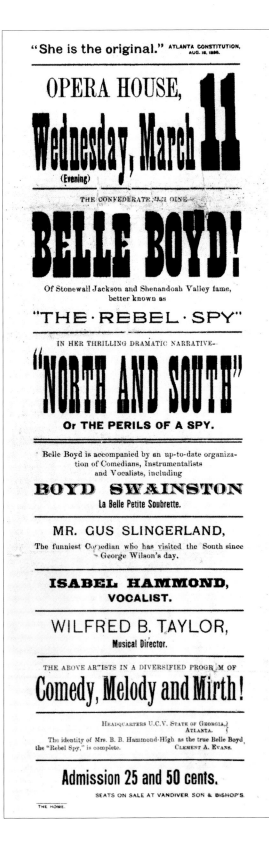

"She is the original." ATLANTA CONSTITUTION, AUG. 18, 1896.

OPERA HOUSE, 11

Wednesday, March

(Evening)

THE CONFEDERATE HEROINE

BELLE BOYD!

Of Stonewall Jackson and Shenandoah Valley fame,
better known as

"THE·REBEL·SPY"

IN HER THRILLING DRAMATIC NARRATIVE--

"NORTH AND SOUTH"

Or THE PERILS OF A SPY.

Belle Boyd is accompanied by an up-to-date organization of Comedians, Instrumentalists
and Vocalists, including

BOYD SWAINSTON

La Belle Petite Soubrette.

MR. GUS SLINGERLAND,

The funniest Comedian who has visited the South since
George Wilson's day.

ISABEL HAMMOND,

VOCALIST.

WILFRED B. TAYLOR,

Musical Director.

THE ABOVE ARTISTS IN A DIVERSIFIED PROGRAM OF

Comedy, Melody and Mirth!

HEADQUARTERS U.C.V. STATE OF GEORGIA,
ATLANTA.

The identity of Mrs. B. B. Hammond-High as the true Belle Boyd,
the "Rebel Spy," is complete.   CLEMENT A. EVANS.

Admission 25 and 50 cents.

SEATS ON SALE AT VANDIVER, SON & BISHOP'S.

THE HOME.

Belle Boyd (1844–1900)

Belle Boyd was born in Martinsburg, Virginia (now West Virginia), and attended school in Baltimore. In July 1861 she claimed to have shot a drunken Union soldier who was trying to raise the Stars and Stripes over their Martinsburg home. Early in the war she was carrying messages to Rebel troops about Union movements around Martinsburg and Winchester. In March 1862 she was arrested for the first time, and a hearing in Baltimore dismissed charges for lack of evidence. From here she went to Front Royal, where family members kept a small hotel. She was consequently well-placed to gather intelligence for Stonewall Jackson's Shenandoah campaign. At one point, she claimed she was able to overhear a conference of Union officers, and then escaped to Jackson's camp with the information thus gathered. In July 1862 she was arrested and held in a the city of Washington prison for a month. After this Boyd was exchanged for Union prisoners. When she made the mistake of returning to Martinsburg in June 1863, she was arrested again. This time Boyd fell ill with typhoid, and was sent to Europe to convalesce. She spent most of the rest of the war in Britain. After the Civil War, she made a point of capitalizing on her reputation, writing her best-selling memoirs and conducting speaking tours around the country. Boyd died in Wisconsin on one such tour and is buried there.

Below: Belle Boyd made considerable claims for her efforts as a spy during the war, and afterward made frequent lecture tours, appearing here along with series of musical and comedy acts.

WASHINGTON

"The folks at home will never be able to comprehend what we have seen."

—Ambrose Edwards, Union soldier, 1864

In 1860, Washington was part of the Washington Territory. The land occupied by Washington was originally known as the Oregon country. The United States claimed the territory during the Washington administration when a fur trader sailed up the Columbia River. Britain also had strong claims to the area, based in part by the visits of the explorer George Vancouver around the same time, when there was nearly naval conflict with Spanish ships in the area. Spain ceded its "discovery rights" to the United States by treaty in 1819. Russian claims were removed by a treaty with the United States in 1824. The settlement of the region by Americans following trails across the Great Plains and over the Rocky Mountains helped to finally resolve the matter in 1846, when Britain and the United States defined their boundary along the forty-ninth parallel by treaty.

In 1843 settlers in Oregon formed a provisional government for themselves under the Stars and Stripes. Formal territorial government from the city of Washington came in 1848. The provisional legislature had defined Oregon to be a Free-Soil territory in 1843. The legislation instituting territorial government extended the provisions of the Northwest Ordinance of 1787 (which had banned slavery) to the Oregon Territory. Thus there was never any possibility of the territory entering the United States as anything other than a Free State. In 1853, the northern and western portions of the Oregon Territory were separated by Congress and established as the Washington Territory. This covered the modern states of Washington, Idaho, and part of Montana and Wyoming. In 1863 the western portion of this territory was given separate status as the Idaho Territory, but its Civil War history will be covered here.

The most significant development occurred right at the start of the war when the regular army garrisons of

Left: *Fort Walla Walla took its name from the valley in which it was built in 1853. It became one of many army posts that during the Civil War were occupied by volunteer units raised from state or territorial residents in the West.*

forts in the Washington Territory were withdrawn. These troops were eventually replaced by volunteer forces under Brigadier General Benjamin Alvord. The main purpose was to protect prospectors and settlers already in the territory, and emigrants using the Oregon Trail.

The only major battle in the Pacific Northwest during the Civil War had no relation to the great war and rebellion in the East. The western Shoshonis had been especially restive in recent years, so in January 1863 Colonel Patrick Connor led out a Union column of California volunteers from Fort Douglas in the Utah Territory to engage the Native Americans. Connor was from Stockton, California, and had served in the Mexican War of 1846–48. Connor was a feisty individual who took his task of protecting the Overland Mail route extremely seriously, and regarded the Mormons just as dangerous to the Union cause as any other. The Shoshoni war chief, Bear Hunter, had prepared a camp with defensive positions along the Bear River on the border between the Utah and Washington territories, and Connor and his men attacked this on January 27, 1863. A frontal attack on the Native American camp was beaten back with heavy losses. Connor then sent parties to high ground overlooking the campsite. Enfilading fire shattered the warriors. Most of the three hundred warriors present at the battle, including Bear Hunter, were killed. The Shoshonis no longer posed such a threat to the Oregon Trail.

Having tackled the worst of the Shoshoni raiders, Connor kept up the pressure on them throughout 1863. He sent a company to Soda Springs, a well-known Oregon Trail landmark, to establish Camp Connor. From here, and from the existing forts Bridger and Douglas, patrols harried the scattered bands. One by one the chiefs came to terms with Connor and ceased their raiding of the Oregon Trail.

WISCONSIN

"The backbone of the Rebellion is this day broken."

—Captain Ira Miltimore, 33rd Wisconsin, July 4, 1863

The Treaty of Paris, which ended the Revolutionary War in 1783, added the territory that today makes up the state of Wisconsin. This region remained unorganized for four years, until Congress made it part of the Northwest Territory. Wisconsin then began a somewhat tortuous jurisdictional march to statehood. In 1800, when the Northwest Territory was divided into two, Wisconsin was included in Indiana Territory. In 1809, the land of Wisconsin became part of newly created Illinois Territory, a situation that only lasted until Illinois became a state in 1818. Wisconsin territory was then added to Michigan Territory. Then, in 1836, in preparation for Michigan's statehood, Wisconsin became its own territory, including part of Minnesota and the East of the Missouri River region. That only lasted two years when the East of the Missouri River area became Iowa Territory. Wisconsin finally gained admission as a state in 1848 within its current boundaries.

Wisconsin's Civil War experience will forever be associated with the tale of the Iron Brigade—the First Brigade, First Division, I Corps, whose first commander was General John Gibbon. It was Gibbon's idea for the brigade to wear the characteristic black Hardee hats that gave the brigade a uniform identity. This brigade was originally formed of four western regiments, the 2nd, 6th, and 7th Wisconsin, plus the 19th Indiana. In October 1862 the 24th Michigan was added. The brigade gained its nickname during the battle of South Mountain in September 1862 when it displayed great steadiness under fire. Three days later at Antietam, the Iron Brigade held firm against a Rebel attack across the cornfield, and the guns of its battery, Battery B of the 4th US artillery, were especially effective in firing canisters at the charging Rebels.

At Gettysburg on July 1, 1863, the brigade advanced to McPherson's Ridge on the banks of Willoughby Run to halt an attack by Heth's division of Rebels. Almost immediately on occupying their position, the Iron Brigade was subjected to a terrific volley of Rebel musketry, which caused about 30 percent casualties immediately. The brigade not only held its position, but counterattacked, stopping the Rebel attack and capturing the brigade commander and 250 men.

Some two hours later the Confederates, heavily reinforced, came on again. This time there were too many for the Iron Brigade's men to hold on to their position without heavy reinforcements, and eventually the Westerners were forced to give ground as their ammunition ran low. The Iron Brigade had lost so heavily that it played a minor role in the rest of the battle of Gettysburg.

In March 1864, General Grant reorganized the army. The Iron Brigade had suffered heavy losses, so it was amalgamated with some other units and transferred to V Corps, where its regiments remained for the rest of the war.

Of the Wisconsin regiments in the Iron Brigade, the 2nd Wisconsin suffered most heavily. It had been the first three-year regiment to arrive in the city of Washington in the summer of 1861, and fought in Sherman's brigade at the first battle of Bull Run. The gray uniforms it wore led to some dangerous confusion during the combat, and the 2nd Wisconsin was actually shot at by both sides. At Gettysburg, the 2nd Wisconsin captured the Rebel General Archer.

At Gettysburg on July 1, the 6th Wisconsin attacked a Rebel force that was advancing across the unfinished railroad with two other Union regiments. Such was the ferocity of the attack that an entire Rebel regiment surrendered to them.

Left: *A six-pound gun marks the site of the position of the 12th battery, Wisconsin Light Artillery, at Vicksburg. It was commanded by Captain William Zickerick, and was attached to the 7th Division, XVII Army Corps.*

INDEX

PICTURE CREDITS